# Norwegian
*phrase book*

**Berlitz Publishing / APA Publications GmbH & Co.
Verlag KG, Singapore Branch, Singapore**

NO part of this book may be reproduced, stored in a retrieval system or transmitted in any form or means electronic, mechanical, photocopying, recording or otherwise, without prior written permission from Apa Publications.

**Contacting the Editors**
Every effort has been made to provide accurate information in this publication, but changes are inevitable. The publisher cannot be responsible for any resulting loss, inconvenience or injury. We would appreciate it if readers would call our attention to any errors or outdated information by contacting Berlitz Publishing, 95 Progress Street, Union, NJ 07083, USA. Fax: 1-908-206-1103
e-mail: comments@berlitzbooks.com

**Satisfaction guaranteed**—If you are dissatisfied with this product for any reason, send the complete package, your dated sales receipt showing price and store name, and a brief note describing your dissatisfaction to: Berlitz Publishing, Langenscheidt Publishing Group, Dept. L, 46-35 54th Rd., Maspeth, NY 11378. You'll receive a full refund.

*All Rights Reserved*
© *2004 Berlitz Publishing/Apa Publications GmbH & Co. Verlag KG, Singapore Branch, Singapore*

Printed in Singapore by Insight Print Services (Pte) Ltd., October 2004.

*Berlitz Trademark Reg. U.S. Patent Office and other countries. Marca Registrada. Used under license from Berlitz Investment Corporation*

Layout: Media Marketing Inc.
Cover photo: ©Peter Langone Inc./International Stock

# Contents

## Travelling around 65

## Sightseeing 80

## Relaxing 86

## Making friends 92

## Shopping guide 97

Acknowledgments
We are particularly grateful to Dr. T.J.A. Bennett who devised the
phonetic transcription of this book.

# Guide to pronunciation

You'll find the pronunciation of Norwegian letters and sounds—based on the Oslo accent—explained below, as well as the symbols we use in the transcriptions. The imitated pronunciation should be read as if it were English, with exceptions as indicated below. It is based on Standard British pronunciation, though we have tried to take into account General American pronunciation as well. If you follow the instructions carefully, you'll have no difficulty in reading our transcriptions so as to make yourself understood.

In the phonetic transcription, some letters are placed in parentheses, e.g. meh(d). In daily conversation, these are rarely pronounced, although it is certainly not incorrect to do so. A bar over a vowel symbol indicates a long sound, usually a pure vowel, not a diphthong (see explanations below). Syllables printed in **bold type** should be stressed.

## Consonants

| Letter | Approximate pronunciation | Symbol | Example | |
|---|---|---|---|---|
| b, c, d, f, h, l, m, n, p, q, t, v, x | as in English | | | |
| g | 1) before **ei**, **i** and **y**, generally like **y** in yes | y | **gi** | yee |
| | 2) before **e** and **i** in some words of French origin, like **sh** in shut | sh | **geni** | sheh**nee** |
| | 3) elsewhere, like **g** in go | g | **gått** | got |
| gj | like **y** in yes | y | **gjest** | yehst |
| j | like **y** in yes | y | **ja** | yaa |
| k | 1) before **i**, and **y**, generally like **ch** in German ich (quite like **h** in huge, but with the tongue raised a little higher) | kh | **kino** | **khee**noo |
| | 2) elsewhere, like **k** in kit | k | **kaffe** | **kah**fer |

| kj | like **ch** in German ich (quite like **h** in huge, but with the tongue raised a little higher) | kh | **kjøre** | **kh**ū̄rrer |
| r | rolled near the front of the mouth (except in south-western Norway, where it's pronounced in the back of the mouth, like in French) | r | **rare** | **r**aarer |
| rs | like **sh** in shut | sh | **norsk** | no**sh**k |
| s | like **s** in sit | s/ss | **spise** | **s**pee**ss**er |
| sj | generally like **sh** in shut | sh | **stasjon** | stah**sh**ōōn |
| sk | 1) before **i**, **y** and **ø**, generally like **sh** in shut | sh | **ski** | **sh**ee |
|  | 2) elsewhere, like **sk** in skate | sk | **skole** | **sk**ōōler |
| skj | like **sh** in shut | sh | **skje** | **sh**āy |
| w | like **v** in vice | v | **whisky** | **v**iski |
| z | like **s** in sit | s | **zoom** | **s**ōōm |

If preceded by **r**, the consonants **l**, **n** and **t** (and sometimes **d**) are pronounced with the tip of the tongue turned up well behind the front teeth. The **r** then ceases to be pronounced, but influences the tone of the following consonant. We indicate this pronunciation by printing a small **r** above the line (e.g. pah^r t). (This "retroflex" pronunciation also occurs in words ending with an **r** if the following word begins with a **d**, **l**, **n**, **s** or **t**.)

### Silent consonants

1. The letter **d** is generally silent after **l**, **n** or **r** (e.g. holde, land, gård).
2. The letter **g** is silent in the endings -**lig** and -**ig**.
3. The letter **h** is silent when followed by a consonant (e.g. **h**jem, **h**va).
4. The letter **t** is silent in the definite form ("the") of neuter nouns (e.g. eple**t**) and in the pronoun de**t**.
5. The letter **v** is silent in certain words (e.g. sel**v**, tol**v**, hal**v**).

## Vowels

In Norwegian, a vowel is generally long in stressed syllables when it's the final letter or followed by one consonant only, and short if followed by two or more consonants.

| a | 1) when long, like a in car | aa | **dag** | daag |
| | 2) when short, between a in cat and u in cut | ah | **takk** | tahk |
| e | 1) when long, like ay in say, but a pure vowel, not a diphthong | $\overline{ay}$ | **sent** | sāynt |
| | 2) when followed by r, often like a in man (long or short) | $\overline{æ}$ | **her** | hǣr |
| | | æ | **herre** | hǣrer |
| | 3) when short, like e in get | eh | **penn** | pehn |
| | 4) when unstressed, like a in about | er * | **betale** | bertaaler |
| i | 1) when long, like ee in bee | ee | **hit** | heet |
| | 2) when short, like i in sit | i | **sitt** | sit |
| o | 1) when long, often like oo in soon, but with the lips more tightly rounded | $\overline{oo}$ | **ord** | ōor |
| | 2) the same sound can be short, like oo in foot | oo | **ost** | oost |
| | 3) when long, sometimes like aw in saw | aw | **·tog** | tawg |
| | 4) when short, sometimes like o in got (British pronunciation) | o | **stoppe** | stopper |
| u | 1) something like ew in few, or Scottish oo in good (long or short); since it is very close to the Norwegian y-sound, we use the same symbol for both | $\overline{ew}$ | **mur** | mēwr |
| | | ew | **busk** | bewsk |
| | 2) occasionally like oo in foot | oo | **nummer** | noommerr |
| y | very much like the sound described under u (1) above (long or short); put your tongue in the position for the ee in bee, and then round your lips as for the oo in pool | $\overline{ew}$ | **by** | bēw |
| | | ew | **bygge** | bewger |

---

* The r should not be pronounced when reading this transcription.

| æ | like a in act (long or short) | ē͞æ | lære | lē͞ærer |
| | | æ | færre | færrer |
| ø | like ur in fur, but with the lips rounded (long or short) | u͞r * | dør | du͞rr |
| | | ur * | sønn | surn |
| å | 1) when long, like aw in saw | aw | såpe | sawper |
| | 2) when short, like o in got (British pronunciation) | o | sånn | son |

### Diphthongs

| au | rather like ou in loud, though the first part is the Norwegian æ-sound | ou | sau | sou |
| ei, eg, egn | like ai in wait, though the first part is the Norwegian æ-sound | æi | geit | yæit |
| | | | jeg | yæi |
| | | | tegne | tæiner |
| øy | rather like oy in boy, though the first part is the Norwegian ø-sound | oy | gøy | goy |

### Intonation

Norwegian uses intonation (tones) to distinguish between certain words. Since no one expects a foreigner to master such subtleties, these tones are not shown in our transcriptions.

| Pronunciation of the Norwegian alphabet | | | | | | | |
|---|---|---|---|---|---|---|---|
| A | aa | I | ee | Q | ke͞w | X | ehkss |
| B | ba͞y | J | yod | R | ær | Y | e͞w |
| C | sa͞y | K | kaw | S | ehss | Z | seht |
| D | da͞y | L | ehl | T | ta͞y | Æ | æ͞ |
| E | a͞y | M | ehm | U | e͞w | Ø | u͞r |
| F | ehf | N | ehn | V | va͞y | Å | aw |
| G | ga͞y | O | o͞o | W | dobberlt-va͞y | | |
| H | haw | P | pa͞y | | | | |

---

* The r should not be pronounced when reading this transcription.

# Some basic expressions

| | | |
|---|---|---|
| Yes. | **Ja.** | yaa |
| No. | **Nei.** | næi |
| Please. | **Vær (så) snill å ... /** | vǣr (saw) snil aw/ |
| | **..., takk.** | ... tahk |
| Thank you. | **Takk.** | tahk |
| Thank you very much. | **Mange takk.** | **mahng**er tahk |
| That's all right/ You're welcome. | **Ingen årsak.** | **ing**ern **aw**shaak |

## Greetings  *Hilsning*

| | | |
|---|---|---|
| Good morning. | **God morgen.** | goo**maw**er$^r$n |
| Good afternoon. | **God dag.** | goo**daag** |
| Good evening. | **God aften/God kveld.** | goo(d)**ahf**tern/goo**kvehl** |
| Good night. | **God natt.** | goo**naht** |
| Goodbye. | **Adjø.** | ah**dyūr** |
| See you later. | **På gjensyn/Vi ses.** | paw **yehn**sēwn/vee **sāy**ss |
| Hello/Hi! | **Hallo/Hei!** | hah**lōō**/hæi |
| How do you do? (Pleased to meet you.) | **God dag.** | goo**daag** |
| How are you? | **Hvordan står det til?** | **voo**$^r$dahn stawr deh til |
| Very well, thanks. And you? | **Bare bra, takk. Og med deg?** | **baar**er braa tahk. o(g) meh(d) dæi |
| Fine. | **Bra, takk.** | braa tahk |
| I beg your pardon? | **Unnskyld?** | **ewn**shewl |
| Excuse me. (May I get past?) | **Unnskyld.** | **ewn**shewl |
| Sorry! | **Beklager!** | ber**klaa**gerr |

INTRODUCTIONS, see page 92

**Questions**  *Spørsmål*

| Where? | **Hvor?** | voor |
|---|---|---|
| How? | **Hvordan/Hvor?** | voo<sup>r</sup>dahn/voor |
| When? | **Når?** | nor |
| What? | **Hva?** | vaa |
| Why? | **Hvorfor?** | voorfor |
| Who? | **Hvem?** | vehm |
| Which? | **Hvilken\*?** | vilkern |
| Where is ...? | **Hvor er ...?** | voor ær |
| Where are ...? | **Hvor er ...?** | voor ær |
| Where can I find ...? | **Hvor finner jeg ...?** | voor finnerr yæi |
| Where can I get ...? | **Hvor kan jeg få tak i ...?** | voor kahn yæi faw taak ee |
| How far? | **Hvor langt?** | voor lahngt |
| How long? | **Hvor lenge?** | voor lehnger |
| How much? | **Hvor mye?** | voor mēwer |
| How many? | **Hvor mange?** | voor mahnger |
| How much does this cost? | **Hvor mye koster dette\*\*?** | voor mēwer kosterr dehter |
| How do I get to ...? | **Hvordan kommer jeg til ...?** | voo<sup>r</sup>dahn kommerr yæi til |
| When does ... open/close? | **Når åpner/ stenger ...?** | nor awpnerr/ stehngerr |
| What do you call this/that in Norwegian? | **Hva heter dette/ det på norsk?** | vaa hāyterr dehter/ deh paw noshk |
| What does this/ that mean? | **Hva betyr dette/ det?** | vaa bertēwr dehter/deh |
| Who's that? | **Hvem er det?** | vehm ær deh |
| Which bus goes to ...? | **Hvilken buss går til ...?** | vilkern bewss gawr til |

---

\* Common gender; neuter = *hvilket*; plural = *hvilke*.
\*\* Neuter; common gender = *denne*; plural = *disse* (see also grammar section, page 161).

**Do you speak ...?** *Snakker du ...?*

| | | |
|---|---|---|
| Do you speak English? | **Snakker du engelsk?** | snahkerr dew ehngerlsk |
| Does anyone here speak English? | **Er det noen her som snakker engelsk?** | ær deh nōōern hǣr som snahkerr ehngerlsk |
| I don't speak (much) Norwegian. | **Jeg snakker ikke (så bra) norsk.** | yæi snahkerr ikker (saw braa) noshk |
| Could you speak more slowly? | **Kan du snakke litt langsommere?** | kahn dew snahker lit lahngsommerrer |
| Could you repeat that? | **Kan du gjenta det?** | kahn dew yehntah deh |
| Could you spell it? | **Kan du stave det?** | kahn dew staaver deh |
| How do you pronounce this? | **Hvordan uttaler du dette?** | voo<sup>r</sup>dahn ēwtahlerr dew dehter |
| Could you write it down, please? | **Kan du skrive det ned, er du snill?** | kahn dew skreever deh nāy(d) ær dew snil |
| Can you translate this for me/us? | **Kan du oversette dette for meg/oss?** | kahn dew awversheter dehter for mæi/oss |
| Could you point to the ... in the book? | **Kan du peke på ... i boken?** | kahn dew pāyker paw ... ee bōōkern |
| phrase | **uttrykket** * | ēwtrewker |
| sentence | **setningen** | sehtningern |
| word | **ordet** | ōōrer |
| Just a moment. | **Et øyeblikk.** | eht oyerblik |
| I'll see if I can find it in this book. | **Jeg skal se om jeg kan finne det i denne boken.** | yæi skahl sāy om yæi kahn finner deh ee dehner bōōkern |
| I understand. | **Jeg forstår.** | yæi foshtawr |
| I don't understand. | **Jeg forstår ikke.** | yæi foshtawr ikker |
| Do you understand? | **Forstår du?** | foshtawr dew |

**Can/May ...?** *Kan ...?*

| | | |
|---|---|---|
| Can I have ...? | **Kan jeg få ...?** | kahn yæi faw |
| Can we have ...? | **Kan vi få ...?** | kahn vee faw |

---

* For information on the definite article, see grammar section, page 159.

| Can you show me ...? | **Kan du vise meg ...?** | kahn dew **vee**sser mæi |
| I can't. | **Jeg kan ikke.** | yæi kahn **ikk**er |
| Can you tell me ...? | **Kan du si meg ...?** | kahn dew **see** mæi |
| Can you help me? | **Kan du hjelpe meg?** | kahn dew **yehl**per mæi |
| Can I help you? | **Kan jeg hjelpe deg?** | kahn yæi **yehl**per dæi |
| Can you direct me to ...? | **Kan du vise meg veien til ...?** | kahn dew **vee**sser mæi **væi**ern til |

**Do you want ...?** *Ønsker du ...?*

| I'd like to ... | **Jeg vil gjerne ...** | yæi vil **yæ$^r$**ner |
| We'd like to ... | **Vi vil gjerne ...** | vee vil **yæ$^r$**ner |
| I'd like a ... | **Jeg vil gjerne ha en/et ...** | yæi vil **yæ$^r$**ner haa ehn/eht |
| Could you bring/ give me ...? | **Kan du gi meg ...?** | kahn dew **yee** mæi |
| Could you show me ...? | **Kan du vise meg ...?** | kahn dew **vee**sser mæi |
| I'm looking for ... | **Jeg ser etter ...** | yæi **sāȳr eh**terr |
| I'm searching for ... | **Jeg leter etter ...** | yæi **lāȳterr eh**terr |
| I'm hungry. | **Jeg er sulten.** | yæi ær **sewl**tern |
| I'm thirsty. | **Jeg er tørst.** | yæi ær **tursht** |
| I'm tired. | **Jeg er trett.** | yæi ær **treht** |
| I'm lost. | **Jeg hat gått meg bort.** | yæi haar **got** mæi boo$^r$t |
| It's important. | **Det er viktig.** | deh ær **vikti** |
| It's urgent. | **Det haster.** | deh **hahs**terr |

**It is/There is ...** *Det er ...*

| It is ... | **Det er ...** | deh ær |
| Is it ...? | **Er det ...?** | ær deh |
| It isn't ... | **Det er ikke ...** | deh ær **ikk**er |
| Here it is. | **Her er det/den.** | hāēr ær deh/dehn |
| Here they are. | **Her er de.** | hāēr ær dee |

| There it is. | **Der er det.** | dær ær deh |
| There they are. | **Der er de.** | dær ær dee |
| There is/are ... | **Det er ...** | deh ær |
| Is/Are there ...? | **Er det ...?** | ær deh |
| There isn't/aren't ... | **Det er ikke ...** | deh ær ikker |
| There isn't any. | **Det er ikke noe.** | deh ær ikker nōōer |
| There aren't any. | **Det er ikke noen.** | deh ær ikker nōōern |

## Opposites   *Motsetninger*

| beautiful/ugly | **pen/stygg** * | pāyn/stewg |
| better/worse | **bedre/verre** | bāydrer/værer |
| big/small | **stor/liten** | stōōr/leetern |
| cheap/expensive | **billig/dyr** | billi/dewr |
| early/late | **tidlig/sen** | teeli/sāyn |
| easy/difficult | **lett/vanskelig** | leht/vahnskerli |
| free (vacant)/ occupied | **ledig/opptatt** | lāydi/optaht |
| full/empty | **full/tom** | fewl/tom |
| good/bad | **bra/dårlig** | braa/dāw'li |
| heavy/light | **tung/lett** | toong/leht |
| here/there | **her/der** | hær/dær |
| hot/cold | **varm/kald** | vahrm/kahl |
| near/far | **nær/fjern** | nær/fyæ'rn |
| next/last | **neste/siste** | nehster/sister |
| old/new | **gammel/ny** | gahmerl/nēw |
| old/young | **gammel/ung** | gahmerl/oong |
| open/shut | **åpen/stengt** | awpern/stehngt |
| quick/slow | **rask/sakte** | rahsk/sahkter |
| right/wrong | **riktig/feil** | rikti/fæil |

## Quantities   *Mengde*

| a little/a lot | **lite/mye** | leeter/mēwer |
| few/a few | **få/noen (få)** | faw/nōōern (faw) |
| much/many | **mye/mange** | mēwer/mahnger |
| more/less | **mer/mindre** | māyr/mindrer |
| more than/less than | **mer enn/mindre enn** | māyr ehn/mindrer ehn |

* For neuter and plural forms, see grammar section, page 160 (adjectives).

| enough/too much | nok/for mye | nok/for mewer |
| some/any | litt, noe(n)/noe(n) | lit, nōōer(n)/nōōer(n) |

## A few more useful words  *Noen flere nyttige ord*

| above | over | awverr |
| after | etter | ehterr |
| and | og | o(g) |
| at | ved | veh(d) |
| before | før | fūrr |
| behind | bak | baak |
| below | under | ewnerr |
| between | mellom | mehlom |
| but | men | mehn |
| down/downstairs | ned/nede | nāy(d)/nāyder |
| during | i løpet av | ee lūrper(t) ahv |
| for | for | for |
| from | fra | fraa |
| in | i | ee |
| inside | inne | inner |
| never | aldri | ahldri |
| next to | ved siden av | veh(d) seedern ahv |
| none | ingen | ingern |
| not | ikke | ikker |
| nothing | ingenting, ikke noe | ingernting, ikker nōōer |
| now | nå | naw |
| on | på | paw |
| only | bare | baarer |
| or | eller | ehlerr |
| outside | ute | ēwter |
| perhaps | kanskje | kahnsher |
| since | siden | seedern |
| soon | snart | snaaᵉt |
| then | da | dah/daa |
| through | gjennom | yehnom |
| to | til | til |
| too (also) | også | osso |
| towards | mot | mōōt |
| under | under | ewnerr |
| until | til | til |
| up/upstairs | opp/oppe | op/opper |
| very | meget | māygert |
| with | med | meh(d) |
| without | uten | ēwtern |
| yet | ennå | ehnaw |

# Arrival

**Passport control**  *Passkontroll*

| | | |
|---|---|---|
| Here's my passport. | **Her er passet mitt.** | hæer ær **pahss**er mit |
| I'll be staying ... | **Jeg kommer til å bli ...** | yæi **komm**err til aw blee |
| a few days | **noen dager** | **nōō**ern **daa**gerr |
| a week | **en uke** | ehn **ēw̄**ker |
| a month | **en måned** | ehn **maw**nerd |
| I don't know yet. | **Jeg vet ikke ennå.** | yæi vāyt **ikk**er **ehn**naw |
| I'm here on holiday (vacation). | **Jeg er her på ferie.** | yæi ær hæer paw **fāy**ryer |
| I'm here on business. | **Jeg er her i forretninger.** | yæi ær hæer ee for**reht**ningerr |
| I'm just passing through. | **Jeg er bare på gjennomreise.** | yæi ær **baa**rer paw **yeh**nomrǣisser |

If things become difficult:

| | | |
|---|---|---|
| I'm sorry, I don't understand. | **Jeg beklager, men jeg forstår ikke.** | yæi ber**klaa**gerr mehn yæi **fosh**tawr **ikk**er |
| Does anyone here speak English? | **Er det noen her som snakker engelsk?** | ær deh **nōō**ern hæer som **snah**kerr **ehng**erlsk |

```
TOLL
CUSTOMS
```

After collecting your baggage at the airport (*flyplassen—* **flew**plahssern), you have a choice: use the green exit if you have nothing to declare, or leave via the red exit if you have items to declare.

```
varer å fortolle
goods to declare
```

```
ingenting å fortolle
nothing to declare
```

The chart below shows what you can bring in duty (tax) free.

| Cigarettes | Cigars | Tobacco | Spirits | Wine |
|---|---|---|---|---|
| 200 | or 250 g. | or 250 g. | 1 l. | and 1 l. |

| I have nothing to declare. | **Jeg har ikke noe å fortolle.** | yæi haar ikker nōōer aw fo'toller |
|---|---|---|
| I have ... | **Jeg har ...** | yæi haar |
| a carton of cigarettes | **en kartong sigaretter** | ehn kah'tong siggahrehterr |
| a bottle of whisky | **en flaske whisky** | ehn flahsker viski |
| That's for my personal use. | **Det er til personlig bruk.** | deh ær til pæshōōnli brewk |
| This is a gift. | **Dette er en gave.** | dehter ær ehn gaaver |

| | |
|---|---|
| **Passet, takk.** | Your passport, please. |
| **Har du noe å fortolle?** | Do you have anything to declare? |
| **Vær snill å åpne denne bagen.** | Please open this bag. |
| **Du må betale toll for dette.** | You'll have to pay duty (tax) on this. |
| **Har du mer bagasje?** | Do you have any more luggage? |

---

* All allowances are subject to change.

## Baggage—Porter    *Bagasje – Bærer*

| | | |
|---|---|---|
| Where are the luggage trolleys (carts)? | **Hvor er bagasje-trallene?** | voor ær bahgaasher-trahlerner |
| Porter! | **Bærer!** | bǣrerr |
| Please take this luggage. | **Vær så snill å ta denne bagasjen.** | vǣr saw snil aw taa **deh**ner bahgaashern |
| That's my suitcase/bag. | **Det er min koffert/bag.** | deh ær meen **koo**fferᵣt/''bag'' |
| That one is mine. | **Den der er min.** | dehn dǣr ær meen |
| Please take this to the ... | **Vær så snill å ta dette til ...** | vǣr saw snil aw taa **deh**ter til |
| bus | **bussen** | **bew**ssern |
| information desk | **informasjons-skranken** | informah**shoon**s-skrahngkern |
| luggage lockers | **oppbevarings-boksene** | **op**bervaaringsbokserner |
| taxi | **drosjen** | **dro**shern |
| How much is that? | **Hvor mye blir det?** | voor **mēw**er bleer deh |
| There's one suitcase missing. | **Det mangler en koffert.** | deh **mahng**lerr ehn **koo**fferᵣt |

## Changing money    *Valutaveksling*

| | | |
|---|---|---|
| Where's the currency exchange office? | **Hvor er vekslings-kontoret?** | voor ær **vehk**shlings-koont**oo**rer |
| Can you change these traveller's cheques (checks)? | **Kan du veksle disse reisesjekkene?** | kahn dew **vehk**shler **dis**ser **ræi**ssershehkerner |
| I'd like to change some ... | **Jeg vil gjerne veksle noen ...** | yæi vil **yǣ**rner **vehk**shler **noo**ern |
| dollars | **dollar** | **dol**lahr |
| pounds | **pund** | pewn |
| Can you change this into Norwegian kroner? | **Kan du veksle dette til norske kroner?** | kahn dew **vehk**shler **deh**ter til **no**shker **kroo**nerr |
| What's the exchange rate? | **Hva er vekslings-kursen?** | vaa ær **vehk**shlings-kewshern |

BANK—CURRENCY, see page 129

## Where ...?  *Hvor ...?*

| Where is the ...? | Hvor er ...? | voor ær |
|---|---|---|
| booking office | billettkontoret | billehtkoontöörer |
| duty (tax)-free shop | tax-free-butikken | tahks-free-bewtikkern |
| newsstand | aviskiosken | ahveeskhyoskern |
| restaurant | restauranten | rehstewrahngern |
| Where can I hire (rent) a car? | Hvor kan jeg leie en bil? | voor kahn yæi læier ehn beel |
| Where can I get a taxi? | Hvor kan jeg få tak i en drosje? | voor kahn yæi faw taak ee ehn drosher |
| How do I get to ...? | Hvordan kommer jeg til ...? | voo<sup>r</sup>dahn kommerr yæi til |
| Is there a bus into town? | Går det en buss inn til byen? | gawr deh ehn bewss in til bēwern |

## Hotel reservation  *Værelsesbestilling*

| Do you have a hotel guide (directory)? | Har du en hotell-fortegnelse? | haar dew ehn hootehl-fo<sup>r</sup>tæinerlser |
|---|---|---|
| Could you reserve a room for me? | Kan du bestille et rom til meg? | kahn dew berstiller eht room til mæi |
| in the centre | i sentrum | ee sehntrewm |
| near the airport | i nærheten av flyplassen | ee nærrhehtern ahv flewplahssern |
| near the railway station | i nærheten av jernbanestasjonen | ee nærrhehtern ahv yæ<sup>r</sup>nbaanerstah-shōonern |
| a single room | et enkeltrom | eht ehngkerltroom |
| a double room | et dobbeltrom | eht dobberltroom |
| not too expensive | ikke for dyrt | ikker for dēw<sup>r</sup>t |
| I'll be staying from ... to ... | Jeg kommer til å bli fra ... til ... | yæi kommerr til aw blee fraa ... til |
| Where is the hotel? | Hvor er hotellet? | voor ær hootehler |
| Can you recommend a guesthouse? | Kan du anbefale et pensjonat? | kahn dew ahnberfahler eht pahngshoonaat |
| Are there any flats (apartments) vacant? | Fins det noen ledige leiligheter? | finss deh nōoern læy-deeyer læilihehterr |
| Do you have a street map? | Har du et kart over byen? | haar dew eht kah<sup>r</sup>t awverr bēwern |

HOTEL/ACCOMMODATION, see page 22

## Car hire (rental) *Bilutleie*

To hire a car you must produce a valid driving licence, that you have held for at least one year, and your passport. Some firms set a minimum age of 21, others 23, 25 or 30 depending on the vehicle's engine size. Most companies require a deposit, but this is waived if you present a recognized credit card.

| | | |
|---|---|---|
| I'd like to hire (rent) a car. | **Jeg vil gjerne leie en bil.** | yæi vil yǣʳner læier ehn beel |
| small | **liten** | leetern |
| medium-sized | **mellomstor** | mehlomsto͞or |
| large | **stor** | sto͞or |
| automatic | **med automatgir** | meh(d) outoomaatgeer |
| I'd like it for ... | **Jeg vil ha den ...** | yæi vil haa dehn |
| a day | **en dag** | ehn daag |
| a week | **en uke** | ehn ēͧwker |
| Are there any weekend arrangements? | **Fins det noen weekend-tilbud?** | finss deh noͦoern veekehnd-tilbēͧwd |
| Do you have any special rates? | **Har dere noen spesialpriser?** | haar dāyrer noͦoern spehsseeaalpreesserr |
| What's the charge ...? | **Hvor mye koster det ...?** | voor mēͧwer kosterr deh |
| per day | **pr. dag** | pær daag |
| per week | **pr. uke** | pær ēͧwker |
| Is mileage included? | **Er kjørelengden inkludert?** | ær khūrrerlehngdern inklewdāyʳt |
| What's the charge per kilometre? | **Hvor mye koster det pr. kilometer?** | voor mēͧwer kosterr deh pær khilloomayterr |
| I'd like to leave the car in ... | **Jeg vil gjerne levere bilen tilbake i ...** | yæi vil yǣʳner lehvāyrer beelen tilbaaker ee |
| I'd like full insurance. | **Jeg vil ha full forsikring.** | yæi vil haa fewl foshikring |
| How much is the deposit? | **Hvor mye må jeg betale i depositum?** | voor mēͧwer maw yæi bertaaler ee dehpoͦo-ssitewm |
| I have a credit card. | **Jeg har kredittkort.** | yæi haar krehditkoʳt |
| Here's my driving licence. | **Her er førerkortet mitt.** | hǣr ær fūrrerkoʳter mit |

CAR, see page 75

## Taxi  *Drosje/Taxi*

All taxis are metered. When they are free, the "Taxi" sign on the roof is illuminated. Drivers rarely cruise for passengers and are not allowed to pick up customers within 100 metres of a taxi rank (those waiting at the rank have priority).

| Where can I get a taxi? | Hvor kan jeg få tak i en drosje? | voor kahn yæi faw taak ee ehn drosher |
|---|---|---|
| Where is the taxi rank (stand)? | Hvor er drosje-holdeplassen? | voor ær drosher-hollerplahssern |
| Could you get me a taxi? | Kan du skaffe meg en drosje? | kahn dew skahfer mæi ehn drosher |
| What's the fare to ...? | Hva koster det til ...? | vaa kosterr deh til |
| How far is it to ...? | Hvor langt er det til ...? | voor lahngt ær deh til |
| Take me to ... | Kjør meg til ... | khūrr mæi til |
| this address | denne adressen | dehner ahdrehssern |
| the airport | flyplassen | flēwplahssern |
| the town centre | sentrum | sehntrewm |
| the ... Hotel | ... hotell | ... hootehl |
| the railway station | jernbanestasjonen | yæᶺnbaanerstahshōōnern |
| Turn ... at the next corner. | Sving til ... ved neste gatehjørne. | sving til ... veh(d) nehster gaateryūrᶺner |
| right/left | høyre/venstre | hoyrer/vehnstrer |
| Go straight ahead. | Kjør rett frem. | khūrr reht frehm |
| Please stop here. | Stans her. | stahnss hær |
| I'm in a hurry. | Jeg har det travelt. | yæi haar deh traaverlt |
| Could you drive more slowly? | Kan du kjøre litt saktere? | kahn dew khūrrer lit sahkterrer |
| Could you help me carry my luggage? | Kan du hjelpe meg å bære bagasjen? | kahn dew yehlper mæi aw bǣrer bahgaashern |
| Could you wait for me? | Kan du vente på meg? | kahn dew vehnter paw mæi |
| I'll be back in 10 minutes. | Jeg er tilbake om 10 minutter. | yæi ær tilbaaker om 10 minnewter |
| How much do I owe you? | Hvor mye skylder jeg? | voor mēwer shewlerr yæi? |

# Hotel—Other accommodation

Early reservation and confirmation are essential in most major tourist centres during high season. Most towns and arrival points have a tourist information office (*turist-kontor*—tew**rist**koontoor) with an accommodation service (*innkvarterings-service*—**in**kvah<sup>r</sup>tayrings-surrviss); that's the place to go to if you're stuck for a room.

Although there is no official rating system, there are different classes of accommodation.

| | |
|---|---|
| **Hotell**<br>(hootehl) | Hotel; simple or deluxe, your room will be spotless. Facilities—and prices—vary across a wide range. Breakfast is usually included; half- and full-board accommodation is also available. |
| **Turisthotell**<br>(tewristhootehl) | Tourist hotel; high-standard resort establishments mostly located in the fjord country. Most offer only half- or full-board accommodation. |
| **Hytte**<br>(hewter) | Hut/Chalet; self-catering accommodation that can be hired by the week. |
| **Høyfjellshotell**<br>(hoyfyehls-hootehl) | Mountain hotel; first-class or deluxe establishments in winter-sports resorts. Most offer only full-board accommodation. |
| **Fjellstue**<br>(fyehlstewer) | Mountain inn; unpretentious but scrupulously clean establishments. Most offer only full-board accommodation, serving wholesome food. |
| **Pensjonat**<br>(pahngshoonaat) | Guesthouse; offers full- or half-board accommodation. |
| **Turisthytte**<br>(tewristhewter) | Tourist hut; simple hostels, some with a café in the grounds. Most bedrooms are for four to six people. |
| **Vandrerhjem**<br>(vahndrerryehm) | Youth and family hostel; for the backpack brigade. Sleeping arrangements may be in dormitories. |

## Checking in—Reception   *Ankomst – Resepsjon*

| My name is ... | **Mitt navn er ...** | mit nahvn ær |
|---|---|---|
| I have a reservation. | **Jeg har bestilt rom.** | yæi haar berstilt room |
| We've reserved 2 rooms. | **Vi har bestilt 2 rom.** | vee haar berstilt 2 room |
| Here's the confirmation. | **Her er bekreftelsen.** | hær ær berkrehfterlsern |
| Do you have any vacancies? | **Har dere noen ledige rom?** | haar dāyrer nōōern lāydeeyer room |
| I'd like a ... | **Jeg vil gjerne ha et ...** | yæi vil yǣ'ner haa eht |
| single room | **enkeltrom** | ehngkerltroom |
| double room | **dobbeltrom** | dobberltroom |
| We'd like a room ... | **Vi vil gjerne ha et rom ...** | vee vil yǣ'ner haa eht room |
| with twin beds | **med to senger** | meh(d) tōō sehngerr |
| with a double bed | **med dobbeltseng** | meh(d) dobberltsehng |
| with a bath | **med bad** | meh(d) baad |
| with a shower | **med dusj** | meh(d) dewsh |
| with a balcony | **med balkong** | meh(d) bahlkong |
| with a view | **med utsikt** | meh(d) ēwtsikt |
| at the front | **på forsiden** | paw fosheedern |
| at the back | **på baksiden** | paw baakseedern |
| It must be quiet. | **Det må være rolig.** | deh maw værer rōōli |
| What floor is it on? | **I hvilken etasje er det?** | ee vilkern ehtaasher ær deh |
| Is there ...? | **Fins det ...?** | finss deh |
| air conditioning | **air-conditioning** | āyr-kondisherning |
| a conference room | **konferanserom** | koonferrahngserroom |
| a gymnasium | **trimrom** | trimroom |
| heating | **varme** | vahrmer |
| hot water | **varmt vann** | vahrmt vahn |
| a laundry service · | **vaskeri-service** | vahskerree-sūrrviss |
| a radio/television in the room | **radio/TV på rommet** | raadyoo/tāyveh paw roommer |
| running water | **rennende vann** | rehnerner vahn |
| a sauna | **badstue/sauna** | bahstew/sounah |
| a swimming pool | **badebasseng** | baaderbahssehng |
| a private toilet | **toalett på rommet** | tooahleht paw roommer |

CHECKING OUT, see page 31

| Could you put an extra bed/a cot in the room? | **Kan du sette inn en ekstra seng/barne- seng på rommet?** | kahn dew sehter in ehn ehkstrah sehng/baa'ner- sehng paw roommer |

## How much? *Hvor mye?*

| How much does it cost ...? | **Hvor mye koster det ...?** | voor mēwer kosterr deh |
|---|---|---|
| per night | **pr. natt** | pær naht |
| per week | **pr. uke** | pær ēwker |
| for bed and break- fast | **for rom med frokost** | for room meh(d) frōokost |
| excluding meals | **uten måltider** | ēwtern mawlteederr |
| for full board (A.P.) | **for helpensjon** | for hāylpahngshōon |
| for half board (M.A.P.) | **for halvpensjon** | for hahlpahngshōon |
| Is ... included? | **Er ... inkludert?** | ær ... inklewdāy't |
| breakfast | **frokost** | frōokost |
| value-added tax (sales tax) | **moms** | moomss |
| Do you have reduced rates for the weekend? | **Er det lavere pris i helgen?** | ær deh laaverer preess ee hehlgern |
| Is there any reduc- tion for children? | **Er det reduksjon for barn?** | ær deh rehdewkshōon for baa'n |
| Do you charge for the baby? | **Koster det noe for babyen?** | kosterr deh nōoer for bāybyern |
| That's too expensive. | **Det er for dyrt.** | deh ær for dēw't |
| Do you have anything cheaper? | **Har dere noe rimeligere?** | haar dāyrer nōoer reemerleeyerrer |

## How long? *Hvor lenge?*

| We'll be staying ... | **Vi blir ...** | vee bleer |
|---|---|---|
| overnight only | **bare natten over** | baarer nahtern awverr |
| a few days | **et par dager** | eht pahr daagerr |
| until Sunday morning | **til søndag morgen** | til surndah(g) mawer'n |
| a week (at least) | **en uke (minst)** | ehn ēwker (minst) |
| I don't know yet. | **Jeg vet ikke ennå.** | yæi vāy't ikker ehnaw |

NUMBERS, see page 147/DAYS OF THE WEEK, see page 150

### Decision *Beslutning*

| | | |
|---|---|---|
| May I see the room? | **Kan jeg få se rommet?** | kahn yæi faw sāy roommer |
| That's fine. I'll take it. | **Det er bra. Jeg tar det.** | deh ær braa. yæi taar deh |
| No. I don't like it. | **Nei. Jeg liker det ikke.** | næi. yæi **lee**kerr deh ikker |
| It's too ... | **Det er for ...** | deh ær for |
| cold/hot | **kaldt/varmt** | kahlt/vahrmt |
| dark/small/noisy | **mørkt/lite/støyende** | murrkt/**lee**ter/**stoy**erner |
| I asked for a room with a bath. | **Jeg ba om et rom med bad.** | yæi baa om eht room meh(d) baad |
| Do you have anything ...? | **Har dere noe ...?** | haar **dāy**rer **nōo**er |
| better | **bedre** | **bāy**drer |
| bigger | **større** | **stū**rrer |
| cheaper | **rimeligere** | **ree**merlee**yerr**er |
| quieter | **roligere** | **rōo**lee**yerr**er |
| Do you have a room with a (better) view? | **Har dere et rom med (bedre) utsikt?** | haar **dāy**rer eht room meh(d) (**bāy**drer) **ēwt**sikt |

### Registration *Innskriving*

Upon arrival at a hotel or guesthouse you'll be asked to fill in a registration form (*meldeskjema*—**meh**lersh**āy**mah).

| | |
|---|---|
| **Etternavn/Fornavn** | Surname/First name |
| **Fødselsdato/Fødested** | Date of birth/Place of birth |
| **Yrke** | Occupation |
| **Hjemsted** | Home town |
| **Nasjonalitet** | Nationality |
| **Passnummer** | Passport No. |
| **Passutstedende myndighet** | Issuing passport authority |
| **Dato for ankomst til Skandinavia/Norge** | Date of arrival in Scandinavia/Norway |
| **Hensikt med oppholdet** | Reason for visit |
| **Underskrift** | Signature |

| What does this mean? | **Hva betyr dette?** | vaa bertewr dehter |

| **Kan jeg få se passet, takk?** | May I see your passport, please? |
| **Kan du fylle ut dette skjemæt?** | Would you mind filling in this form? |
| **Undertegn her.** | Please sign here. |
| **Hvor lenge kommer du til å bli?** | How long will you be staying? |

| What's my room number? | **Hvilket romnummer har jeg?** | vilkert roomnoommerr haar yæi |
| Will you have our luggage sent up? | **Kan jeg få brakt opp bagasjen?** | kahn yæi faw brahkt op bahgaashern |
| Where can I park my car? | **Hvor kan jeg parkere bilen?** | voor kahn yæi pahrkayrer beelern |
| Does the hotel have a garage? | **Har hotellet egen garasje?** | haar hootehlert aygern gahraasher |
| I'd like to leave this in the hotel safe. | **Jeg vil gjerne deponere dette i hotellets safe.** | yæi vil yærner dehpoonayrer dehter ee hootehlerss "safe" |

## Hotel staff  *Hotellpersonale*

| hall porter (bell captain) | **portier** | poortyay |
| maid | **værelsespike** | værerlserspeeker |
| manager | **direktør** | dirrehkturr |
| porter (bellman) | **bærer** | bærerr |
| receptionist | **resepsjonist** | rehsehpshoonist |
| switchboard operator | **sentralbordbetjent** | sehntraalboorbertyaynt |
| waiter | **kelner/servitør** | kehlnerr/særveeturr |
| waitress | **serveringsdame/servitør** | særvayringsdaamer/særveeturr |

To attract the attention of staff members say "Excuse me" —*Unnskyld* (**ewn**shewl).

TELLING THE TIME, see page 153

## General requirements  *Allmenne forespørsler*

| | | |
|---|---|---|
| The key to room ..., please. | **Nøkkelen til rom ..., takk.** | nurkerlern til room ... tahk |
| Could you wake me at ..., please? | **Kan du vekke meg kl. ...?** | kahn dew vehker mæi klokkern |
| When is breakfast/lunch/dinner served? | **Når serveres det frokost/lunsj/middag?** | nor særvayrerss deh frookost/lurnsh/middah(g) |
| May we have breakfast in our room, please? | **Kan vi få frokosten servert på rommet?** | kahn vee faw frookostern særvayrt paw roommer |
| Is there a bath on this floor? | **Fins det bad i denne etasjen?** | finss deh baad ee dehner ehtaashern |
| Where's the shaver socket (outlet)? | **Hvor er stikk-kontakten for barbermaskinen?** | voor ær stikkoontahktern for bahrbayrmahsheenern |
| Can you find me a ...? | **Kan du skaffe meg en ...?** | kahn dew skahfer mæi ehn |
| babysitter | **barnevakt** | baarnervahkt |
| secretary | **sekretær** | sehkrertær |
| typewriter | **skrivemaskin** | skreevermahsheen |
| May I have a/an/some ...? | **Kan jeg få ...?** | kahn yæi faw |
| bath towel | **et badehåndkle** | eht baaderhongkler |
| (extra) blanket | **et (ekstra) ullteppe** | eht (ehkstrah) ewltehper |
| hangers | **noen hengere** | nooern hengerer |
| hot-water bottle | **en varmeflaske** | ehn vahrmerflahsker |
| ice cubes | **noen isbiter** | nooern eesbeeterr |
| needle and thread | **nål og tråd** | nawl o(g) traw |
| (extra) pillow | **en (ekstra) pute** | ehn (ehkstrah) pewter |
| (extra) quilt | **en (ekstra) dyne** | ehn (ehkstrah) dewner |
| reading lamp | **en leselampe** | ehn laysserlahmper |
| soap | **en såpe** | ehn sawper |
| Where's the ...? | **Hvor er ...?** | voor ær |
| bathroom | **badet** | baader |
| dining room | **spisesalen** | speessersssaalern |
| emergency exit | **nødutgangen** | nurdewtgahngern |
| hairdresser | **frisørsalongen** | frissurshahlongern |
| lift (elevator) | **heisen** | hæissern |
| telephone | **telefonen** | tehlerfoonern |
| Where are the toilets? | **Hvor er toalettet?** | voor ær tooahlehter |

BREAKFAST, see page 38

## Telephone—Post (Mail) *Telefon − Post*

| | | |
|---|---|---|
| Can you get me Tromsø 123456? | **Kan jeg få Tromsø 123456?** | kahn yæi faw **troomsur** 123456 |
| Do you have any stamps? | **Har du frimerker?** | haar dew **freemærkerr** |
| Would you post (mail) this for me, please? | **Kan du poste dette for meg?** | kahn dew **poster dehter** for mæi |
| Are there any letters for me? | **Er det noen brev til meg?** | ær deh nōōern brāyv til mæi |
| Are there any messages for me? | **Er det noen beskjed til meg?** | ær deh nōōern bershāy til mæi |
| How much is my telephone bill? | **Hvor stor er telefon-regningen min?** | voor stōōr ær tehlerfōōn-ræiningern meen |

## Difficulties *Vanskeligheter*

| | | |
|---|---|---|
| The ... doesn't work. | **... virker ikke.** | ... virkerr ikker |
| air conditioning | **air-conditioningen** | āyr-kondisherningern |
| bidet | **bidetet** | beedāyer |
| heating | **varmen** | vahrmern |
| light | **lyset** | lēwsser |
| radio | **radioen** | raadyooern |
| refrigerator | **kjøleskapet** | khūrlerskaaper |
| television | **TV'en** | tāyvehern |
| The tap (faucet) is dripping. | **Kranen drypper.** | kraanern drewperr |
| There's no hot water. | **Det er ikke noe varmt vann.** | deh ær ikker nōōer vahrmt vahn |
| The washbasin (sink) is blocked. | **Vasken er tett.** | vahskern ær teht |
| The window is jammed. | **Vinduet sitter fast.** | vindewer sitterr fahst |
| The curtains are stuck. | **Gardinene henger fast.** | gahʳdeenerner hehngerr fahst |
| The bulb is burned out. | **Lyspæren har gått.** | lēwspærern haar got |
| My bed hasn't been made up. | **Sengen min er ikke blitt redd opp.** | sehngern meen ær ikker blit rehd op |

| The ... is/are broken. | ... er i stykker. | ... ær ee **stewker**r |
|---|---|---|
| blind | **rullegardinen** | rewlergah<sup>r</sup>deenern |
| lamp | **lampen** | **lahmp**ern |
| plug | **støpslet** | **sturp**shler |
| switch | **bryteren** | br**ew**terrern |
| venetian blinds | **persiennen** | pæshy**eh**nern |
| Can you get it repaired? | **Kan du få det reparert?** | kahn dew faw deh rehpahr**ay**<sup>r</sup>t |

## Laundry—Dry cleaner's   *Vask – Rens*

| I'd like these clothes ... | **Jeg vil gjerne ha disse klærne ...** | yæi vil y**ææ**<sup>r</sup>ner haa disser klæ<sup>r</sup>ner |
|---|---|---|
| dry-cleaned | **renset** | **rehn**sert |
| ironed | **strøket** | str**ur**kert |
| pressed | **presset** | **preh**ssert |
| washed | **vasket** | **vah**skert |
| I need them ... | **Jeg trenger dem ...** | yæi **treh**ngerr dehm |
| today | **i dag** | ee daag |
| tonight | **i kveld** | ee kvehl |
| tomorrow | **i morgen** | ee **maw**er<sup>r</sup>n |
| before Friday | **før fredag** | fürr fr**ay**dah(g) |
| Can you ... this? | **Kan du ... dette?** | kahn dew ... **deh**ter |
| mend/stitch | **lappe/sy sammen** | **lahp**er/s**ew** **sah**mern |
| Can you sew on this button? | **Kan du sy i denne knappen?** | kahn dew s**ew** ee **deh**ner **knah**pern |
| Can this be invisibly mended? | **Kan du kunststoppe dette?** | kahn dew **kewnst**stopper **deh**ter |
| Can you get this stain out? | **Kan du få bort denne flekken?** | kahn dew faw boo<sup>r</sup>t **deh**ner **fleh**kern |
| Is my laundry ready? | **Er vasken min klar?** | ær **vah**skern meen klaar |
| This isn't mine. | **Dette er ikke mitt.** | **deh**ter ær **ikk**er mit |
| There's something missing. | **Det er noe som mangler.** | deh ær n**oo**er som **mah**nglerr |
| There's one item missing. | **Det mangler et plagg.** | deh **mah**nglerr eht plahg |
| There's a hole in this. | **Det er gått hull i dette.** | deh ær got hewl ee **deh**ter |

## Hairdresser—Barber  *Damefrisør – Herrefrisør*

| | | |
|---|---|---|
| Is there a ... in the hotel? | Fins det en ... på hotellet? | finss deh ehn ... paw hoo**teh**ler |
| hairdresser beauty salon | frisørsalong skjønnhetssalong | fris**sūr**shahlong shurn**heht**ssahlong |
| Can I make an appointment for Thursday? | Kan jeg få time på torsdag? | kahn yæi faw **tee**mer paw **tawsh**dah(g) |
| Could you ... my hair, please? | Kan du ... håret mitt? | kah dew ... **haw**rer mit |
| blow-dry | føne | **fūr**ner |
| cut | klippe | **klip**per |
| dye | farge | **fahr**gger |
| tint | tone | **tōō**ner |
| with a fringe (bangs) | med lugg | meh(d) lewg |
| I'd like a/some ... | Jeg vil gjerne ha ... | yæi vil **yæ**<sup>r</sup>ner haa |
| colour rinse | fargeskylling | **fahr**ggershewling |
| face massage | ansiktsmassasje | **ahn**siktsmahsaasher |
| face pack | ansiktsmaske | **ahn**siktsmahsker |
| manicure | manikyr | mahni**kewr** |
| perm(anent wave) | permanent | pærmah**nehnt** |
| setting lotion | leggevann | **leh**gervahn |
| shampoo and set | vask og legg | vahsk o(g) lehg |
| I'd like a shampoo for ... hair. | Jeg vil ha en sjampo for ... hår. | yæi vil haa en **sham**poo for ... hawr |
| normal | normalt | noor**maalt** |
| dry | tørt | tur<sup>r</sup>t |
| greasy (oily) | fett | feht |
| Do you have a colour chart? | Har du et farge-kart? | haar dew eht **fahr**gger-kah<sup>r</sup>t |
| I don't want any hair spray. | Jeg vil ikke ha hårlakk. | yæi vil **ik**ker haa **haw**<sup>r</sup>lahk |
| I'd like a haircut. please. | Klipping, takk. | **klip**ping tahk |
| Don't cut it too short. | Klipp det ikke for kort. | klip deh **ik**ker for ko<sup>r</sup>t |
| A little more off the ... | Ta litt mer ... | taa lit mā̄yr |
| back | bak | baak |

DAYS OF THE WEEK, see page 150

| top | **på issen** | paw issern |
| neck | **i nakken** | ee nahkern |
| sides | **på sidene** | paw seederner |
| I'd like a shave. | **Barbering, takk.** | bahrbāyring tahk |
| Would you trim my ..., please? | **Kan du stusse ...?** | kahn dew **stewss**er |
| beard | **skjegget** | **sheh**ger |
| moustache | **barten** | **bah**ʳtern |
| sideboards (sideburns) | **kinnskjegget** | **khin**shehger |

.

## Checking out  *Avreise*

| May I have my bill, please? | **Kan jeg få regningen?** | kahn yæi faw **ræi**ningern |
| I'm leaving early in the morning. | **Jeg reiser i morgen tidlig.** | yæi ræisserr ee **maw**erʳn teeli |
| Please have my bill ready. | **Kan du ha regningen klar?** | kahn dew haa **ræi**ningern klaar |
| We'll be checking out around noon. | **Vi reiser ved tolv-tiden.** | vee ræisserr veh(d) **tol**-teedern |
| I must leave at once. | **Jeg må reise med én gang.** | yæi maw ræisser meh(d) āyn gahng |
| Can I pay by credit card? | **Kan jeg betale med kredittkort?** | kahn yæi ber**taal**er meh(d) **krehd**itkoʳt |
| I think there's a mistake in the bill. | **Jeg tror det er en feil på regningen.** | yæi trōōr deh ær ehn fæil paw **ræi**ningern |
| Can you get us a taxi? | **Kan du skaffe oss en drosje?** | kahn dew **skah**fer oss ehn **dros**her |
| Could you have our luggage brought down? | **Kan vi få båret ned bagasjen?** | kahn vee faw **baw**rert nāy(d) bah**gaa**shern |
| Here's the forwarding address. | **Her er etter-sendingsadressen.** | hāār ær **ehterr**-sehningsahdrehssern |
| You have my home address. | **Du har min hjem-stedsadresse.** | dew haar meen **yehm**-stāydsahdrehsser |
| It's been a very enjoyable stay. | **Det har vært et meget hyggelig opphold.** | deh haar væʳt eht **māy**gert **hew**gerli **op**hold |

## Camping *Camping*

Norway has some 1,500 registered camp sites, classified by one, two or three stars according to facilities offered. Many have cabins for rent. The camping season is normally from mid-May or early June to the end of August. Camping outside organized sites is permitted, but you will have to ask permission from the landowner or tenant.

| | | |
|---|---|---|
| Is there a camp site nearby? | **Er det en camping-plass i nærheten?** | ær deh ehn **kæm**ping-plahss ee **næ**rhehtern |
| Can we camp here? | **Kan vi campe her?** | kahn vee **kæm**per hær |
| Do you have room for a ...? | **Har dere plass til ...?** | haar **day**rer plahss til |
| tent | **et telt** | eht tehlt |
| caravan (trailer) | **en campingvogn** | ehn **kæm**pingvongn |
| What's the charge ...? | **Hva koster det ...?** | vaa **kos**terr deh |
| per day | **pr. dag** | pær daag |
| per person | **pr. person** | pær pæsh**oo**n |
| for a car | **for en bil** | for ehn beel |
| for a tent | **for et telt** | for eht tehlt |
| for a caravan | **for en campingvogn** | for ehn **kæm**pingvongn |
| Is there/Are there (a) ...? | **Fins det ...?** | finss deh |
| cabins | **hytter** | **hew**terr |
| cafeteria | **kafeteria** | kahfert**ay**reeah |
| cooking facilities | **kokemuligheter** | **koo**kermewlihehterr |
| drinking water | **drikkevann** | **drik**kervahn |
| electricity | **elektrisitet** | ehlehktrissit**ayt** |
| playground | **lekeplass** | **lay**kerplahss |
| restaurant | **restaurant** | rehstew**rahng** |
| shopping facilities | **shoppingmuligheter** | **shop**pingmewlihehterr |
| sauna | **badstue/sauna** | **bah**stew/**sou**nah |
| swimming pool | **badebasseng** | **baa**derbahssehng |
| Where are the showers/toilets? | **Hvor er dusjene/toalettet?** | voor ær **dew**sherner/tooahl**eh**ter |
| Where can I get butane gas? | **Hvor kan jeg få tak i butangass?** | voor kahn yæi faw taak ee bewt**aan**gahss |
| Is there a youth hostel nearby? | **Er det et vandrer-hjem i nærheten?** | ær deh eht **vahn**drerr-yehm ee **næ**rhehtern |

CAMPING EQUIPMENT, see page 106

# Eating out

The following rundown of places to eat will help you decide
what to look for.

**Bar**
(baar)

Only found in hotels in large towns.

**Bistro**
(**bis**troo)

Small, informal restaurant.

**Brasserie**
(brahsser**ree**)

Normally a simple but welcoming medium-
priced establishment.

**Fiskerestaurant**
(**fis**kerrehstewrahng)

Fish and seafood specialities.

**Gatekjøkken**
(**gaa**terkhurkern)

"Kitchen on the street". Serves fast food like
sausages and hamburgers with mashed
potatoes or chips (French fries); *pølse med
lompe*, frankfurter (wienerwurst) in a small
potato pancake; ice cream and soft drinks.

**Kafé**
(kah**fay**)

Café, also called *kaffebar* (**kah**ferbaar); serves
pastries and open sandwiches, coffee, tea and
soft drinks.

**Kafeteria**
(kahfert**ay**reeah)

Cafeteria.

**Konditori**
(koondit**too**ree)

Teashop (coffee shop); often a bakery, serving pastries, ice cream and sandwiches.

**Kro**
(kr**oo**)

Usually a road-side diner; mostly self service.

**Lunsjbar**
(**lurnsh**baar)

Lunch bar; usually self service.

**Pizzapub/-bar**
(**pit**sah"pub"/-baar)

Pizzas in different sizes or by the slice.

**Pølsebod**
(**purl**serbood)

Hot-dog stand.

**Restaurant**
(rehstew**rahng**)

Up-market establishment serving Norwegian
and international food with all the trimmings.

**Rotisserie**
(rotisser**ree**)

Specializes in grilled meat; can be expensive.

| Salatbar | Salad bar. |
|---|---|
| (sahl**aat**baar) | |
| Vertshus | Normally a small and informal neighbourhood |
| (væ$^r$tsh**ew**ss) | restaurant. |

## Eating habits  *Spisevaner*

Most Norwegians start the day with a meal that is somewhat more substantial than the typical continental breakfast—coffee or tea and open sandwiches (*smørbrød*). Country hotels and some places in the city offer breakfast buffets. Lunch is usually a fast-food snack, but many hotels and restaurants serve hot meals, and some feature a smorgasbord (*koldtbord*). Dinner is the main meal of the day.

Norwegians often drink plain tap water with their meals. Most restaurants are licensed to serve beer, and many offer wine, too; only the more elegant ones have a licence to serve spirits (liquor).

## Meal times  *Spisetider*

Breakfast ( *frokost*—**fro**okost) is usually served from 7 or 8 to 10 a.m. and is often included in the hotel arrangement.

Lunch (*lunsj*—lurnsh) is normally served from 11 a.m. and dinner (*middag*—**mid**dah[g]) from around 6 p.m. (much earlier in smaller establishments).

## Norwegian cuisine  *Det norske kjøkken*

Some of the best food in Norway comes from the sea, which is to be expected in one of the world's leading fishing nations. You can dine on lobster or salmon in elegant surroundings, or go down to the waterfront and buy a picnic lunch of prawns (shrimp) right off the trawler. But you'll also find beef, pork, mutton and game dishes.

Norwegians go berserk over berries. They love scouring the countryside in search of wild berries, to eat them fresh or in jams. The supreme delicacy is *multer med krem*, arctic cloud-berries with cream.

For those who enjoy a slice of bread with their meal, Norway offers a wide variety ranging from white, black, unleavened and wholemeal to crispy crackers and delicate wafers in all shapes and sizes. You'll probably see the full range at break-fast or when having *koldtbord*—the traditional self-service buffet.

| | |
|---|---|
| Hva skal det være? | What would you like? |
| Jeg kan anbefale dette. | I recommend this. |
| Hva vil du/dere* ha å drikke? | What would you like to drink? |
| Vi har ikke ... | We don't have ... |
| Vil du ha ...? | Would you like ...? |

### Hungry?  *Sulten?*

| | | |
|---|---|---|
| I'm hungry/I'm thirsty. | Jeg er sulten/ Jeg er tørst. | yæi ær **sewl**tern/ yæi ær tursht |
| Can you recommend a good restaurant? | Kan du anbefale en bra restaurant? | kahn dew **ahn**berfaaler ehn braa rehs**tew**rahng |
| Are there any inexpensive restaurants around here? | Fins det noen rimelige restauranter i nærheten? | finss deh **nōō**ern **ree**merleeyer rehs**tew**rahngerr ee **nær**hehtern |

If you want to be sure of getting a table in a popular restaurant, it's better to book in advance.

| | | |
|---|---|---|
| I'd like to reserve a table for 4. | Jeg vil gjerne bestille et bord til 4. | yæi vil **yǣ**rner ber**stiller** eht bōōr til 4 |
| We'll come at 8. | Vi kommer kl. 8. | vee **kommerr klokkern** 8 |

* *du* = singular, *dere* = plural

| Could we have a ...? | **Kan vi få et ...?** | kahn vee faw eht |
|---|---|---|
| table in the corner | **hjørnebord** | yūr'nerbōōr |
| table by the window | **vindusbord** | vindewsbōōr |
| table outside | **bord ute** | bōōr ēwter |

| Could we have a table in a ...? | **Kan vi få et bord ...?** | kahn vee faw eht bōōr |
|---|---|---|
| non-smoking area | **for ikke-røykere** | for ikker-roykerrer |
| smoking area | **for røykere** | for roykerrer |

## Asking and ordering  *Spørsmål og bestilling*

| Waiter/Waitress! | **Unnskyld! \*** | ewnshewl |
|---|---|---|
| We'd like to eat. | **Vi vil gjerne spise.** | vee vil yǣr'ner speesser |
| I'd like something to eat/drink. | **Jeg vil gjerne ha noe å spise/drikke.** | yæi vil yǣr'ner haa nōōer aw speesser/drikker |
| May I have the menu, please? | **Kan jeg få se spisekartet?** | kahn yæi faw sāy speesserkah'ter |
| Do you have a ...? | **Har dere en ...?** | haar dāyrer ehn |
| set menu | **meny** | mehnēw |
| children's menu | **barnemeny** | baa'nermehnēw |
| local speciality | **lokal spesialitet** | lookaal spehsseeahlitāyt |
| What do you recommend? | **Hva kan du anbefale?** | vaa kahn dew ahnberfaaler |
| Could we have a/ an ..., please? | **Kan vi få ...?** | kahn vee faw |
| ashtray | **et askebeger** | eht ahskerbāygerr |
| cup | **en kopp** | ehn kop |
| extra chair | **en stol til** | ehn stōōl til |
| fork | **en gaffel** | ehn gahferl |
| glass | **et glass** | eht glass |
| knife | **en kniv** | ehn kneev |
| napkin (serviette) | **en serviett** | ehn sehrvyeht |
| plate | **en tallerken** | ehn tahlærkern |
| spoon | **en skje** | ehn shāy |
| May I have some ...? | **Kan jeg få litt ...?** | kahn yæi faw lit |
| bread | **brød** | brūr |
| butter | **smør** | smurr |

---

\* *Unnskyld*: Excuse me

NUMBERS, see page 147

| oil/vinegar | olje/eddik | olyer/ehdik |
| salt/pepper | salt/pepper | sahlt/pehperr |
| seasoning | krydder | krewderr |
| sugar | sukker | sookkerr |

Some useful expressions for those with special requirements:

| I'm on a special diet. | Jeg holder diett. | yæi hollerr deeyeht |
| I mustn't eat food containing ... | Jeg kan ikke spise mat som inneholder ... | yæi kahn ikker speesser maat som innerhollerr |
| fat/flour | fett/mel | feht/māyl |
| salt/sugar | salt/sukker | sahlt/sookkerr |
| Do you have any ... dishes? | Har dere retter med ...? | haar dāyrer rehterr meh(d) |
| low-fat | lavt fettinnhold | laavt fehtinhol |
| low-cholesterol | lavt kolesterolinnhold | laavt koolehsterrōōlinhol |
| Is there alcohol in it? | Er det alkohol i det? | ær deh ahlkoohōōl ee deh |
| Do you have ... for diabetics? | Har dere ... for diabetikere? | haar dāyrer ... for deeahbāytikkerrer |
| cakes | kaker | kaakerr |
| a fruit juice | en juice | ehn yēwss |
| a special menu | en spesialmeny | ehn spehsseeaalmehnēw |
| Do you have any vegetarian dishes? | Har dere noen vegetariske retter? | haar dāyrer nōōern vehgertaarisker rehterr |
| Could I have ... instead of dessert? | Kan jeg få ... i stedet for dessert? | kahn yæi faw ... ee stāyder for dehssǣr |
| Can I have an artificial sweetener? | Kan jeg få et søtningsmiddel? | kahn yæi faw eht sūrtningsmidderl |

And ...

| I'd like some more. | Jeg vil gjerne ha litt mer. | yæi vil yǣʳner haa lit māyr |
| Can I have more ...? | Kan jeg få litt mer ...? | kahn yæi faw lit māyr |
| Just a small portion. | Bare en liten porsjon. | baarer ehn leetern pooshōōn |
| Nothing more, thanks. | Takk, ikke mer. | tahk ikker māyr |

## Breakfast *Frokost*

Most hotels offer a continental breakfast as well as a buffet, consisting of a variety of breads, butter, cheese, cold cuts, eggs, herring, jam, cereals, fruit juice, milk, coffee and tea.

| | | |
|---|---|---|
| I'd like breakfast, please. | **Jeg vil gjerne ha frokost.** | yæi vil yæᵣner haa froökost |
| I'll have a/an/some ... | **Jeg tar ...** | yæi taar |
| bacon and eggs | **egg og bacon** | ehg o(g) bæikern |
| boiled egg | **et kokt egg** | eht kookt ehg |
| soft/hard | **bløtkokt/hardkokt** | blūrtkookt/haarkookt |
| cereal | **frokostblanding** | froökostblahning |
| cheese | **ost** | oost |
| eggs | **egg** | ehg |
| fried egg | **et speilegg** | eht spæilehg |
| scrambled eggs | **eggerøre** | ehgerrūrer |
| fruit juice | **juice** | yēwss |
| grapefruit | **grapefrukt-** | grāypfrewkt- |
| orange | **appelsin-** | ahperlseen- |
| ham and eggs | **egg og skinke** | ehg o(g) shingker |
| jam | **syltetøy** | sewltertoy |
| marmalade | **appelsinmarmelade** | ahperlseenmahrmerlaader |
| omelet | **omelett** | oomerleht |
| porridge | **grøt** | grūrt |
| roll | **et rundstykke** | eht rewnstewker |
| toast | **litt ristet brød** | lit ristert brūr |
| yoghurt | **en yoghurt** | ehn yogewᵣt |
| May I have some ...? | **Kan jeg få ...?** | kahn yæi faw |
| bread | **litt brød** | lit brūr |
| butter | **litt smør** | lit smurr |
| (hot) chocolate | **(varm) sjokolade** | (vahrm) shookoolaader |
| coffee | **kaffe** | kahfer |
| decaffeinated | **koffeinfri** | koffeheenfree |
| black | **svart** | svahᵣt |
| with cream | **med fløte** | meh(d) flūrter |
| honey | **litt honning** | lit honning |
| (cold/hot) milk | **litt (kald/varm) melk** | lit (kahl/vahrm) mehlk |
| pepper | **litt pepper** | lit pehperr |
| salt | **litt salt** | lit sahlt |
| tea | **te** | tāy |
| with milk/lemon | **med melk/sitron** | meh(d) mehlk/sitroön |
| (hot) water | **litt (varmt) vann** | lit (vahrmt) vahn |

### What's on the menu? *Hva står på menyen?*

Many restaurants display their menu (*spisekart/meny*) outside. In addition to the à la carte menu, some restaurants offer a dish of the day (*dagens rett*).

Under the headings below you'll find alphabetical lists of dishes that might be offered on a Norwegian menu, with their English equivalent. You can simply show the book to the waiter. If you want some cheese, for instance, let *him* point to what's available on the appropriate list. Use pages 36 and 37 for ordering in general.

|  | page |  |
|---|---|---|
| Open sandwiches | 41 | Smørbrød |
| Smorgasbörd | 41 | Koldtbord |
| Starters (Appetizers) | 43 | Forretter |
| Soups | 44 | Supper |
| Salads | 44 | Salater |
| Egg dishes | 45 | Eggeretter |
| Fish and seafood | 45 | Fisk og skalldyr |
| Meat | 47 | Kjøtt |
| Game and poultry | 50 | Vilt og fugl |
| Vegetables | 51 | Grønnsaker |
| Potatoes, rice, pasta | 52 | Poteter, ris, pasta |
| Sauces | 52 | Sauser |
| Cheese | 53 | Ost |
| Fruit | 54 | Frukt |
| Dessert | 55 | Dessert |
| Drinks | 56 | Drikkevarer |
| Nonalcoholic drinks | 59 | Alkoholfrie drikker |
| Snacks | 62 | Småretter |
| Pastries and cakes | 63 | Bakverk og kaker |
| Picnic | 64 | Picnic |

## Reading the menu   Å lese spisekartet

| Dagens rett/suppe/ grønnsaker | Dish/Soup/Vegetables of the day |
|---|---|
| Barnemeny | Children's menu |
| Vegetar ... | Vegetarian ... |
| Kjøkkensjefen anbefaler ... | The chef proposes ... |
| Som vår kjøkkensjef liker det | As our chef likes it |
| (Husets) Spesialiteter | Specialities (of the house) |
| Serveres/Servert med ... | Served with ... |
| Velg mellom ... | Choice of ... |
| Valgfritt tilbehør | Choice of side dishes |
| På bestilling | Made on request |
| ... med ass. ... | ... with assorted ... |
| ... m/ ... | ... with ... |
| ... inkl. | ... included |

| | | |
|---|---|---|
| dessert | dehss**ǣr** | dessert |
| drikker | **drikk**err | drinks |
| fisk | fisk | fish |
| forretter | **for**rehterr | starters (appetizers) |
| frukt | frewkt | fruit |
| fugl | fēwl | poultry |
| hovedretter | **hōō**verdrehterr | main courses (entrees) |
| is(krem) | **ees**(krāym) | ice cream |
| kaker | **kaa**kerr | pastries/cakes |
| kjøtt | khurt | meat |
| koldtbord | **kolt**bōōr | smorgasbord |
| leskedrikk | **lehsk**erdrik | soft drinks |
| ost | oost | cheese |
| pastaretter | **pahs**tahrehterr | pasta dishes |
| risretter | **rees**rehterr | rice dishes |
| salatbar | **sah**laatbaar | salad bar |
| smørbrød | **smurr**brūr | open sandwiches |
| supper | **sew**perr | soups |
| varme smørbrød | **vahr**mer **smurr**brūr | sandwiches with hot meat, fish, etc. |
| varmretter | **vahrm**rehterr | hot dishes |
| vilt | vilt | game |

## Open sandwiches *Smørbrød*

*Smørbrød* means bread and butter, which is quite an understatement when you consider Scandinavia's reputation for elaborate open sandwiches. Almost anything may turn up on one of these appetizing *smørbrød*, most of which are served cold. Two or three open sandwiches will generally satisfy most appetites. *Landgang* (**lahn**gahng), literally "gangway", is a halved French loaf with several different toppings (fish, egg, meat, cheese, etc.).

| | | |
|---|---|---|
| I'd like an open sandwich with ... | **Jeg vil gjerne ha et smørbrød med ...** | yæi vil yæ<sup>r</sup>ner haa eht smurrbrur meh(d) |

| | |
|---|---|
| **egg og ansjos** (ehg o[g] ahngsh**ōo**ss) | sliced egg and marinated sprats |
| **italiensk salat** (eetahlee**ay**nsk sah**laat**) | "Italian" salad; sliced ham, apple, potato, onion, carrot, peas in mayonnaise dressing |
| **reker** (r**ay**kerr) | prawns (shrimp) with mayonnaise |
| **rekesalat** (r**ay**kersahlaat) | prawn (shrimp) salad; prawns, apple, celery, sometimes in a tomato dressing, sometimes in a mayonnaise dressing |
| **roastbiff** (rostbif) | sliced roast beef, often served with a herb-flavoured mayonnaise sauce |
| **røkelaks** (r**ū**rkerlahkss) | sliced smoked salmon, often served with scrambled eggs |
| **sildesalat** (sillersahlaat) | herring salad; pickled herring, potato, beetroot, apple, egg, onion in cream-and-beetroot dressing |

## Smorgasbord *Koldtbord*

The Swedish name, *smørgåsbord* ("sandwich table"), is better known than its Norwegian equivalent, *koldtbord* ("cold table"). Some restaurants and mountain hotels specialize in this bountiful self-service buffet. A scaled-down version of the *koldtbord* is often prepared in Norwegian homes for special occasions, particularly during the Christmas season.

Dishes may vary according to season, but there is always a variety of fish (marinated and smoked herring, herring salads, cold salmon, trout or halibut in aspic) and seafood, meat (cold cuts, pâtés, hot sausages, meatballs), vegetables, egg dishes, salads, fruit, cheese and bread.

One of the mainstays of *koldtbord*, particularly in summer and early autumn, is *spekemat* (**spay**kermaat) or cured meat. Norway has a long tradition of curing meat, originating from the time when there was no other way of conserving food. Usually *spekemat* is eaten with scrambled eggs and a crisp, paper-thin barley-and-wheat or barley-and-rye cracker called *flatbrød* (**flaht**brūr).

Another speciality that may be found among *koldtbord* dishes is *rømmegrøt* (**rur**mergrūrt), a tasty, refreshing and filling porridge made from thick sour cream, flour and milk, which is topped with butter, sugar and cinnamon.

Start with the fish dishes. Use a fresh plate for meat, salad and egg dishes, and another for cheese and fruit. Don't hurry yourself; the whole point of *koldtbord* is to enjoy a large meal with as many trips back to the buffet as desired, and all at a leisurely pace.

Aquavit and beer go particularly well with this spread. It is rare to drink wine with *koldtbord*.

| | | |
|---|---|---|
| I'd like to try some Norwegian specialities. | **Jeg vil gjerne prøve noen norske spesialiteter.** | yæi vil yǣ<sup>r</sup>ner prūrver nōōern noshker speh-sseeahlitāyterr |
| What do you recommend? | **Hva anbefaler du?** | vaa **ahn**berfaalerr dew |
| **fenalår**<br>(fāynahlawr) | cured leg of mutton | |
| **spekepølse**<br>(spāykerpurlser) | slices of smoked, cured sausage made from different meats that range in colour from pinkish to black | |
| **spekeskinke**<br>(spāykershingker) | smoked, cured ham, as a main dish often served with thick sour cream (*rømme*) and boiled potatoes | |

## Starters (Appetizers) *Forretter*

Except on special occasions, Norwegians are usually content with soup as a starter. In more elegant restaurants, however, there will be a choice of appetizing hors d'œuvres; maybe one of the dishes from the *koldtbord*, a mixed salad or a selection of scaled-down *smørbrød* called *snitter* (**snitt**err).

| | | |
|---|---|---|
| I'd like a starter (an appetizer). | **Jeg vil gjerne ha en forrett.** | yæi vil yæ<sup>r</sup>ner haa ehn forreht |
| **blåskjell** | **blawshehl** | mussels |
| **froskelår** | **froskerlawr** | frogs' legs |
| **gåselever** | **gawsserlehverr** | goose liver |
| **hummer** | **hoommerr** | lobster |
| **kaviar** | **kahveeaar** | caviar |
| **krabbe** | **krahber** | crab |
| **laks** | **lahkss** | salmon |
|   gravet |   graavert |   cured |
|   røkt/røkelaks |   rurkt/rūrkerlahkss |   smoked |
| **rekecocktail** | **rāykerkoktæil** | prawn (shrimp) cocktail |
| **(speke)skinke** | **(spāyker)shingker** | (smoked, cured) ham |
| **skinke med melon** | **shingker meh(d) mehlōōn** | ham with melon |
| **snegler** | **snæilerr** | snails |
| **sursild** | **sēwshil** | marinated herring |
| **tomatjuice** | **toomaatyēwss** | tomato juice |
| **østers** | **urstersh** | oysters |
| **ål i gelé** | **awl ee shehlāy** | jellied eel |

| | |
|---|---|
| **fiskekabaret** (fiskerkahbahrāy) | assorted seafood and vegetables in aspic, usually served with bread, butter and a mayonnaise sauce |
| **gravlaks** (graavlahkss) | salt-and-sugar-cured salmon (same as *gravet laks*), often served with a sweet mustard-and-dill sauce |
| **rakørret** (raakurreht) | specially processed, salt-cured and fermented trout, often served with small potatoes, sour cream and *flatbrød* |
| **(ferske) reker** ([fæshker] rāykerr) | (unshelled) prawns (shrimp), usually served with lemon, toast and butter |
| **sildebrikke** (sillerbrikker) | a variety of herring, served with bread and butter |
| **sjømannsskjell** (shūrmahnssshehl) | mussels simmered in white wine with onion and parsley |

## Soups *Supper*

| | | |
|---|---|---|
| I'd like some soup. | **Jeg vil gjerne ha en suppe.** | yæi vil yǣ<sup>r</sup>ner haa ehn sewper |
| What do you recommend? | **Hva foreslår du?** | vaa fawrerslawr dew |

| | | |
|---|---|---|
| **aspargessuppe** | ahspahrggerssewper | asparagus soup |
| **betasuppe** | bāytahsewper | thick meat-and-vegetable soup |
| **blomkålsuppe** | blomkawlsewper | cauliflower soup |
| **buljong** | bewlyong | consommé |
| **fiskesuppe** | fiskersewper | fish soup |
| **fransk løksuppe** | frahnsk lūrksewper | French onion soup |
| **grønnsaksuppe** | grurnsaaksewper | vegetable soup |
| **gul ertesuppe** | gewl æ<sup>r</sup>tersewper | yellow pea soup |
| **hummersuppe** | hoommerrsewper | lobster soup |
| **kjøttsuppe** | khurtsewper | meat soup |
| **løksuppe** | lūrksewper | onion soup |
| **neslesuppe** | nehshlersewper | nettle soup |
| **oksehalesuppe** | ookserhahlersewper | oxtail soup |
| **rekesuppe** | rāykersewper | prawn (shrimp) soup |
| **sellerisuppe** | sehlerreesewper | celery soup |
| **sjampinjongsuppe** | shahmpinyongsewper | button mushroom soup |
| **soppsuppe** | sopsewper | field mushroom soup |
| **tomatsuppe** | toomaatsewper | tomato soup |

## Salads *Salater*

Many restaurants offer an appetizing self-service salad bar (*salatbar*—sah**laat**baar).

| | | |
|---|---|---|
| What salads do you have? | **Hva slags salater har dere?** | vaa shlahkss sahlaater haar dāyrer |

| | |
|---|---|
| **agurksalat** (ahgewrksahlaat) | cucumber salad, usually with a vinegar-sugar dressing |
| **blandet salat** (blahnert sahlaat) | mixed salad (lettuce, tomatoes, cucumber, etc., with oil-and-vinegar dressing); accompanies many main courses |
| **størje-/tunfisksalat** (sturryer-/tēwnfisk-sahlaat) | tuna fish salad—Norwegian version of salad Niçoise |
| **skalldyrsalat** (skahldēwrsahlaat) | seafood salad (mostly mussels and prawns, but also lobster or crab) |

## Egg dishes   *Eggeretter*

| | | |
|---|---|---|
| eggerøre | ehgerrurrer | scrambled eggs |
| forlorent egg | forloorernt ehg | poached egg |
| omelett | oomerleht | omelet |
|   med kryddergrønt | meh(d) krewderr-grurnt | with fine herbs |
|   med ost | meh(d) oost | with cheese |
|   med skinke | meh(d) shingker | with ham |
|   med sjampinjong | meh(d) shahmpinyong | with button mush-rooms |
|   med sopp | meh(d) sop | with mushrooms |
|   med -stuing | meh(d) -stewing | with ... sauce |
| pannekake | pahnerkaaker | pancake |
| speilegg/stekt egg | spæilehg/stehkt ehg | fried egg |

## Fish and seafood (shellfish)   *Fisk og skalldyr*

Fish plays no less an important part in the diet of Norwegians today than it did a thousand years ago. Nowadays, however, visitors will be offered a much wider choice of fish and seafood, prepared in a variety of imaginative and interesting ways.

| What kind of ...<br>do you have? | **Hva slags ... har<br>dere?** | vaa shlahkss ... haar<br>dayrer |
|---|---|---|
| fish | **fisk** | fisk |
| seafood (shellfish) | **skalldyr** | skahldewr |
| **abbor** | ahbor | perch |
| **ansjos** | ahngshooss | marinated sprats |
| **blekksprut** | blehksprewt | octopus |
| **blåskjell** | blawshehl | mussels |
| **brasme** | brahsmer | bream |
| **brisling** | brishling | sprat/brisling |
| **flyndre** | flewndrer | flounder |
| **gjedde** | yehder | pike |
| **hellefisk** | hehlerfisk | halibut |
| **hummer** | hoommerr | lobster |
| **hvitting** | vitting | whiting |
| **hyse** | hewsser | haddock |
| **kamskjell** | kahmshehl | scallop |
| **karpe** | kahrper | carp |
| **klippfisk** | klipfisk | salted and dried cod |
| **knurr** | knewr | gurnard |

| kolje | kolyer | haddock |
| krabbe | krahber | crab |
| kreps | krehpss | freshwater crayfish |
| kveite | kvæiter | halibut |
| lake | laaker | burbot |
| laks | lahkss | salmon |
| lysing | lēwssing | hake |
| makrell | mahkrehl | mackerel |
| piggvar | pigvaar | turbot |
| regnbueørret | ræinbēwerurreht | rainbow trout |
| reker | rāykerr | prawns (shrimp) |
| rogn | rongn | roe |
| rødspette | rūrspehter | plaice |
| røye | royer | char |
| sardell | sah⸢dehl | anchovy |
| sardin | sah⸢deen | sardine |
| sei | sæi | coalfish (pollack) |
| sik | seek | whitefish |
| sild | sil | herring |
| sjøtunge | shūrtoonger | sole |
| sjøørret | shūrurreht | sea trout |
| slettvar | shlehtvaar | brill |
| steinbit | stæinbeet | catfish |
| stør | stūrr | sturgeon |
| størje | sturryer | tuna |
| torsk | toshk | cod |
| tunfisk | tēwnfisk | tuna |
| uer | ēwehr | rosefish |
| ørret | urreht | trout |
| østers | urstersh | oysters |
| åbor | awboor | perch |
| ål | awl | eel |

| au gratin | gratinert | grahtināy⸢t |
| boiled | kokt | kookt |
| breaded | griljert/panert | grilyāy⸢t/pahnāy⸢t |
| deep fried | fritert/frityrstekt | fritāy⸢t/fritēwshtehkt |
| fried | stekt | stehkt |
| grilled (broiled) | grillet/grillstekt | grillert/grilstehkt |
| marinated | marinert | mahrināy⸢t |
| poached | pochert/kokt | pooshāy⸢t/kookt |
| simmered | lettkokt | lehtkookt |
| smoked | røkt | rurkt |
| steamed | dampet/dampkokt | dahmpert/dahmpkookt |

| | | |
|---|---|---|
| **fiskeboller /**<br>**fiskepudding**<br>(fiskerbollerr /<br>fiskerpewding) | fish balls / fish pudding; served poached and<br>laid in a béchamel or shrimp sauce, or fried,<br>with boiled potatoes and vegetables | |
| **fritert flyndrefilet**<br>(fritay$^r$t flewndrerfillay) | (deep) fried fillets of flounder; usually served<br>with boiled potatoes or chips (French fries), a<br>cucumber or mixed salad and a herb-flavoured<br>mayonnaise sauce | |
| **gravet laks / gravlaks**<br>(graavert lahkss /<br>graavlahkss) | salt-and-sugar-cured salmon flavoured with<br>dill; often served with sliced potatoes in a<br>white sauce | |
| **kokt torsk**<br>(kookt toshk) | poached cod; normally served with cod liver,<br>boiled potatoes, lemon and melted butter | |
| **kokt / dampet ørret**<br>(kookt / dahmpert<br>urrert) | poached trout; usually served with boiled<br>potatoes, hollandaise sauce or thick sour<br>cream and cucumber salad | |
| **lutefisk**<br>(lewterfisk) | stockfish soaked in lye; simmered and served<br>with boiled potatoes, peas, mustard, pepper<br>and melted butter or dripping or alternatively<br>a béchamel sauce (a traditional Christmas<br>dish) | |
| **seibiff med løk**<br>(sæibif meh[d] lurk) | fried fillets of coalfish (pollack) with onions,<br>served with boiled potatoes and vegetables or<br>salad | |
| **spekesild**<br>(spaykersil) | salted herring; served with boiled potatoes,<br>onion rings, pickled beetroot, butter and often<br>cabbage or mashed swedes (rutabaga) | |

## Meat  *Kjøtt*

| | | |
|---|---|---|
| What kind of meat<br>is this? | **Hva slags kjøtt er**<br>**dette?** | vaa shlahkss khurt ær<br>dehter |
| beef | **oksekjøtt** | ookserkhurt |
| lamb | **lammekjøtt** | lahmerkhurt |
| mutton | **fårekjøtt** | fawrerkhurt |
| pork | **svinekjøtt** | sveenerkhurt |
| veal | **kalvekjøtt** | kahlverkhurt |
| I'd like some ... | **Jeg vil gjerne ha ...** | yæi vil yæ$^r$ner haa |
| **biff** | bif | beef steak |
| **frikadeller** | frikahdehlerr | meat balls |
| **fårestek** | fawrerstayk | roast leg of mutton<br>or lamb |

| | | |
|---|---|---|
| kalvebrissel | kahlverbrisserl | sweetbread |
| kalverlever | kahlverlehverr | calf's liver |
| kalvemedaljonger | kahlvermehdahlyongerr | small round fillets of veal |
| kalvenyrestek | kahlvernēwrerstāyk | roast loin of veal |
| karbonade(kake) | kahrboonaader(kaaker) | hamburger |
| kjøttboller | khurtbollerr | meat balls |
| kjøttkaker | khurtkaakerr | small hamburgers |
| kjøttpudding | khurtpewding | meat loaf |
| -knoke | -knōōker | ... bone |
| -kotelett | -kotterleht | ... chop |
| lammebog | lahmerbōōg | shoulder of lamb |
| lammebryst | lahmerbrewst | brisket of lamb |
| lammelår | lahmerlawr | leg of lamb |
| lammesadel | lahmersaaderl | saddle of lamb |
| lammestek | lahmerstāyk | roast lamb |
| -lever | -lehverr | ... liver |
| lungemos | loongermōōs | minced pork lungs and onions |
| medisterkaker | mehdisterrkaakerr | small pork-and-veal hamburgers |
| medisterpølse | mehdisterrpurlser | pork-and-veal sausage |
| mørbradstek | mūrrbraadstāyk | roast sirloin |
| -nyrer | -nēwrerr | ... kidneys |
| oksebryst | ookserbrewst | brisket of beef |
| oksefilet | ookserfillāy | fillet of beef |
| oksekam | ookserkahm | loin |
| okserulader | ookserrewlaaderr | braised beef rolls |
| oksestek | ookserstāyk | roast beef |
| pølse | purlser | sausage |
| -ragu | -rahgēw | ... ragout |
| roastbiff | rostbif | roast beef |
| skinke | shingker | ham |
|   kokt |   kookt |   boiled |
|   røkt |   rurkt |   smoked |
| spekeskinke | spāykershingker | smoked, cured ham |
| -stek | -stāyk | roast ... |
| svinefilet | sveenerfillāy | fillet of pork |
| svinekam | sveenerkahm | loin of pork |
| svineribbe | sveenerribber | sparerib |
| svinestek | sveenerstāyk | roast pork |
| svor | svōōr | crackling |
| sylte | sewlter | brawn (headcheese) |
| tartarbiff | tahˈtaarbif | steak tartare |
| T-benstek | tāy-bāynstāyk | T-bone steak |
| -tunge | -toonger | ... tongue |
| wienerschnitzel | veenershnitserl | breaded veal escalope |

| boiled | **kokt** | kookt |
|---|---|---|
| braised | **braisert** | brahssāy<sup>r</sup>t |
| breaded | **griljert/panert** | grilyāy<sup>r</sup>t/pahnāy<sup>r</sup>t |
| fried | **stekt** | stehkt |
| grilled (broiled) | **grillet/grillstekt** | grillert/grilstehkt |
| roast | **ovnsstekt** | ovnsstehkt |
| sautéed | **sautert/brunet** | sotāy<sup>r</sup>t/brēwnert |
| smoked | **røkt** | rurkt |
| stuffed | **fylt** | fewlt |
| whole roasted | **helstekt** | hāylstehkt |
| underdone (rare) | **råstekt** | rawstehkt |
| medium | **medium stekt** | māydiewm stehkt |
| well-done | **godt stekt** | got stehkt |

**benløse fugler**
(bāynlürsser fēwlerr)
fried rolled slices of veal or beef stuffed with forcemeat, served with gravy, potatoes and vegetables or salad

**biff med løk**
(bif meh[d] lūrk)
thick beef steak topped with fried onion, usually served with chips (French fries) and salad

**fårikål**
(fawrikawl)
mutton or lamb in cabbage stew, cooked in a big pot and served with boiled potatoes (a national dish)

**kjøttkaker med løk**
(khurtkaakerr meh[d] lūrk)
small hamburgers with fried onions, boiled potatoes and vegetables

**lapskaus**
(lahpskouss)
a tasty stew that comes either "brown" (*brun* or *bifflapskaus*), with diced fried beef, potatoes and onions, or "white" (*lys* or *saltkjøttlapskaus*), with diced, salted boiled meat (usually pork), potatoes and different root vegetables; traditionally eaten with *flatbrød*

**pinnekjøtt**
(pinnerkhurt)
salted and dried ribs of mutton steamed on twigs; usually served with boiled potatoes and mashed swedes (rutabaga) or as a *koldtbord* dish (a Christmas speciality)

**stekt ribbe/juleribbe**
(stehkt ribber/yēwlerribber)
roast spareribs; usually served with sweet-and-sour cabbage stew and boiled potatoes or as a *koldtbord* dish (a Christmas speciality)

## Game and poultry   *Vilt og fugl*

Game is normally served with a rich and heavy cream sauce, boiled potatoes, vegetables and cranberries.

| I'd like some game. | **Jeg vil gjerne ha en viltrett.** | yæi vil yǣᵣner haa ehn viltreht |
|---|---|---|
| What poultry dishes do you serve? | **Hva slags fugleretter har dere?** | vah shlahkss fewlerrehterr haar dǟyrer |

| | | |
|---|---|---|
| **and** | ahn | duck |
| **bekkasin** | berkahseen | snipe |
| **broiler** | broylerr | chicken |
| **dyrestek** | dēwrerstāȳk | roast venison |
| **elg** | ehlg | elk |
| **elgbiff** | ehlgbif | elk steak |
| **elgfilet** | ehlgfillāȳ | fillet of elk |
| **elgstek** | ehlgstāȳk | roast elk |
| **fasan** | fahssaan | pheasant |
| **gås** | gawss | goose |
| **hane** | haaner | cock |
| **hare** | haarer | hare |
| **harestek** | haarerstāȳk | roast hare |
| **hjort** | yoᵗt | deer |
| **hjortesadel** | yoᵣtersaaderl | saddle of deer |
| **høne** | hūrner | hen |
| **jerpe** | yærper | hazelhen |
| **kalkun** | kahlkēwn | turkey |
| **kanin** | kahneen | rabbit |
| **kylling** | khewling | chicken |
| **orre / orrfugl** | orrer / orfewl | black grouse |
| **rapphøne** | rahphūrner | partridge |
| **reinsdyr / rensdyr** | ræinsdēwr / rāȳnsdēwr | reindeer |
| **reinsdyrmedaljonger** | ræinsdēwrmehdahl-yongerr | small, round fillets of reindeer |
| **reinsdyrstek** | ræinsdēwshtāȳk | roast reindeer |
| **rugde** | rewgder | woodcock |
| **rype** | rēwper | ptarmigan |
| **rådyr** | rawdēwr | venison |
| **rådyrsadel** | rawdēwshaaderl | saddle of venison |
| **rådyrstek** | rawdēwshtāȳk | roast venison |
| **tiur** | teeēwr | woodgrouse (caper-caillie) |
| **vaktel** | vahkterl | quail |
| **villand** | vilahn | wild duck |
| **årfugl** | awrfēwl | black grouse |

### Vegetables *Grønnsaker*

| Could I have some vegetables? | **Kan jeg få litt grønnsaker?** | kahn yæi faw lit **grurnsaakerr** |
|---|---|---|
| **agurk** | ahgewrk | cucumber |
| **artisjokker** | ah'tishokkerr | artichokes |
| **asparges** | ahspahrggers | asparagus |
| **aubergine** | obæsheen | aubergine (eggplant) |
| **blomkål** | blomkawl | cauliflower |
| **brekkbønner** | brehkburnerr | French (cut green) beans |
| **bønner** | burnerr | beans |
| **erter** | æ'terr | peas |
| **gresskar** | grehskaar | marrow |
| **grønnkål** | grurnkawl | curly kale |
| **gulrøtter** | gewlrurterr | carrots |
| **hodesalat** | hōōdersahlaat | lettuce |
| **kantareller** | kahntahrehlerr | chanterelle mushrooms |
| **kål** | kawl | cabbage |
| **kålrabi/kålrot** | kawlraabi/**kawlrōōt** | swede (rutabaga) |
| **løk** | lūrk | onions |
| **linser** | linserr | lentils |
| **mais** | maayss | sweet corn (corn) |
| **maiskolbe** | **maays**kolber | corn on the cob |
| **nepe** | nāyper | turnips |
| **paprika** | **paa**prikkah | sweet pepper |
| **purre** | pewrer | leeks |
| **reddiker** | rehdikkerr | radishes |
| **rosenkål** | rōōssernkawl | Brussels sprouts |
| **rødbeter** | rūrbehterr | beetroot |
| **rødkål** | rūrkawl | red cabbage |
| **salat** | sahlaat | salad |
| **selleri** | sehlerree | celery |
| **sjampinjonger** | shahmpinyongerr | button mushrooms |
| **sopp** | sop | mushrooms |
| **sylteagurk** | **sewl**terahgewrk | pickled gherkin |
| **tomater** | toomaaterr | tomatoes |
| **spinat** | spinnaat | spinach |

| baked | **bakte** | bahkter |
|---|---|---|
| boiled | **kokte** | kookter |
| au gratin | **gratinerte** | grahtinäy'ter |
| in a sauce | **stuede** | stewerder |
| stuffed | **fylte** | fewlter |

## Potatoes, rice and pasta  *Poteter, ris og pasta*

| | | |
|---|---|---|
| bakt potet | bahkt poot**ay**t | baked potato |
| komper | koomperr | potato dumplings |
| kokte poteter | kookter poot**ay**terr | boiled potatoes |
| kumler | koomlerr | potato dumplings |
| nudler | newdlerr | noodles |
| nypoteter | n**ew**poot**ay**terr | new potatoes |
| pommes frites | pom frit | chips (French fries) |
| potet | poot**ay**t | potato |
| potetgull | poot**ay**tgewl | potato crisps (chips) |
| potetkroketter | poot**ay**tkrookehterr | potato croquettes |
| potetmos/-puré/ -stappe | poot**ay**tm**oo**ss/-pewr**ay**/ -stahper | mashed potatoes |
| potetsalat | poot**ay**tsahlaat | potato salad |
| raspeball | rahsperbahl | potato dumplings |
| ris | reess | rice |
| stekte poteter | stehkter poot**ay**terr | sautéed potatoes |
| stuede poteter | st**ew**erder poot**ay**terr | potatoes in a white sauce |

| | |
|---|---|
| sildeball (sillerbahl) | potato dumplings with a filling of minced salted herring, onion, bacon and flour; served with melted butter and pickled beetroot |

## Sauces  *Sauser*

| | | |
|---|---|---|
| ansjossmør | ahng**shoo**ssmurr | butter with chopped marinated sprats |
| brun saus | br**ur**n souss | gravy |
| dillsaus | dilsouss | sweet-and-sour béchamel sauce with dill |
| fløtesaus | fl**ur**tersouss | cream sauce |
| hvitløksmør | veetl**ur**ksmurr | garlic butter |
| hvit saus | veet souss | béchamel sauce |
| kryddersmør | krewderrsmurr | herb butter |
| løksaus | l**ur**ksouss | onion sauce |
| majones | mahyoon**ay**ss | mayonnaise |
| pepperrotsaus | pehperr**oo**tsouss | horseradish sauce |
| persillesmør | pæshillersmurr | parsley butter |
| rekesaus | r**ay**kersouss | prawn (shrimp) sauce |
| rømme | rurmer | thick sour cream |
| smeltet smør | smehltert smurr | melted butter |
| viltsaus | viltsouss | rich cream sauce served with game |

Some of the herbs, *urter*, and spices, *krydder*, you may come across:

| | | |
|---|---|---|
| **dill** | dil | dill |
| **eine(r)bær** | æiner(r)bǣr | juniper berries |
| **gressløk** | grehslürk | chives |
| **hvitløk** | veetlürk | garlic |
| **ingefær** | ingerfǣr | ginger |
| **kanel** | kahnāyl | cinnamon |
| **kapers** | kaapersh | capers |
| **karri** | kahri | curry seasoning |
| **karve** | kahrver | caraway seeds |
| **nellik** | nehlik | clove |
| **persille** | pæshiller | parsley |
| **pepper** | pehperr | pepper |
| **salvie** | sahlvee | sage |
| **salt** | sahlt | salt |
| **timian** | teemeeahn | thyme |

## Cheese   *Ost*

Cheese is mostly eaten on *smørbrød*. Some cheeses are home-grown versions of well-known continental cheeses, while others are indigenous Norwegian.

| | |
|---|---|
| **gammelost** (gahmerloost) | ''old-fashioned'' pungent ''cheese'' made with skimmed milk |
| **Jarlsbergost** (yaaᵣlsbærgoost) | mild, slightly sweet, semi-hard; a taste that falls between Gouda and Emmental |
| **normannaost** (noormahnahoost) | blue-veined cow's milk cheese; sharp taste |
| **ridderost** (ridderroost) | semi-hard with nutty flavour; eaten young or mature |

The square brown (goat's) cheeses found on Norwegian breakfast and lunch tables come in different varieties:

| | |
|---|---|
| **ekte geitost** (ehkter yæitoost) | ''real'' goat's cheese, the most pungent, is made from the whey of goat's milk |
| **Gudbrandsdalsost** (gewdbrahnsdaalsoost) | milder, consists of goat's and cow's milk |
| **fløtemysost** (flürtermēwssoost) | mild and sweet, made from the whey of cow's milk with cream added |

## Fruit  *Frukt*

| Do you have (fresh) fruit? | **Har dere (frisk) frukt?** | haar dāyrer (frisk) frewkt |
| I'd like a fruit salad. | **Jeg vil gjerne ha en fruktsalat.** | yæi vil yǣ'ner haa ehn **frewkt**sahlaat |
| **ananas** | **ahnahnahss** | pineapple |
| **appelsin** | **ahper|seen** | orange |
| **aprikos** | **ahprikkooss** | apricot |
| **banan** | **bahnaan** | banana |
| **bjørnebær** | **byūr'nerbær** | blackberries |
| **blåbær** | **blawbær** | bilberries (blueberries) |
| **bringebær** | **bringerbær** | raspberries |
| **dadler** | **dahdlerr** | dates |
| **druer** | **drēwerr** | grapes |
| blå | blaw | black |
| grønne | grurner | white |
| **eple** | **ehpler** | apple |
| **fersken** | **fæshkern** | peach |
| **fikener** | **feekernerr** | figs |
| **grapefrukt** | **grāypfrewkt** | grapefruit |
| **hasselnøtter** | **hahsserlnurterr** | hazelnuts |
| **jordbær** | **yoorbær** | strawberries |
| **kastanjer** | **kahstahnyerr** | chestnuts |
| **kirsebær** | **khisherbær** | cherries |
| **kokosnøtt** | **kookoosnurt** | coconut |
| **korinter** | **koorinterr** | currants |
| **mandler** | **mahndlerr** | almonds |
| **markjordbær** | **mahrkyoorbær** | wild strawberries |
| **melon** | **mehlōōn** | melon |
| **moreller** | **moorehlerr** | morello cherries |
| **multer** | **mewlterr** | arctic cloudberries |
| **nøtter** | **nurterr** | nuts |
| **plommer** | **ploommerr** | plums |
| **pære** | **pǣrer** | pear |
| **rabarbra** | **rahbahrbrah** | rhubarb |
| **rips** | ripss | redcurrants |
| **rognebær** | **rongnerbær** | rowanberries |
| **rosiner** | **roosseenerr** | raisins |
| **sitron** | **sitrōōn** | lemon |
| **solbær** | **sōōlbær** | blackcurrants |
| **stikkelsbær** | **stikkerlsbær** | gooseberries |
| **svisker** | **sviskerr** | prunes |
| **tyttebær** | **tewterbær** | cranberries |
| **valnøtter** | **vaalnurterr** | walnuts |
| **vannmelon** | **vahnmehlōōn** | watermelon |

### Dessert *Dessert*

| English | Norwegian | Pronunciation |
|---|---|---|
| I'd like a dessert, please. | **Jeg vil gjerne ha en dessert.** | yæi vil yǣ<sup>r</sup>ner haa ehn dehssǣr |
| Something light, please. | **Noe lett, takk.** | nōōer leht tahk |
| With/Without ... | **Med/Uten ...** | meh(d)/ēwtern |
| cream | **fløte** | flūrter |
| whipped cream | **krem** | krāym |
| jam | **syltetøy** | sewltertoy |
| (varm) eplekake med krem | (vahrm) ehplerkaaker meh(d) krāym | (hot) apple pie with whipped cream |
| frityrstekt camembert med solbær- syltetøy | fritēwshtehkt kahmang- bǣr meh(d) sōōlbǣr- sewltertoy | deep-fried camembert with blackcurrant jam |
| fruktkompott | frewktkoompot | stewed fruit |
| is(krem) | eess(krāym) | ice cream |
| jordbær- | yoorbǣr- | strawberry |
| sjokolade- | shookoolaader- | chocolate |
| vanilje- | vahnilyer- | vanilla |
| karamellpudding | kahrahmehlpewding | creme caramel |
| mandelkake | mahnderlkaaker | almond cake |
| multer med krem | mewlterr meh(d) krāym | arctic cloudberries with whipped cream |
| pannekaker | pahnerkaaker | pancakes |
| riskrem | reeskrāym | creamed rice with red berry sauce |
| rødgrøt | rūrgrūrt | fruit pudding with cream |
| sjokoladepudding | shookoolaaderpewding | chocolate mousse |
| sorbett | sorbeht | sorbet (sherbet) |
| sufflé | sewflāy | soufflé |
| terte | tæ<sup>r</sup>ter | fruit cake |
| vafler med syltetøy | vahflerr meh(d) sewltertoy | waffles with jam |

| | |
|---|---|
| **Hoffdessert** (hofdehssǣr) | layers of meringue and whipped cream, topped with chocolate sauce and toasted almonds |
| **pære Belle Helene** (pǣrer behl hehlāyn) | poached pears with vanilla ice cream and chocolate |
| **tilslørte bondepiker** (tilshlūr<sup>r</sup>ter boonnerpeekerr) | layers of stewed apples, biscuit (cookie) crumbs, sugar and whipped cream |

## Drinks *Drikkevarer*

Alcohol* is expensive because of high taxes. Elegant restaurants are licensed to serve spirits (liquor), but only after 3 p.m., and never on Sundays. Beer and wine are served in a larger number of restaurants — but by no means all of them — even on Sundays, after 12 noon.

## Beer *Øl*

Norwegian beer meets international standards. *Pils* (pilss) is the generic term for lager, *bayerøl* (**bah**yerrurl) is medium-strong and dark, *bokkøl* (**book**url) is strong and dark, and *exportøl* (ehks**po<sup>r</sup>**turl) is strong and light-coloured. If you're driving, stick to low-alcohol beer (*lettøl*—**leht**url or *lagerøl*—**laa**gerrurl) or the nonalcoholic *Zero* (s**āy**roo). *Vørterøl* (vur<sup>r</sup>-terrurl) is a nonalcoholic dark and rather sweet "beer".

| I'd like a beer, please. | **Jeg vil gjerne ha en øl.** | yæi vil yǣ<sup>r</sup>ner haa ehn url |
| Do you have ...? | **Har dere ...?** | haar d**āy**rer |
| bottled beer | **flaskeøl** | **flahs**kerurl |
| draught (tap) beer | **fatøl** | **faa**turl |
| foreign beer | **utenlandsk øl** | **ēw**ternlahnsk url |
| light/dark beer | **lyst/mørkt øl** | l**ēw**st/**murrkt** url |
| A bottle of ... | **En flaske ...** | ehn **flahs**ker |
| A glass of ... | **Et glass ...** | eht glahss |
| Half a litre of lager, please. | **En halv pils, takk.** | ehn hahl pilss tahk |

## Aquavit *Akevitt*

This traditional Norwegian drink is served ice-cold in tiny glasses and goes well with herring hors d'œuvres, *spekemat* and rich food. *Akevitt* (ahker**vit**), which is usually served with a beer chaser, contains about 40% pure alcohol. It is distilled from potatoes or grain, flavoured with aromatic seeds (mostly

---

* If you want to buy wine or spirits, a branch of *Vinmonopolet* (**veen**moonoop**ōō**ler), the State Wine Monopoly, is the place to go to.

caraway) and spices and matured in oak casks. *Linjeakevitt* (**lin**yerahkervit—"line" aquavit) is aquavit which has crossed the equator circle stored in the holds of a Norwegian ship; the rolling motion of the ship is said to produce a unique taste.

### Wine  *Vin*

Wine is imported from many countries. You'll find excellent Bordeaux and Burgundy vintages in better hotels and restaurants, together with less expensive wines which can be ordered by the carafe or the glass.

| | | |
|---|---|---|
| Do you have a wine list? | **Har dere et vinkart?** | haar dāȳrer eht veenkahʳt |
| May I have the wine list, please? | **Kan jeg få se vinkartet?** | kahn yæi faw sāȳ veenkahʳter |
| Do you have any open wines? | **Har dere åpne viner?** | haar dāȳrer awpner veenerr |
| I'd like to try a glass of ... | **Jeg vil gjerne prøve et glass ...** | yæi vil yǣʳner prūrver eht glahss |
| Can you recommend a good white wine? | **Kan du anbefale en god hvitvin?** | kahn dew ahnberfaaler ehn gōō(d) veetveen |
| I'd like a ... of red wine. | **Jeg vil gjerne ha ... rødvin.** | yæi vil yǣʳner haa ... rūrveen |
| bottle | **en flaske** | ehn flahsker |
| carafe | **en karaffel** | ehn kahrahferl |
| glass | **et glass** | eht glahss |
| half bottle | **en halv flaske** | ehn hahl flahsker |
| A bottle of champagne, please. | **En flaske champagne, takk.** | ehn flahsker shahmpahnyer tahk |
| Please bring me another ... | **Kan jeg få en ... til?** | kahn yæi faw ehn ... til |
| Where does this wine come from? | **Hvor kommer denne vinen fra?** | voor kommerr dehner veenern fraa |
| It's excellent. | **Den er meget god.** | dehn ær māȳgert gōō(d) |
| Do you have any nonalcoholic wines? | **Har dere alkoholfrie viner?** | haar dāȳrer ahlkoohōōlfreeyer veenerr |

| red | **rødvin** | rûrveen |
| white | **hvitvin** | veetveen |
| rosé | **rosévin** | roossāyveen |
| dry | **tørr** | turr |
| full-bodied | **fyldig** | fewldi |
| sparkling | **musserende** | mewssāyrehner |
| very dry | **meget tørr** | māygert turr |
| sweet | **søt** | sūrt |
| chilled | **avkjølt** | aavkhurlt |
| at room temperature | **værelsestemperert** | vāˈrerlserstehmperrāyˈt |

## Other alcoholic drinks   *Andre alkoholholdige drikker*

You can get almost all the drinks you're used to at home. The customary international names are used, and the drinks are mixed the same way.

| I'd like a/an ..., please. | **Jeg vil gjerne ha ...** | yæi vil yāˈner haa |
| aperitif | **en aperitiff** | ehn ahperritif |
| brandy | **brandy** | "brandy" |
| cognac | **et glass konjakk** | eht glahss konyahk |
| gin and tonic | **en gin tonic** | ehn "gin tonic" |
| liqueur | **et glass likør** | eht glahss likûrr |
| port | **et glass portvin** | eht glahss pooˈrtveen |
| rum | **rom** | room |
| sherry | **et glass sherry** | eht glahss shæri |
| vermouth | **et glass vermut** | eht glahss værmewt |
| vodka | **vodka** | vodkah |
| whisky | **whisky** | viski |
| neat (straight) | **bar** | baar |
| on the rocks | **med is** | meh(d) eess |
| with water | **med vann** | meh(d) vahn |
| with soda water | **med soda** | me(h)d soōdah |

**SKÅL!**
(skawl)
CHEERS!

## Nonalcoholic drinks  *Alkoholfrie drikker*

Of course, you don't have to order wine or spirits. If you prefer, ask for a soft drink.

| | | |
|---|---|---|
| I don't drink alcohol. | Jeg drikker ikke alkohol. | yæi **drik**kerr **ik**ker ahlkoo**hōōl** |
| A bottle of mineral (spring) water, please. | En flaske naturlig mineralvann, takk. | ehn **flahsk**er nah**tēw**ʳli minerr**aal**vahn tahk |
| fizzy (sparkling) | med kullsyre | meh(d) **kewls**ēwrer |
| still (natural) | uten kullsyre | **ēw**tern **kewls**ēwrer |
| I'd like a/an ... | Jeg vil gjerne ha ... | yæi vil **yǣ**ʳner haa |
| apple juice | eplesaft | **ehp**lersahft |
| grapefruit juice | grapefruktjuice | **grāyp**frewkt**yēw**ss |
| iced tea | iste | **ees**tāy |
| lemonade | sitronbrus | si**trōōn**brewss |
| (glass of) milk | (et glass) melk | (eht glahss) mehlk |
|    low-fat milk |    lettmelk |    **leht**mehlk |
| milkshake | en milkshake | ehn ''milkshake'' |
| orange juice | appelsinjuice | ahperl**seen**yēwss |
| pineapple juice | ananasjuice | ah**nahns**yēwss |
| soft drink | leskedrikk | **lehsk**erdrik |

## Hot drinks  *Varme drikker*

The best place to go for your afternoon tea or coffee is a *konditori*, teashop (coffee shop). Pay for your cake or pastry at the counter and then take it through to the seating area. In more elegant or old-fashioned cafés you'll be served at the table.

| | | |
|---|---|---|
| I'd like a/an ... | Jeg vil gjerne ha ... | yæi vil **yǣ**ʳner haa |
| (hot) chocolate | (varm) sjokolade | (vahrm) shookoo**laad**er |
| coffee | kaffe | **kah**fer |
|    a pot of |    en kanne |    ehn **kahn**er |
|    decaffeinated |    koffeinfri |    koffer**een**free |
|    espresso |    en espresso |    ehn ehs**preh**ssoo |
|    with cream |    med fløte |    meh(d) **flür**ter |
| tea | te | tāy |
|    a cup of |    en kopp |    ehn kop |
|    with lemon |    med sitron |    meh(d) si**trōōn** |
|    with milk |    med melk |    meh(d) mehlk |

## Complaints *Klager*

| English | Norwegian | Pronunciation |
|---|---|---|
| There's a ... missing. | **Det mangler ...** | deh **mahng**lerr |
| plate | **en tallerken** | ehn tah**lær**kern |
| glass | **et glass** | eht glahss |
| I don't have a ... | **Jeg har ikke noen ...** | yæi haar ikker nōōern |
| knife | **kniv** | kneev |
| fork | **gaffel** | **gah**ferl |
| spoon | **skje** | shāy |
| That's not what I ordered. | **Dette er ikke det jeg bestilte.** | **deh**ter ær **ik**ker deh yæi ber**stil**ter |
| I asked for ... | **Jeg ba om ...** | yæi baa om |
| There must be a mistake. | **Det må være en misforståelse.** | deh maw **vær**er ehn misfoshta**werl**ser |
| May I change this? | **Kan jeg få byttet dette?** | kahn yæi faw **bew**tert **deh**ter |
| I asked for a small portion (for the child). | **Jeg ba om en liten porsjon (til barnet).** | yæi baa om ehn **lee**tern poo**shōōn** (til **baar**ner) |
| The meat is ... | **Kjøttet er ...** | **khur**ter ær |
| overdone | **for mye stekt** | for **mēw**er stehkt |
| underdone | **for lite stekt** | for **lee**ter stehkt |
| too rare | **for blodig** | for **blōō**di |
| too tough | **for seigt** | for sæit |
| This is too ... | **Dette er for ...** | **deh**ter ær for |
| bitter | **beskt** | behskt |
| salty | **salt** | sahlt |
| sweet | **søtt** | surt |
| This doesn't taste right. | **Dette smaker ikke godt.** | **deh**ter **smaa**kerr **ik**ker got |
| The food is cold. | **Maten er kald.** | **maa**tern ær kahl |
| This isn't fresh. | **Dette er ikke ferskt.** | **deh**ter ær **ik**ker fæshkt |
| What's taking so long? | **Hvorfor tar det så lang tid?** | **voor**for taar deh saw lahng teed |
| Have you forgotten our drinks? | **Har du glemt drinkene våre?** | haar du glehmt **dring**kerner **vaw**rer |
| The wine doesn't taste right. | **Vinen smaker ikke godt.** | **vee**nern **smaa**kerr **ik**ker got |

| This isn't clean. | **Dette er ikke rent.** | dehter ær ikker rāynt |
| I'd like to speak to the head waiter/ manager. | **Kan jeg få snakke med hovmesteren/ bestyreren?** | kahn yæi faw **snahk**er meh(d) **hawv**mehsterrern/ berst**ēw**rerren |

## The bill (check) *Regningen*

The service charge is automatically included in restaurant bills. You can add a little extra if you are satisfied with the meal and the service.

| The bill, please. | **Regningen, takk.** | **ræi**ningern tahk |
| I'd like to pay. | **Jeg vil gjerne betale.** | yæi vil y**æ**ʳner bertaaler |
| We'd like to pay separately. | **Vi vil gjerne betale hver for oss.** | vee vil y**æ**ʳner bertaaler v**æ**r for oss |
| I think there's a mistake in this bill. | **Jeg tror det er en feil på regningen.** | yæi tr**ōō**r deh ær ehn fæil paw **ræi**ningern |
| What's this amount for? | **Hva står dette beløpet for?** | vah stawr **deh**ter ber**lū**rper for |
| Is everything included? | **Er alt inkludert?** | ær ahlt inklewd**ay**ʳt |
| Do you accept traveller's cheques/ Eurocheques? | **Tar dere reisesjekker/ eurosjekker?** | taar **day**rer **ræi**ssershehkerr/ y**ēw**rooshehkerr |
| Can I pay with this credit card? | **Kan jeg betale med dette kreditt-kortet?** | kahn yæi bertaaler meh(d) **deh**ter krehdit-ko**ʳ**ter |
| This is for you. | **Vær så god.** | vær saw g**ōō**(d) |
| Keep the change. | **Behold veksle-pengene.** | berhol **vehk**shler-pehngerner |
| That was a delicious meal. | **Det var et utsøkt måltid.** | deh vaar eht **ēw**tsurkt **maw**lteed |
| We enjoyed it, thank you. | **Det var meget godt.** | deh vaar m**āy**gert got |

**SERVICE INKLUDERT**
SERVICE INCLUDED

## Snacks  *Småretter*

For a quick snack, go to a *gatekjøkken*, "street kitchen", where
you can get everything from a hot dog to chicken and spring
rolls, ice cream and soft drinks. At cafés and cafeterias, you
can have pastries, open sandwiches and maybe a salad.

| | | |
|---|---|---|
| I'll have one of those. | **Jeg vil gjerne ha en av dem.** | yæi vil yāēᵣner haa ehn ahv dehm |
| Can I have two of these, please? | **Kan jeg få to av disse?** | kahn yæi faw tōō ahv disser |
| to the right/left above/below | **til høyre/venstre ovenfor/nedenfor** | til hoyrer/**vehn**strer **aw**vernfor/**nāy**dernfor |
| It's to take away. | **Jeg tar det med meg.** | yæi taar deh meh(d) mæi |
| I'll eat it here. | **Jeg spiser det her.** | yæi **spee**serr deh hǣr |
| A frankfurter with ..., please. | **En pølse med ...** | ehn **pur**lser meh(d) |
| mashed potatoes a potato pancake | **potetstappe lompe** | poo**tāyt**stahper **loom**per |
| I'd like a/an/ some ... | **Jeg vil gjerne ha ...** | yæi vil yāēᵣner haa |
| fried sausage in a roll with chips (fries) with onion | **en grillpølse med brød med pommes frites med løk** | ehn **gril**purlser meh(d) brūr meh(d) pom frit meh(d) lūrk |
| ice cream | **en is(krem)** | ehn eess(krāym) |
| (slice of) pizza | **en (skive) pizza** | ehn (**shee**ver) pitsah |
| soft ice cream with nuts with chocolate | **en softis med nøtter med sjokolade** | ehn **soft**eess meh(d) **nur**terr meh(d) shookoo**laa**der |
| spring (egg) roll | **vårrull** | **vawr**rewl |
| water ice | **en fruktis** | ehn **frewk**teess |
| Can I have an open sandwich with eggs and marinated sprats? | **Kan jeg få et smørbrød med egg og ansjos?** | kahn yæi faw eht **smurr**brūr meh(d) ehg o(g) ahng**shōōs** |
| cheese | **ost** | oost |
| cod roe | **torskerogn** | **tosh**kerrongn |
| fish pudding | **fiskepudding** | **fisker**pewding |
| ham | **kokt skinke** | kookt **shing**ker |
| liver paté | **leverpostei** | **leh**verrpoostæi |

## Pastries and cakes   *Bakverk og kaker*

| | | |
|---|---|---|
| I'd like a piece of ... | **Jeg vil gjerne ha et stykke ...** | yæi vil yæᶠner haa eht stewker |
| gâteau (layer cake) with marzipan | **bløtkake** **med marsipan** | blūᵣtkaaker meh(d) mahshippaan |
| I'd like a/an/ some... | **Jeg vil gjerne ha ...** | yæi vil yæᶠner haa |
| apple pie | **en eplekake** | ehn ehplerkaaker |
| biscuits (cookies) | **noen småkaker** | nōōern smawkkaakerr |
| bun with raisins | **en bolle** **med rosiner** | ehn boller meh(d) roosseenerr |
| chocolate cake | **en sjokoladekake** | ehn shookoolaaderkaaker |
| coconut macaroons | **noen kokos- makroner** | nōōern kookooss- mahkrōōnerr |
| cream horn | **et fløtehorn** | eht flūᵣterhōōᶠn |
| custard slice (napoleon) | **en napoleonskake** | ehn nahpōōlehonskaaker |
| Danish pastry | **et wienerbrød** | eht veenerrbrūr |
| doughnut | **en smultring** | ehn smewltring |
| fruit tart | **en fruktterte** | ehn frewktttæᶠter |
| meringues | **noen marengs** | nōōern mahrehngss |
| shortbread | **en sandkake** | ehn sahnkaaker |
| sponge cake | **et sukkerbrød** | eht sookkerrbrūr |
| Swiss roll with vanilla butter with jam with chocolate cream | **en rullekake** **med vaniljefyll** **med syltetøy** **med sjokoladefyll** | ehn rewlerkaaker meh(d) vahnilyerfewl meh(d) sewltertoy meh(d) shookoolaader- fewl |

**fastelavnsbolle**
(fahsterlaavns-
boller)

lenten bun; bun cut in half, filled with whipped cream and topped with icing (confectioners') sugar

**julekake**
(yēwlerkaaker)

rich fruit cake (a Christmas speciality)

**kransekake**
(krahnserkaaker)

cone-shaped pile of almond-macaroon rings decorated with icing (frosting), marzipan flowers, etc.

**kringle**
(kringler)

twisted sweet yeast-bread ring

**krumkake**
(kroomkaaker)

wafer cone filled with whipped cream and jam or berries

**vaniljebolle**
(vahnilyerboller)

bun filled with vanilla custard and topped with icing sugar

## Picnic   *Picnic*

Here's a basic list of food and drink that might come in useful when shopping for a picnic.

| I'd like a/an/some ... | Jeg vil gjerne ha ... | yæi vil yǣ'ner haa |
|---|---|---|
| apples | epler | ehpler |
| bananas | bananer | bahnaanerr |
| beer | øl | url |
| bread | brød | brur |
| rye | rug | rewg |
| white | loff | loof |
| butter | smør | smurr |
| cake | en kake | ehn kaaker |
| cheese | ost | oost |
| cheese spread | smøreost | smurreroost |
| chips (Am.) | potetgull | pootaytgewl |
| chocolate bar | en sjokoladeplate | ehn shookoolaaderplaater |
| coffee | kaffe | kahfer |
| instant coffee | pulverkaffe | pewlverrkahfer |
| cold cuts | kjøttpålegg | khurtpawlehg |
| crackers | salte kjeks | sahlter khehkss |
| crisps | potetgull | pootaytgewl |
| eggs | egg | ehg |
| grapes | druer | drewerr |
| ham | skinke | shingker |
| lemon | en sitron | ehn sitroon |
| liver paté | leverpostei | lehverrpoostæi |
| liver sausage | leverpølse | lehverrpurlser |
| milk | melk | mehlk |
| mustard * | sennep | sehnerp |
| oranges | appelsiner | ahperlseenerr |
| pastries | kaker | kaakerr |
| pepper | pepper | pehperr |
| pickled gherkins | sylteagurker | sewlterahgewrkerr |
| rolls | rundstykker | rewnstewkerr |
| salt | salt | sahlt |
| sausage | pølse | purlser |
| soft drink | leskedrikk | lehskerdrik |
| sugar | sukker | sookkerr |
| tea | te | tay |
| wine | vin | veen |

---

* Norwegian mustard is sweet; if you want a sharp one, ask for French mustard (*fransk sennep* – frahnsk **seh**nerp).

# Travelling around

### Plane  *Fly*

| | | |
|---|---|---|
| Is there a flight to Tromsø? | **Går det et fly til Tromsø?** | gawr deh eht flew til troomsur |
| Is it a direct flight? | **Er det et direkte fly?** | ær deh eht deerehkter flew |
| When's the next flight to Alta? | **Når går neste fly til Alta?** | nor gawr nehster flew til ahltah |
| Is there a connection to Kirkenes? | **Fins det en forbindelse til Kirkenes?** | finss deh ehn forbinerlser til khirkernæyss |
| I'd like to make a reservation for Stavanger. | **Jeg vil gjerne reservere en plass til Stavanger.** | yæi vil yæᵣner rehssærvæyrer ehn plahss til stahvahngerr |
| I'd like a ticket to Bergen. | **Jeg vil gjerne ha en billett til Bergen.** | yæi vil yæᵣner haa ehn billeht til bærgern |
| single (one-way) | **enkeltbillett** | ehngkerltbilleht |
| return (round-trip) | **tur-returbillett** | tewr-rehtewrbilleht |
| aisle seat | **plass ved midtgangen** | plahss veh(d) mitgahngern |
| window seat | **vindusplass** | vindewsplahss |
| What time ...? | **Når ...?** | nor |
| do we take off | **går flyet** | gawr flewer |
| should I check in | **må jeg sjekke inn** | maw yæi shehker in |
| do we arrive | **er vi fremme** | ær vee frehmer |
| This is cabin luggage. | **Dette er håndbagasje.** | dehter ær honbahgaasher |
| Is there a bus to/from the airport? | **Går det buss til/fra flyplassen?** | gawr deh bewss til/fraa flewplahssern |
| I'd like to ... my reservation. | **Jeg vil gjerne ... reservasjonen.** | yæi vil yæᵣner ... rehssærvahshoonern |
| cancel/change confirm | **annullere/endre bekrefte** | ahnewlæyrer/ehndrer berkrehfter |
| How long is the ticket valid? | **Hvor lenge er billetten gyldig?** | voor lehnger ær billehtern yewldi |

| ANKOMST | AVGANG |
|---|---|
| ARRIVAL | DEPARTURE |

## Train  *Tog*

Trains in Norway are operated by Norwegian State Railways—Norges Statsbaner (NSB). From Oslo central station (*Oslo Sentralstasjon*) there are connections to Sweden and the Continent via Copenhagen. The main inland destinations are Stavanger, Bergen and Trondheim, with connections to Bodø, Norway's northernmost station (apart from Narvik, which has connections to Sweden only).

Children under four years old travel free. Travellers under 16 pay half price.

Except on local trains, food is available either from a snack trolley (cart; *serveringsvogn*), a kiosk (*togkiosk*), a buffet car (*kafeteriavogn*) or a dining car (*restaurantvogn*). In sleeping cars, men and women can be accommodated separately; there are also family compartments. Most long-distance trains have carriages specially equipped for parents with babies and for disabled people. It's worth reserving a seat, particularly on long-distance trains.

| | |
|---|---|
| **EuroCity-tog (EC)** (yēwroositti-tawg) | International express train with first and second class |
| **Inter-City-tog** ("intercity"-tawg) | Day train connecting major towns in southern Norway with Oslo |
| **Ekspresstog** (ehksprehstawg) | Long-distance express train stopping at few stations |
| **Hurtigtog** (hewᵣtitawg) | Long-distance express train stopping at more stations than the *ekspresstog* |
| **Lokaltog** (lookaaltawg) | Local train stopping at all stations |

### Coach (Long-distance bus)  *Rutebil/Ekspressbuss*

Areas not served by NSB are covered by regional and local bus companies. Tourist information offices and travel agencies have timetables and other details.

*Note:* Most of the phrases on the following pages can be used for both train and coach travel.

## To the railway station  *Til jernbanestasjonen*

| Where's the railway station? | **Hvor er jernbanestasjonen?** | voor ær yǣʳnbaanerstahshoōonern |
| Where's the coach station? | **Hvor er bussstasjonen?** | voor ær bewsstahshoōonern |
| Taxi! | **Drosje!** | drosher |
| Take me to the ..., please. | **Kjør meg til ...** | khǖrr mæi til |

| INNGANG | ENTRANCE |
| UTGANG | EXIT |
| TIL TOGENE | TO THE TRAINS |
| INFORMASJON | INFORMATION |

## Where's the ...?  *Hvor er ...?*

| Where is/are (the) ...? | **Hvor er ...?** | voor ær |
| booking office | **billettkontoret** | billehtkoontoōorer |
| cafeteria | **kafeteriaen** | kahfertāyreeahern |
| currency exchange office | **vekslingskontoret** | vehkshlingskoontoōorer |
| left-luggage office (checkroom) | **bagasjeoppbevaringen** | bahgaasheropbervaaringern |
| lost property (lost and found) office | **hittegodskontoret** | hittergoodskoontoōorer |
| luggage (baggage) lockers | **oppbevaringsboksene** | opbervaaringsbokserner |
| newsstand | **aviskiosken** | ahveeskhyoskern |
| platform 2 | **perrong 2** | pehrong 2 |
| reservations office | **billettkontoret** | billehtkoontoōorer |
| restaurant | **restauranten** | rehstewrahngern |
| snack bar | **snackbaren** | snækbaarern |
| ticket office | **billettluken** | billehtlēwkern |
| track 5 | **spor 5** | spoōr 5 |
| waiting room | **ventesalen** | vehntersaalern |
| Where are the toilets? | **Hvor er toalettet?** | voor ær tooahlehter |

TAXI, see page 21

## Inquiries  *Forespørsler*

In Norway the sign $\boxed{i}$ means information office.

| | | |
|---|---|---|
| When is the ....train to Halden? | **Når går ... tog til Halden?** | nor gawr ... tawg til **hahl**dern |
| first/last | **første/siste** | **fursh**ter/**sis**ter |
| When is the next train to Hamar? | **Når går neste tog til Hamar?** | nor gawr **nehs**ter tawg til **haa**mahr |
| What time does the train to Oslo leave? | **Når går toget til Oslo?** | nor gawr **taw**ger til **oosh**loo |
| What's the fare to Trondheim? | **Hvor mye koster det til Trondheim?** | voor **mew**er **kos**terr deh til **tron**hæim |
| Is it a through train? | **Er det et gjennom-gående tog?** | ær deh eht **yeh**nom-gawehner tawg |
| Is there a connection to Elverum? | **Fins det en forbin-delse til Elverum?** | finss deh ehn forbin-erlser til **ehl**verrewm |
| Do I have to change trains? | **Må jeg bytte tog?** | maw yæi **bew**ter tawg |
| Is there enough time to change? | **Rekker jeg å bytte tog?** | **reh**kerr yæi aw **bew**ter tawg |
| Is the train running on time? | **Er toget i rute?** | ær **taw**ger ee **rew**ter |
| What time does the train arrive in Åndalsnes? | **Når er toget fremme i Åndalsnes?** | nor ær **taw**ger **freh**mer ee **on**dahls**nä**yss |
| Is there a dining car/sleeping car on the train? | **Er det en spise-vogn/sovevogn i toget?** | ær deh ehn **spees**ser-vongn/**saw**vervongn ee ...er |
| Does the train stop in Asker? | **Stanser toget i Asker?** | **stahn**serr **taw**ger ee **ah**skerr |
| Which platform does the train to Skien leave from? | **Fra hvilken perrong går toget til Skien?** | fraa **vil**kern pehr**rong** gawr **taw**ger til **shä**yern |
| Which track does the train from Gjøvik arrive at? | **På hvilket spor kommer toget fra Gjøvik inn?** | paw **vil**kert spoor **kom**merr **taw**ger fraa **yur**veek in |
| I'd like a time-table, please. | **Jeg vil gjerne ha en rutetabell.** | yæi vil **yæ**rner haa ehn **rew**tertahbehl |

| | |
|---|---|
| Det er et gjennomgående tog. | It's a through train. |
| Du må bytte i ... | You have to change at ... |
| Bytt i ... og ta lokaltoget. | Change at ... and get a local train. |
| Perrong 2 er ... | Platform 2 is ... |
| der borte/opp trappen | over there/upstairs |
| til høyre/til venstre | on the right/on the left |
| Det går et tog til Tønsberg kl. 16.00. | There's a train to Tønsberg at 16.00 (4 p.m.). |
| Toget går fra spor 8. | Your train will leave from track 8. |
| Det er ... minutter forsinket. | It's running ... minutes late. |
| Første klasse er foran/i midten/bakerst. | First class at the front/in the middle/at the rear. |

## Tickets—Reservation    *Billetter – Bestilling*

| I'd like a ticket to ... | Jeg vil gjerne ha en billett til ... | yæi vil yǣ'rner haa ehn billeht til |
|---|---|---|
| single (one-way) | enkeltbillett | ehngkerltbilleht |
| return (round-trip) | tur-returbillett | tewr-rehtewrbilleht |
| first class | første klasse | furshter klahsser |
| second class | andre/annen klasse | ahndrer/aaern klahsser |
| half price | halv pris | hahl preess |
| Must the child pay full fare? | Må barnet betale full takst? | maw baa'ner bertaaler fewl tahkst |
| I'd like a window seat. | Jeg vil gjerne ha vindusplass. | yæi vil yǣ'rner hah vindewsplahss |
| I'd like to reserve a ... | Jeg vil gjerne reservere en ... | yæi vil yǣ'rner rehssærvǣyrer ehn |
| couchette | køye i liggevognen | koyer ee liggervongnern |
| berth in the sleeping car | køye i sovevognen | koyer ee sawvervongnern |
| upper berth | overkøye | awverrkoyer |
| middle berth | midtkøye | mitkoyer |
| lower berth | underkøye | ewnerrkoyer |

TIME, see page 153

## On the platform  *På perrongen*

| | | |
|---|---|---|
| Is this the platform for the train to Kongsberg? | **Er dette perrongen for toget til Kongsberg?** | ær **deh**ter pehrongern for **taw**ger til **kongs**bærg |
| Is this the train to Geilo? | **Er dette toget til Geilo?** | ær **deh**ter **taw**ger til **yæi**loo |
| Is the train from Levanger late? | **Er toget fra Levanger forsinket?** | ær **taw**ger fraa ler**vahng**err fo**shing**kert |
| What track does the train to Gol arrive on? | **På hvilket spor kommer toget til Gol inn?** | paw **vil**kert **spoor** **kom**merr **taw**ger til gool in |

## All aboard  *Ta plass*

| | | |
|---|---|---|
| Excuse me. Could I get by? | **Unnskyld. Kan jeg få komme forbi?** | **ewn**shewl. kahn yæi faw **kom**mer for**bee** |
| Is this seat taken? | **Er denne plassen opptatt?** | ær **deh**ner **plahs**sern **op**taht |

| | |
|---|---|
| **RØYKING TILLATT** SMOKER | **RØYKING FORBUDT/ RØYKING IKKE TILLATT** NONSMOKER |

| | | |
|---|---|---|
| I think that's my seat. | **Jeg tror at det er min plass.** | yæi **troor** aht deh ær meen **plahss** |
| Would you let me know before we get to Røros? | **Kan du si fra før vi kommer til Røros?** | kahn dew see fraa **fürr** vee **kom**merr til **rü****rawss** |
| What station is this? | **Hvilken stasjon er dette?** | **vil**kern stah**shoon** ær **deh**ter |
| How long does the train stop here? | **Hvor lenge står toget her?** | voor **lehng**er stawr **taw**ger hær |
| When do we get to Voss? | **Når kommer vi til Voss?** | nor **kom**merr vee til voss |
| Where are we now? | **Hvor er vi nå?** | voor ær vee naw |
| Where's the ...? | **Hvor er ...** | voor ær |
| dining car buffet car kiosk | **spisevognen kafeteriavognen togkiosken** | **spee**sservongnern kahfer**tay**reeahvongnern **tawg**khyoskern |

## Sleeping *I sovevognen*

| | | |
|---|---|---|
| Are there any free compartments in the sleeping car? | **Fins det noen ledige kupéer i sovevognen?** | finss deh nōōern lāy-deeyer kewpāyerr ee sawvervongnern |
| Where's the sleeping car? | **Hvor er sovevognen?** | voor ær sawvervongnern |
| Where's my berth? | **Hvor er min køye?** | voor ær meen koyer |
| I'd like a lower berth. | **Jeg vil gjerne ha en underkøye.** | yæi vil yǣ'ner haa ehn ewnerrkoyer |
| Would you make up our berths? | **Kan du gjøre i stand køyene våre?** | kahn dew yūrrer ee stahn koyerner vawrer |
| Would you wake me at 7 o'clock? | **Kan du vekke meg kl. 7?** | kahn dew vehker mæi klokkern 7 |

## Baggage and porters *Bagasje og bærere*

| | | |
|---|---|---|
| Can you help me with my luggage? | **Kan du hjelpe meg med bagasjen?** | kahn dew yehlper mæi meh(d) bahgaashern |
| Are there any ...? | **Fins det ... her?** | finss deh ... hǣr |
| luggage trolleys (carts) | **bagasjetraller** | bahgaashertrahlerr |
| luggage (baggage) lockers | **oppbevarings-bokser** | opbervaaringsbokserr |
| Where are they? | **Hvor er de?** | voor ær dee |
| Where's the left-luggage office (checkroom)? | **Hvor er bagasje-oppbevaringen?** | voor ær bahgaasher-opbervaaringern |
| I'd like to leave my luggage, please. | **Jeg vil gjerne levere inn bagasjen til oppbevaring.** | yæi vil yǣ'ner lehvayrer in bahgaashern til opbervaaring |
| I'd like to register (check) my luggage. | **Jeg vil gjerne ekspedere bagasjen.** | yæi vil yǣ'ner ehksper-dāyrer bahgaashern |
| I'd like to take out luggage insurance. | **Jeg vil gjerne tegne en reisegods-forsikring.** | yæi vil yǣ'ner tæiner ehn ræissergoods-foshikring |

---

**REISEGODSEKSPEDISJON**
REGISTERING LUGGAGE (BAGGAGE CHECKING)

---

PORTERS, see also page 18

## Bus—Tram (Streetcar) *Buss — Trikk*

Single tickets are available from the driver. In Oslo, it's worth buying a booklet of tickets (valid for transfers within one hour) if you plan to travel around.

| | | |
|---|---|---|
| I'd like a booklet of tickets. | **Jeg vil gjerne ha et billetthefte.** | yæi vil **yæ**ʳner haa eht bill**eht**thehfter |
| Which tram (streetcar) goes to the town centre? | **Hvilken trikk går til sentrum?** | **vil**kern trik gawr til **sehn**trewm |
| Does this bus stop at ...? | **Stanser denne bussen ved ...?** | **stahn**serr **deh**ner **bews**sern veh(d) |
| Where can I get a bus to the Folk Museum? | **Hvorfra går bussen til Folkemuseet?** | **voor**fra gawr **bews**sern til **fol**ker**mews**sāyer |
| Which tram do I take to Vigeland Park? | **Hvilken trikk går til Vigelandsparken?** | **vil**kern trik gawr til **vee**gerlahnspahrkern |
| Where's the ...? | **Hvor er ...?** | voor ær |
| bus stop | **bussholdeplassen** | **bews**hollerplahssern |
| tram stop | **trikkeholdeplassen** | **trik**kerhollerplahssern |
| When is the ... bus to the town centre? | **Når går ... buss til sentrum?** | nor gawr ... bewss til **sehn**trewm |
| first/next/last | **første/neste/siste** | **furh**ster/**neh**ster/**sis**ter |
| How much is the fare to ...? | **Hvor mye koster det til ...?** | voor **mēw**er **kos**terr deh til |
| Do I have to change buses? | **Må jeg bytte buss?** | maw yæi **bew**ter bewss |
| How many stops are there to ...? | **Hvor mange holdeplasser er det til ...?** | voor **mahn**ger **hol**ler-plahsserr ær deh til |
| Will you tell me when to get off? | **Kan du si fra når jeg skal gå av?** | kahn dew see fraa nor yæi skahl gaw ahv |
| I want to get off at ... | **Jeg skal av ved ...** | yæi skahl ahv veh(d) |

**BUSSHOLDEPLASS**
BUS STOP

## Underground (Subway)  *T-bane*

Oslo's underground railway extends from the centre of the city
to the suburbs. Maps of the system are displayed at stations
and aboard trains. You can transfer from bus or tram to
underground (subway) on the same ticket.

| | | |
|---|---|---|
| Where's the near-est underground station? | **Hvor er nærmeste T-banestasjon?** | voor ær **nærmehs**ter tāy-baanerstahshōōn |
| Does this train go to Holmenkollen? | **Går denne banen til Holmenkollen?** | gawr **deh**ner baanern til **hol**mernkollern |
| Where do I change for ...? | **Hvor må jeg bytte for å komme til ...?** | voor maw yæi **bew**ter for aw **kom**mer til |
| Is the next station ...? | **Er neste stasjon ...?** | ær **neh**ster stahshōōn |
| Which line should I take to ...? | **Hvilken linje skal jeg ta til ...?** | **vil**kern **lin**yer skahl yæi taa til |

## Boat—Ship  *Båt – Skip*

Travelling by car in western Norway involves numerous fjord
crossings by ferry. The frequency of services depends on the
season. In rural areas, local hotels will always be able to tell
you exact ferry times. At the height of the summer tourist
season, try to reserve a place for your car or you may find
yourself spending hours in queues. Fares vary according to size
and weight of vehicle.

In Oslo, there are guided cruises of the harbour and around
the islands, as well as regular boat services to the museums
on the Bygdøy peninsula.

| | | |
|---|---|---|
| When does the boat/ferry for ... leave? | **Når går båten/ fergen til ...?** | nor gawr **baw**tern/ **færg**gern til |
| Where's the embarkation point? | **Ved hvilken kai legger båten til?** | veh(d) **vil**kern kahy **leh**gerr **baw**tern til |
| How long does the crossing take? | **Hvor lang tid tar overfarten?** | voor lahng teed taar **aw**verrfah'tern |

| When do we call at Molde? | **Når legger vi til i Molde?** | nor **leh**gerr vee til ee **molder** |
| I'd like to take a boat trip/harbour tour. | **Jeg vil gjerne ta en båttur/havne-rundtur.** | yæi vil yæ$^r$ner taa ehn **bawt**tewr/**hahv**ner-rewntewr |
| boat | **en båt** | ehn bawt |
| cabin | **en lugar** | ehn **lew**gaar |
| single/double | **enkel/dobbel** | **ehng**kerl/**dobb**erl |
| canoe | **en kano** | ehn **kaa**noo |
| cruise | **et cruise** | eht "cruise" |
| deck | **et dekk** | eht dehk |
| ferry | **en ferge/ferje** | ehn **fær**gger/**fær**yer |
| car ferry | **bilferge** | **beel**færgger |
| gangway | **en landgang** | ehn **lahn**gahng |
| hydrofoil | **en hydrofoil** | ehn **hew**droo**foil** |
| jetty | **en brygge** | ehn **brew**ger |
| kayak | **en kajakk** | ehn **kah**yahk |
| life belt | **et livbelte** | eht **leev**behlter |
| life boat | **en livbåt** | ehn **leev**bawt |
| life jacket | **en flytevest** | ehn **flew**tervehst |
| motorboat | **en motorbåt** | ehn **mōō**toorbawt |
| pier | **en pir** | ehn peer |
| port | **en havn** | ehn hahvn |
| rowing boat | **en robåt** | ehn **roo**bawt |
| sailing boat | **en seilbåt** | ehn **sæil**bawt |
| ship | **et skip** | eht sheep |
| steamer | **en dampbåt** | ehn **dahmp**bawt |

## Other means of transport *Andre transportmidler*

| bicycle | **en sykkel** | ehn **sew**kerl |
| cable car | **en taubane** | ehn **tou**baaner |
| helicopter | **et helikopter** | eht hehli**kop**terr |
| moped | **en moped** | ehn moo**pāyd** |
| motorbike | **en motorsykkel** | ehn **mōō**tooshewkerl |
| scooter | **en scooter** | ehn **skēw**terr |
| I'd like to hire (rent) a bicycle. | **Jeg vil gjerne leie en sykkel.** | yæi vil yæ$^r$ner **læ**ier ehn **sew**kerl |

Or perhaps you prefer:

| to hike | **å vandre** | aw **vahn**drer |
| to hitchhike | **å haike** | aw **hah**yker |
| to walk | **å spasere** | aw spah**ssāy**rer |

## Car  *Bil*

All the basic rules for right-hand traffic apply. The use of seat belts (*bilbelte*) is obligatory, and that includes back-seat passengers if the car is so equipped. A red reflector warning triangle must be carried. Crash helmets are compulsory for both drivers and passengers on motorcycles and scooters. Fines for drinking and driving are prohibitive and may involve loss of licence and imprisonment.

| | | |
|---|---|---|
| Where's the nearest filling station? | **Hvor er nærmeste bensinstasjon?** | voor ær **nærmehster** behn**seenstahshōōn** |
| Fill it up, please. | **Full tank, takk.** | fewl tahngk tahk |
| Give me ... litres of petrol (gasoline). | **... liter bensin, takk.** | ... leeterr behn**seen** tahk |
| super (premium) | **super** | **sēw**perr |
| regular | **normal** | noor**maal** |
| unleaded | **blyfri** | **blēw**free |
| diesel | **diesel** | **dees**serl |
| Please check the ... | **Vær snill å kontrollere ...** | vær snil aw koontroo**lāy**rer |
| battery | **batteriet** | bahter**ree**eyer |
| brake fluid | **bremsevæsken** | **brehm**servehskern |
| oil/water | **oljen/vannet** | **ol**yern/**vah**ner |
| Would you check the tyre pressure? | **Kan du kontrollere trykket i dekkene?** | kahn dew koontroo**lāy**rer **trewk**er ee **deh**kerner |
| 1.6 front, 1.8 rear. | **1,6 foran, 1,8 bak.** | 1 **kom**mah 6 **for**ahn 1 **kom**mah 8 baak |
| Could you check the spare tyre, too? | **Kan du kontrollere reservedekket også?** | kahn dew koontroo**lāy**rer reh**sær**verdehker **os**so |
| Can you mend this puncture (fix this flat)? | **Kan du reparere denne punkte-ringen?** | kahn dew rehpah**rāy**rer **deh**ner **poong**tāy-ringern |
| Would you change the ..., please? | **Kan du skifte ...** | kahn dew **shif**ter |
| bulb | **pæren** | **pæ**rern |
| fan belt | **vifteremmen** | **vif**terrehmern |
| spark(ing) plugs | **tennstiftene** | **tehn**stifterner |
| tyre | **dekket** | **deh**ker |
| wipers | **vindusviskerne** | **vin**dewsviskæ^rner |

| Would you clean the windscreen (windshield)? | **Kan du vaske frontruten?** | kahn dew **vah**sker **front**rewtern |
| Where can I get my car cleaned? | **Hvor kan jeg få vasket bilen?** | voor kahn yæi faw **vah**skert **bee**lern |
| Is there a car wash here/nearby? | **Er det en bilvask her/i nærheten?** | ær deh ehn **beel**vahsk hǣr/ee **nær**hehtern |

### Asking the way *Spørre om veien*

| In which direction is ...? | **I hvilken retning ligger ...?** | ee **vil**kern **reht**ning **lig**gerr |
| Can you tell me the way to ...? | **Kan du vise meg veien til ...?** | kahn dew **vee**sser mæi **væi**ern til |
| Can you tell me where ... is? | **Kan du si meg hvor ... ligger?** | kahn dew see mæi voor ... **lig**gerr |
| How do I get to ...? | **Hvordan kommer jeg til ...?** | **voor**dahn **kom**merr yæi til |
| this place this address | **dette stedet denne adressen** | **deh**ter **stay**der **deh**ner ah**dreh**ssern |
| Am I on the right road for ...? | **Er dette veien til ...?** | ær **deh**ter **væi**ern til |
| How far is the next village? | **Hvor langt er det til neste tettsted?** | voor lahngt ær deh til **neh**ster **teht**stay(d) |
| How far is it to ... from here? | **Hvor langt er det til ... herfra?** | voor lahngt ær deh til ... **hær**frah |
| Is there a motor-way (expressway) to ...? | **Fins det en motorvei til ...?** | finss deh ehn **moo**toorvæi til |
| Is there a road with little traffic? | **Fins det en vei med lite trafikk?** | finss deh ehn væi meh(d) **lee**ter trah**fik** |
| Can I drive to the centre of town? | **Kan jeg kjøre inn i sentrum?** | kahn yæi **khur**rer in ee **sehn**trewm |
| How long does it take by car/on foot? | **Hvor lang tid tar det med bil/til fots?** | voor lahng teed taar deh meh(d) beel/til footss |
| Where does this road lead to? | **Hvor fører denne veien?** | voor **fur**rerr **deh**ner **væi**ern |
| Can you show me on the map where I am? | **Kan du vise meg på kartet hvor jeg er?** | kahn dew **vee**sser mæi paw **kah**rter voor yæi ær |

| | |
|---|---|
| Du har kjørt feil. | You're on the wrong road. |
| Kjør rett frem. | Go straight ahead. |
| Det er der borte til høyre/venstre. | It's down there on the right/left. |
| midt imot/bak ... | opposite/behind ... |
| ved siden av/etter ... | next to/after ... |
| nord/sør/øst/vest | north/south/east/west |
| Kjør til første/annet kryss. | Go to the first/second crossroads (intersection). |
| Sving til venstre ved trafikklyset. | Turn left at the traffic lights. |
| Ta til høyre ved neste kryss. | Turn right at the next corner. |
| Ta E 6. | Take the E 6. |
| Det er en enveisgate. | It's a one-way street. |
| Du må kjøre tilbake til ... | You have to go back to ... |
| Følg skiltene til Moss. | Follow signs for Moss. |

## Parking  *Parkering*

| | | |
|---|---|---|
| Where can I park? | **Hvor kan jeg parkere?** | voor kahn yæi pahrkayrer |
| Is there a ... nearby? | **Fins det en ... i nærheten?** | finns deh ehn ... ee nærhehtern |
| car park (parking lot) | **parkeringsplass** | pahrkayringsplahss |
| multistorey car park (parking garage) | **parkeringshus** | pahrkayringshewss |
| May I park here? | **Kan jeg parkere her?** | kahn yæi pahrkayrer hær |
| How long can I park here? | **Hvor lenge kan jeg stå her?** | voor **leh**nger kahn yæi staw hær |
| What's the charge per hour? | **Hvor mye koster det pr. time?** | voor mewer kosterr deh pær teemer |
| Do you have some change for the parking meter? | **Har du vekslepenger til parkometeret?** | haar dew **vehk**shlerpehn-gerr til pahrkoomayterrer |

## Breakdown—Road assistance   *Motorstopp – Hjelp på veien*

| Where's the nearest garage (auto repair shop)? | **Hvor er nærmeste bilverksted?** | voor ær **nærm**ehster **beel**værksteh(d) |
| My car has broken down. | **Jeg har fått motorstopp.** | yæi haar fot **moo**tooshtop |
| I've had a breakdown at ... | **Jeg har fått motorstopp ved ...** | yæi haar fot **moo**tooshtop veh(d) |
| Can you send a mechanic? | **Kan du sende en mekaniker?** | kahn dew **sehn**er ehn meh**kaan**ikkerr |
| My car won't start. | **Bilen starter ikke.** | **beel**ern staa<sup>r</sup>terr **ikk**er |
| The battery is dead. | **Batteriet er flatt.** | bahterr**eey**er ær flaht |
| I've run out of petrol (gas). | **Jeg har kjørt tom.** | yæi haar khür<sup>r</sup>t tom |
| I have a flat tyre. | **Jeg har punktert.** | yæi haar poong**tay**<sup>r</sup>t |
| The engine is overheating. | **Motoren har gått varm.** | **moo**toorern haar got vahrm |
| There is something wrong with the ... | **Det er noe i veien med ...** | deh ær **noo**er ee **væi**ern meh(d) |
| brakes | **bremsene** | **brehm**serner |
| carburettor | **forgasseren** | for**gahss**errern |
| exhaust (tail) pipe | **eksosrøret** | ehk**soos**rürrer |
| ignition | **tenningen** | **teh**ningern |
| indicator | **blinklyset** | **blingk**lewsser |
| radiator | **kjøleren** | **khür**lerrern |
| steering | **styringen** | **stew**ringern |
| wheel | **hjulet** | **yür**ler |
| Can you send a breakdown van (tow truck)? | **Kan du sende en kranbil?** | kahn dew **sehn**er ehn **kraan**beel |
| How long will you be? | **Når kommer du?** | nor **komm**err dew |
| Can you lend me a/some ...? | **Kan du låne meg ...?** | kahn dew **law**ner mæi |
| jack | **en jekk** | ehn yehk |
| jerry can | **en bensinkanne** | ehn behn**seen**kahner |
| pliers | **en tang** | ehn tahng |
| spanner | **en skrunøkkel** | ehn **skrew**nurkerl |
| tools | **noe verktøy** | **noo**er **værk**toy |
| towrope | **et slepetau** | eht **shlay**pertou |

## Accident—Police *Ulykke – Politi*

| | | |
|---|---|---|
| Please call the police. | **Vær så snill å ringe politiet.** | vær saw snil aw **ringer** politt**eey**er |
| There's been an accident. | **Det har skjedd en ulykke.** | deh haar shehd ehn **ēw**lewker |
| It's about 2 km. from ... | **Det er ca. 2 km fra ...** | deh ær **sirr**kah 2 **kh**illoomā**y**terr fraa |
| Where's there a telephone? | **Hvor fins det en telefon?** | voor finss deh ehn tehler**fōōn** |
| Call a doctor/an ambulance quickly. | **Ring etter lege/ sykebil!** | ring **eh**terr **lāy**ger/ **sēw**kerbeel |
| There are people injured. | **Det er noen som er skadet.** | deh ær **nōō**ern som ær **skaa**dert |
| Here's my driving licence. | **Her er førerkortet mitt.** | hær ær **fūr**rerrko'ter mit |
| What's your name and address? | **Kan jeg få navn og adresse?** | kahn yæi faw nahvn o(g) ah**dreh**sser |
| What's your insurance company? | **Hvilket forsikrings- selskap har du?** | vilkert fo**shik**rings- sehlskaap haar dew |

## Road signs *Trafikkskilt*

| | |
|---|---|
| **ALL STANS FORBUDT** | No stopping |
| **DATOPARKERING** | Parking according to date * |
| **FERIST** | Cattle grid |
| **GRUSVEI** | Gravelled road |
| **INNKJØRSEL FORBUDT** | No entry |
| **KJØR SAKTE** | Drive slowly |
| **LØS GRUS** | Gravelled road |
| **MØTEPLASS** | Road passing place |
| **FORBIKJØRING FORBUDT** | No overtaking (passing) |
| **OMKJØRING** | Diversion (Detour) |
| **PARKERING (FORBUDT)** | (No) Parking |
| **RASFARE** | Falling rocks |
| **SVAKE KANTER** | Soft shoulders |
| **TELELØSNING/TELELØYSE** | Potholes due to frost |
| **TOLL** | Customs |
| **UTKJØRSEL** | Exit |
| **VEIARBEID/VEGARBEID** | Roadworks (Men working) |

* Night parking on one side of the street only (even numbers on even days, odd numbers on odd days).

# Sightseeing

| Where's the tourist office? | Hvor er turist-kontoret? | voor ær tewrist-koontōōrer |
| What are the main points of interest? | Hva er hoved-severdighetene? | vah ær hōōverd-sehværdihehterner |
| We're here for ... | Vi skal være her ... | vee skahl værer hær |
| a few hours<br>a day/a week | et par timer<br>en dag/en uke | eht pahr teemerr<br>ehn daag/ehn ēwker |
| Can you recommend a/an ...? | Kan du anbefale en ...? | kan dew ahnberfaaler ehn |
| sightseeing tour<br>excursion | sightseeingtur<br>utflukt | "sightseeing"tēwr<br>ēwtflewkt |
| Where do we leave from? | Hvor starter vi fra? | voor staaʳterr vee fraa |
| Will the bus pick us up at the hotel? | Kommer bussen og henter oss ved hotellet? | kommer bewssern o(g) hehnterr oss veh(d) hootehler |
| How much does the tour cost? | Hvor mye koster turen? | voor mēwer kosterr tēwrern |
| What time does the tour start? | Når starter turen? | nor staaʳterr tēwrern |
| Is lunch included? | Er lunsj inkludert? | ær lunsh inklewdāyʳt |
| What time do we get back? | Når er vi tilbake? | nor ær vee tilbaaker |
| Do we have free time in ...? | Har vi fri tid til disposisjon i ...? | haar vee free teed til dispoosishōōn ee |
| Is there an English-speaking guide? | Fins det en engelsk-talende guide der? | finss deh ehn ehngerlsk-taalerner "guide" dær |
| I'd like to hire a private guide for ... | Jeg vil gjerne ha en privat guide for ... | yæi vil yæʳner haa ehn preevaat "guide" for |
| half a day<br>a day | en halv dag<br>en dag | ehn hahl daag<br>ehn daag |
| I'd like to see the ... | Jeg vil gjerne se ... | yæi vil yæʳner sāy |
| Are there any special events going on? | Foregår det noen spesielle begiven-heter her for tiden? | fawrergawr deh nōōern spehsseeyehler beryee-vernhehterr hær for teedern |

| Where is/are the ...? | Hvor er ...? | voor ær |
|---|---|---|
| amusement park | fornøyelsesparken | fo‘noyerlserspahrkern |
| aquarium | akvariet | ahkvaareeyer |
| art gallery | kunstgalleriet | kewnstgahlerreeyer |
| botanical gardens | den botaniske hagen | dehn bootaanisker haagern |
| bridge | broen | brōoern |
| building | bygningen | bewgningern |
| business district | forretningskvarteret | forrehtningskvah‘tāyrer |
| castle | slottet | shlotter |
| cathedral | domkirken | domkhirkern |
| cave | hulen | hēwlern |
| cemetery | gravlunden | graavlewnern |
| chapel | kapellet | kahpehler |
| church | kirken | khirkern |
| citadel | festningen | fehstningern |
| city centre | sentrum | sehntrewm |
| concert hall | konserthuset | koonsæ‘thewsser |
| conference centre/ congress hall | kongresshallen | konggrehshahlern |
| court house | tinghuset | tinghēwsser |
| downtown area | sentrum | sehntrewm |
| exhibition | utstillingen | ēwtstillingern |
| factory | fabrikken | fahbrikkern |
| fair | messen | mehssern |
| flea market | loppemarkedet | loppermahrkerder |
| fortress | borgen | borggern |
| fountain | fontenen | fontāynern |
| gardens | hagene | haagerner |
| grotto | grotten | grottern |
| harbour | havnen | hahvnern |
| lake | (inn)sjøen | (in)shūrern |
| library | biblioteket | biblyootāyker |
| market | torghandelen | torghahnderlern |
| memorial | minnesmerket | minnersmærker |
| monastery | klostret | klostrer |
| monument | monumentet | moonewmehnter |
| museum | museet | mewssāyer |
| observatory | observatoriet | obsærvahtōoryer |
| old town | gamlebyen | gahmlerbēwern |
| opera house | operahuset | ooperrahhēwsser |
| palace | slottet | shlotter |
| park | parken | pahrkern |
| parliament building | Stortinget | stoō‘tinger |
| planetarium | planetariet | plahnertaaryer |
| royal palace | det kongelige slott | deh kongerleeyer shlot |

| ruins | ruinene | reweenerner |
| shopping area | handlestrøket | hahndlerstrürker |
| square | plassen/torget | plahssern/torgger |
| stadium | stadion | staadyoon |
| statue | statuen | staatewern |
| stave church | stavkirken | staavkhirkern |
| stock exchange | børsen | bürshern |
| theatre | teatret | tayaatrer |
| tomb | graven | graavern |
| tower | tårnet | taw$^r$ner |
| town (city) hall | rådhuset | rawdhewsser |
| university | universitetet | ewnivæshitayter |
| zoo | dyrehagen | dewrerhaagern |

## Admission   Adgang

| Is ... open on Sundays? | Er ... åpent på søndager? | ær ... awpernt paw surndaagerr |
| When is it open? | Når er det åpent? | nor ær deh awpernt |
| When does it open/close? | Når åpner/stenger det? | nor awpnerr/stehngerr deh |
| What's the entrance fee? | Hva koster inngangs-billetten? | vah kosterr ingahngs-billehtern |
| 2 adults and 1 child | 2 voksne og 1 barn | 2 voksner o(g) 1 baa$^r$n |
| Is there any reduction for (the) ...? | Er det noen rabatt for ...? | ær deh nööern rahbaht for |
| children | barn | baa$^r$n |
| disabled | bevegelseshemmede | bervaygerlsershehmerder |
| groups | grupper | grewperr |
| pensioners (senior citizens) | pensjonister | pahngshoonisterr |
| students | studenter | stewdehnterr |
| Do you have a guide-book (in English)? | Har du en guidebok (på engelsk)? | haar dew ehn "guide"-böok (paw ehngerlsk) |
| Can I buy a catalogue? | Kan jeg få kjøpt en katalog? | kahn yæi faw khurpt ehn kahtahlawg |
| Is it all right to take pictures? | Er det tillatt å fotografere? | ær deh tillaht aw footoograhfayrer |

| GRATIS ADGANG | ADMISSION FREE |
| FOTOGRAFERING FORBUDT | NO CAMERAS ALLOWED |

## Who—What—When? *Hvem – Hva – Når?*

| What's that building? | **Hvilken bygning er det?** | vilkern **bewg**ning ær dāy |
| Who was the ...? | **Hvem var ...?** | vehm vaar |
| architect | **arkitekten** | ahrki**tehk**tern |
| artist | **kunstneren** | **kewnst**nerrern |
| painter | **maleren** | **maal**errern |
| sculptor | **billedhuggeren** | **bill**erdhewgerrern |
| Who built it? | **Hvem har bygd den?** | vehm haar bewgd dehn |
| Who painted that picture? | **Hvem har malt det bildet?** | vehm haar maalt dāy **bild**er |
| When did he live? | **Når levde han?** | nor **lehv**der hahn |
| When was it built? | **Når ble det bygd?** | nor bleh deh bewgd |
| Where's the house where ... lived? | **Hvor er huset hvor ... bodde?** | vohr ær **hēw**sser voor ... **bood**der |
| We're interested in ... | **Vi interesserer oss for ...** | vee interrehs**sāy**rerr oss for |
| antiques | **antikviteter** | ahntikvit**tāy**terr |
| archaeology | **arkeologi** | ahrkehoo**loo**gee |
| art | **kunst** | kewnst |
| botany | **botanikk** | boota**nik** |
| ceramics | **keramikk** | khæra**hmik** |
| coins | **mynter** | **mewn**terr |
| folk art | **folkekunst** | **folker**kewnst |
| furniture | **møbler** | **murb**lerr |
| geology | **geologi** | gāyoo**loo**gee |
| handicrafts | **kunsthåndverk** | **kewnst**honværk |
| history | **historie** | hist**ōō**ryer |
| maritime history | **sjøfartshistorie** | shūrfah**r**tshist**ōō**ryer |
| medicine | **medisin** | mehd**iss**een |
| modern art | **moderne kunst** | moodæ**r**ner kewnst |
| music | **musikk** | mews**sik** |
| natural history | **naturhistorie** | naht**ēw**rhist**ōō**ryer |
| ornithology | **ornitologi** | oornitoo**loo**gee |
| painting | **maleri** | mahler**ree** |
| pottery | **pottemakerkunst** | **pott**ermaakerrkewnst |
| religion | **religion** | rehligge**ōōn** |
| sculpture | **skulptur** | skewlpt**ēw**r |
| zoology | **zoologi** | soo**loo**gee |
| Where's the ... department? | **Hvor er avdelingen for ...?** | voor ær ahv**dāy**lingern for |

| It's ... | Det er ... | deh ær |
|---|---|---|
| amazing | **praktfullt** | **prahkt**fewlt |
| awful | **forferdelig** | forf**ær**derli |
| beautiful | **vakkert** | **vahker**ᶠt |
| fantastic | **fantastisk** | fahn**tah**stisk |
| gloomy | **dystert** | **dew**ster^rt |
| impressive | **imponerende** | impoon**ay**rerner |
| interesting | **interessant** | interehss**ahngt** |
| magnificent | **storslagent** | st**oo**shlaagernt |
| pretty | **søtt** | surt |
| romantic | **romantisk** | roo**mahn**tisk |
| strange | **underlig** | **ewn**derli |
| superb | **ypperlig** | **ewp**erli |
| terrible | **forferdelig** | forf**ær**derli |
| tremendous | **forskrekkelig** | fosh**krehk**erli |
| ugly | **stygt** | stewkt |

## Churches—Religious services  *Kirker – Gudstjenester*

Norway has a Lutheran state church, but freedom of religion is assured, and other denominations have their own places of worship.

Most churches are open to visitors except, of course, when a service is being conducted.

| Is there a ... | **Fins det en ...** | finss deh ehn ... |
|---|---|---|
| nearby? | **i nærheten?** | ee n**ær**hehtern |
| Catholic church | **katolsk kirke** | kah**too**lsk khirker |
| Protestant church | **protestantisk kirke** | prooter**stahn**tisk khirker |
| mosque | **moské** | moos**kay** |
| synagogue | **synagoge** | sewnah**goo**gger |
| At what time is ...? | **Når begynner ...?** | nor ber**yew**nerr |
| mass | **messen** | **mehs**sern |
| the service | **gudstjenesten** | **gewd**styehnerstern |
| Where can I find a ... who speaks English? | **Hvor kan jeg få tak i en ... som snakker engelsk?** | voor kahn yæi faw taak ee ehn ... som **snahk**kerr **ehn**gerlsk |
| priest | **katolsk prest** | kah**too**lsk prehst |
| minister | **protestantisk prest** | prooter**stahn**tisk prehst |
| rabbi | **rabbiner** | rah**bee**nerr |
| I'd like to visit the church. | **Jeg vil gjerne se kirken.** | yæi vil y**æ**ᶠner s**ay** **khir**kern |

## In the countryside *På landet*

| | | |
|---|---|---|
| Is there a scenic route to ...? | **Fins det en natur-skjønn vei til ...?** | finss deh ehn nahtēwr-shurn væi til |
| How far is it to ...? | **Hvor langt er det til ...?** | voor lahngt ær deh til |
| Can we walk there? | **Kan man spasere dit?** | kahn mahn spahssāyrer deet |
| How high is that mountain? | **Hvor høyt er det fjellet?** | voor hoyt ær dāy fyehler |
| What kind of ... is that? | **Hva slags ... er det?** | vaa shlahkss ... ær dāy |
| animal/bird | **dyr/fugl** | dēwr/fēwl |
| flower/tree | **blomst/tre** | blomst/trāy |

## Landmarks *Landemerker*

| | | |
|---|---|---|
| cliff | **en klippe** | ehn klipper |
| coast | **en kyst** | ehn khewst |
| farm | **en bondegård** | ehn boonergawr |
| field | **et jorde** | eht yōorer |
| fjord | **en fjord** | ehn fyōor |
| footpath | **en sti** | ehn stee |
| forest | **en skog** | ehn skōog |
| garden | **en hage** | ehn haager |
| hill | **en høyde** | ehn hoyder |
| house | **et hus** | eht hēwss |
| inlet | **en vik** | ehn veek |
| island | **en øy** | ehn oy |
| meadow | **en eng** | ehn ehng |
| mountain | **et fjell** | eht fyehl |
| ocean | **et hav** | eht haav |
| path | **en sti** | ehn stee |
| peak | **en topp** | ehn top |
| pond | **en dam** | ehn dahm |
| ridge | **en ås** | ehn awss |
| river | **en elv** | ehn ehlv |
| sea | **en sjø** | ehn shūr |
| spring | **en kilde** | ehn khilder |
| stream | **en bekk** | ehn behk |
| valley | **en dal** | ehn daal |
| wall | **en mur** | ehn mēwr |
| waterfall | **en foss** | ehn foss |
| well | **en brønn** | ehn brurn |

ASKING THE WAY, see page 76

# Relaxing

### Cinema (Movies)—Theatre   *Kino – Teater*

To find out what's on, check the newspapers and advertizing posters, or the weekly/monthly tourist publication in Oslo and other towns.

All films are shown in the original language with Norwegian subtitles. Advance booking is essential for theatres and the opera.

| | | |
|---|---|---|
| I'd like to ... tonight. | **Jeg har lyst til å ... i kveld.** | yæi haar lewst til aw ... ee kvehl |
| go to the cinema<br>go to the teatre | **gå på kino**<br>**gå i teatret** | gaw paw **khee**noo<br>gaw ee tāȳ**aat**rer |
| What's on at the cinema tonight? | **Hvilke filmer vises på kino i kveld?** | vilker **film**err **vee**ssers paw **khee**noo ee kvehl |
| What's playing at the National Theatre? | **Hva spilles på Nationaltheatret?** | vah **spill**erss paw nahshoo**naal**tāȳaatrer |
| What sort of play is it? | **Hva slags stykke er det?** | vah shlahkss **stew**ker ær deh |
| Who's it by? | **Hvem har skrevet det?** | vehm haar **skrāȳ**vert deh |
| Can you recommend a ...? | **Kan du anbefale en ...?** | kahn dew **ahn**berfaaler ehn |
| good film<br>comedy<br>musical<br>revue | **god film**<br>**komedie**<br>**musikal**<br>**revy** | goo(d) film<br>koo**māy**dyer<br>mewssi**kaal**<br>reh**vēw** |
| Where's that new film directed by ... being shown? | **Hvor går den nye filmen av ...?** | voor gawr dehn **nēw**er **film**ern ahv |
| Who's in it? | **Hvem spiller i den?** | vehm **spill**err ee dehn |
| Who's playing the lead? | **Hvem spiller hovedrollen?** | vehm **spill**err **hoo**verd-rollern |
| Who's the director? | **Hvem har regissert den?** | vehm haar rehshiss**āȳ**'t dehn |

| At which theatre is that new play by … being performed? | **På hvilket teater går det nye stykket av …?** | paw vilkert tāyaaterr gawr deh nēwer stewker ahv |
| What time does it begin/finish? | **Når begynner/ slutter det?** | nor beryewnerr/ shlewterr deh |
| How long does it last? | **Hvor lenge varer det?** | voor lehnger vaarerr deh |
| Are there any tickets for tonight? | **Fins det fremdeles billetter til i kveld?** | finss deh frehmdāylerss billehterr til ee kvehl |
| How much are the tickets? | **Hvor mye koster billettene?** | voor mēwer kosterr billehterner |
| I'd like to reserve 2 tickets for the show on Friday evening. | **Jeg vil gjerne be- stille 2 billetter til forestillingen på fredag kveld.** | yæi vil yǣrner ber- stiller 2 billehterr til fawrerstillingern paw frāydah(g) kvehl |
| Can I have a ticket for the matinée on Tuesday? | **Kan jeg få en billett til matinéen på tirsdag?** | kahn yæi faw ehn billeht til mahtināyern paw teeshdah(g) |
| I'd like a seat in the stalls (orchestra). | **Jeg vil gjerne ha en plass i parkett.** | yæi vil yǣrner haa ehn plahss ee pahrkeht |
| Not too far back. | **Ikke for langt bak.** | ikker for lahngt baak |
| Somewhere in the middle. | **Et sted i midten.** | eht stāy(d) ee mittern |
| How much are the tickets for the circle (mezzanine)? | **Hvor mye koster billettene på bal- kongen?** | voor mēwer kosterr billehterner paw bahl- kongern |
| May I have a pro- gramme, please? | **Kan jeg få et program?** | kahn yæi faw eht proograhm |
| Where's the cloakroom? | **Hvor er garderoben?** | voor ær gahrderrōōbern |

---

| 👉 | 👈 |
| --- | --- |
| **Dessverre, det er utsolgt.** | I'm sorry, we're sold out. |
| **Det er bare noen få plasser igjen på balkongen.** | There are only a few seats left in the circle (mezzanine). |
| **Kan jeg få se billetten?** | May I see your ticket? |
| **Dette er din plass.** | This is your seat. |

DAYS OF THE WEEK, see page 150

## Opera—Ballet—Concert   *Opera – Ballett – Konsert*

| | | |
|---|---|---|
| Can you recommend a/an ...? | **Kan du anbefale en ...?** | kahn dew **ahn**berfaaler ehn |
| ballet/concert opera/operetta | **ballett/konsert opera/operette** | bahl**eht**/koon**sæ**ʳt ooperrah/ooper**reh**ter |
| Where's the opera house/the concert hall? | **Hvor er operahuset/ konserthuset?** | voor ær ooperrah**hew̄**sser/ koon**sæ**ʳt**hew̄**sser |
| What's on at the opera tonight? | **Hva spilles på operaen i kveld?** | vah **spill**erss paw **oo**perrahern ee kvehl |
| Who's singing/ dancing? | **Hvem synger/ danser?** | vehm **sewng**err/ **dahn**serr |
| Which orchestra is playing? | **Hvilket orkester spiller?** | **vil**kert or**keh**sterr **spill**err |
| What are they playing? | **Hva spilles?** | vah **spill**erss |
| Who's the conductor/soloist? | **Hvem er dirigent/ solist?** | vehm ær dirri**ggehnt**/ soo**list** |

## Nightclubs   *Nattklubber*

| | | |
|---|---|---|
| Can you recommend a good nightclub? | **Kan du anbefale en bra nattklubb?** | kahn dew **ahn**berfaaler ehn braa **naht**klewb |
| Is there a floor show? | **Vises det noe show?** | **vee**sserss deh **noo**er ''show'' |
| What time does the show start? | **Når begynner showet?** | nor ber**yew**nerr ''schow''er |
| Do I have to wear a tie? | **Er det slipstvang?** | ær deh **shlips**tvahng |

## Discos   *Diskoteker*

| | | |
|---|---|---|
| Where can we go dancing? | **Hvor kan man gå og danse?** | voor kahn mahn gaw o(g) **dahn**ser |
| Is there a discotheque in town/ nearby? | **Fins det et diskotek i byen/i nærheten?** | finss deh eht disko**tāyk** ee **bew̄**ern/ee **nær**rehtern |
| Would you like to dance? | **Skal vi danse?** | skahl vee **dahn**ser |

## Sports *Sport*

| Are there any sporting events going on? | Holdes det noe sportsstevne her for tiden? | hollerss deh nōōer spoᶜrtsstehvner hǣr for teedern |

| athletics (track-and-field) meeting | friidrettsstevne | freeeedrehtsstehvner |
| bicycle racing | sykkelløp | sewkerllūrp |
| car racing | billøp | beellūrp |
| football (soccer) match | fotballkamp | footbahlkahmp |
| horse racing | hesteveddeløp | hehstervehderlūrp |
| ice hockey match | ishockeykamp | eeshokkikahmp |
| regatta | regatta | rehgahtah |
| speed skating | skøyteløp | shoyterlūrp |
| ski race | skirenn | sheerehn |
| ski jumping | skihopping | sheehopping |
| tennis match | tenniskamp | tehniskahmp |

| Is there a football (soccer) match anywhere this Saturday? | Er det en fotball-kamp noe sted på lørdag? | ær deh ehn footbahl-kahmp nōōer stāy(d) paw lūrᶜdah(g) |
| Which teams are playing? | Hvilke lag spiller? | vilker laag spillerr |
| Can you get me a ticket? | Kan du skaffe meg en billett? | kahn dew skahfer mæi ehn billeht |
| I'd like to see an ice-hockey match. | Jeg vil gjerne se en ishockeykamp | yæi vil yǣᶜner sāy ehn eeshokkikahmp |
| What's the admission charge? | Hva koster inngangs-billetten? | vah kosterr ingahngs-billehtern |
| Where's the race course (track)? | Hvor er heste-veddeløpsbanen? | voor ær hehster-vehderlūrpsbaanern |

And if you want to take a more active part:

| Is there a golf course/tennis court nearby? | Fins det en golf-bane/tennisbane i nærheten? | finss deh ehn golfbaaner/tehnisbaaner ee nǣr-hehtern |
| I'd like to play golf/tennis. | Jeg vil gjerne spille golf/tennis. | yæi vil yǣᶜner spiller golf/tehniss |

| What's the charge per ...? | **Hva koster det pr. ....?** | vah kosterr deh pær |
| day/round/hour | **dag/runde/time** | daag/rewnder/teemer |
| Can I hire (rent) rackets? | **Kan man leie racketer?** | kahn mahn læier rehkeh'terr |
| Is there any good fishing around here? | **Fins det en bra fiske-plass i nærheten?** | finss deh ehn braa fisker-plahss ee nærhehtern |
| Do I need a permit? | **Må man ha fiske-kort?** | maw mahn haa fiskerko'rt |
| Can one swim in the lake/river? | **Kan man bade i (inn)sjøen/elven?** | kahn mahn baader ee (in)shürern/ehlvern |
| Is there a swimming pool here? | **Er det et svømme-basseng her?** | ær deh eht svurmer-bahssehng hær |
| Is it an open-air or indoor pool? | **Er det utendørs eller innendørs?** | ær deh ewterndürsh ehlerr innerndürsh |
| Is it heated? | **Er det oppvarmet?** | ær deh opvahrmert |
| Is there a sandy beach? | **Fins det en sand-strand her?** | finss deh ehn sahn-strahn hær |

| bicycling | **sykling** | sewkling |
| (horse-back) riding | **ridning** | reedning |
| fishing | **fiske** | fisker |
| mountain climbing | **fjellklatring** | fyehlklahtring |
| rowing | **roing** | rooing |
| sailing | **seiling** | sæiling |
| swimming | **svømming** | svurming |

## On the beach  *På stranden*

| Is it safe to swim/dive here? | **Er det trygt å bade/dykke her?** | ær deh trewkt aw baader/dewker hær |
| Is there a lifeguard? | **Fins det badevakt?** | finss deh baadervahkt |
| Is it safe for children? | **Er det trygt for barn?** | ær deh trewkt for baa'n |
| Could I have swim-ming lessons? | **Kan man ta svømme-timer?** | kahn mahn taa svurmer-teemerr |
| Are there any dangerous currents? | **Fins det noen farlige strømmer?** | finss deh nööer faa'r-leeyer strurmerr |
| How deep is it? | **Hvor dypt er det?** | voor dewpt ær deh |

| Is it shallow? | **Er det langgrunt?** | ær deh **lahng**grewnt |
| What's the temperature of the water? | **Hvor mange grader er det i vannet?** | voor **mahng**er graaderr ær deh ee vahner |
| I want to hire (rent) a/some ... | **Jeg vil gjerne leie ...** | yæi vil yæ<sup>r</sup>ner læier |
| bathing hut (cabana) | **et badehus** | eht baaderhewss |
| skin-diving equipment | **et dykkerutstyr** | eht dewkerrewtstewr |
| sunshade | **en parasoll** | ehn pahrah**sol** |
| water-skis | **vannski** | **vahn**shee |
| windsurfer | **et seilbrett** | eht **sæil**breht |

| **BADING FORBUDT** | NO SWIMMING |
| **FISKING FORBUDT** | NO FISHING |

## Winter sports  *Vintersport*

| Is there a skating rink near here? | **Fins det en skøyte-bane i nærheten?** | finss deh ehn **shoy**ter-baaner ee **nær**hehtern |
| I'd like to ski. | **Jeg vil gjerne gå på ski.** | yæi vil yæ<sup>r</sup>ner gaw paw shee |
| downhill | **utforkjøring** | **ewt**forkhurring |
| cross-country skiing | **langrenn** | **lahng**rehn |
| Are there any ski runs for ...? | **Fins det noen skibakker for ...?** | finss deh **noo**ern sheebahkerr for |
| beginners | **begynnere** | ber**yew**nerrer |
| average skiers | **middelsgode skiløpere** | **midd**erlsgoo(d)er sheel**ur**perrer |
| good skiers | **gode skiløpere** | **goo**(d)er sheel**ur**perrer |
| Which way are the ski lifts? | **I hvilken retning ligger skiheisene?** | ee **vil**kern **reht**ning **ligg**err shee**hæis**serner |
| Are there any good ski tracks (trails) nearby? | **Fins det noen gode skiløyper i nærheten?** | finss deh **noo**ern **goo**(d)er shee**loy**perr ee **nær**hehtern |
| Are there floodlit ski tracks? | **Fins det lysløyper?** | finss deh **lews**loyperr |
| I'd like to hire ... | **Jeg vil gjerne leie ...** | yæi vil yæ<sup>r</sup>ner læier |
| skates/skis | **skøyter/ski** | **shoy**terr/shee |
| ski boots/poles | **skistøvler/staver** | **shee**sturvlerr/**staa**verr |

Underholdning

# Making friends

## Introduction *Presentasjon*

| | | |
|---|---|---|
| May I introduce ...? | **Får jeg presentere ...?** | fawr yæi prehssern-tāyrer |
| John, this is ... | **John, dette er ...** * | John dehter ær |
| My name is ... | **Mitt navn er ...** | mit nahvn ær |
| Pleased to meet you! | **Hyggelig å treffes!** | hewgerli aw trehferss |
| What's your name? | **Hva heter du?** | vah hāyterr dew |
| How are you? | **Hvordan står det til?** | voo<sup>r</sup>dahn stawr deh til |
| Fine, thanks. And you? | **Bare bra, takk. Og med deg?** | baarer braa tahk. o(g) meh(d) dæi |

## Follow up *Nærmere bekjentskap*

| | | |
|---|---|---|
| How long have you been here? | **Hvor lenge har du vært her?** | voor lehnger haar dew væ<sup>r</sup>t hǣr |
| I've been here a week. | **Jeg har vært her en uke.** | yæi haar væ<sup>r</sup>t hǣr ehn ēwker |
| We're on a 3-day visit. | **Vi er her på et 3-dagers besøk.** | vee ær hǣr paw eht 3-daagersh bersūrk |
| Is this your first visit to Oslo? | **Er det første gang du er i Oslo?** | ær deh furshter gahng dew ær ee ooshloo |
| How do you like Norway? | **Hva synes du om Norge?** | vah sēwnerss dew om norgger |
| We like it here. | **Vi liker oss her.** | vee leekerr oss hǣr |
| What do you think of the country/the people? | **Hva synes du om landet/folket?** | vah sēwnerss dew om lahner/folker |
| The scenery is beautiful. | **Naturen er vakker.** | nahtēwrern ær vahkerr |
| Where do you come from? | **Hvor kommer du fra?** | voor kommer dew fraa |
| I'm from ... | **Jeg er fra ...** | yæi ær fraa |

---

\* The terms Mr., Mrs. and Miss (*herr* – hærr, *fru* – frēw, *frøken* – frūrkern) are very rarely used. People are introduced by their full name.

COUNTRIES, see page 146

5

5

| What nationality are you? | **Hvilken nasjonalitet har du?** | vilkern nahshoonahlitayt haar dew |
| I'm ... | **Jeg er ...** | yæi ær |
| American | **amerikaner** | ahm(er)rikaanerr |
| British | **brite** | breeter |
| Canadian | **kanadier** | kahnaadyer |
| English | **englender** | ehnglehnder |
| Irish | **irlender** | eerlehnderr |
| Where are you staying? | **Hvor bor du her?** | voor boor dew hær |
| Are you on your own? | **Er du her alene?** | ær dew hær ahlayner |
| I'm with my ... | **Jeg er her med ...** | yæi ær hær meh(d) |
| wife/husband | **min kone/min mann** | meen kooner/meen mahn |
| family | **min familie** | meen fahmeelyer |
| children | **mine barn** | meener baa'n |
| parents | **mine foreldre** | meener forehldrer |
| boyfriend/girlfriend | **min venn/venninne** | meen vehn/vehninner |

| father/mother | **far/mor** | faar/moor |
| son/daughter | **sønn/datter** | surn/dahterr |
| brother/sister | **bror/søster** | broor/sursterr |
| uncle/aunt | **onkel/tante** | oongkerl/tahnter |
| nephew/niece | **nevø/niese** | nehvur/neeaysser |
| cousin | **fetter\*/kusine\*\*** | fehterr/kewsseener |

\* masc., \*\* fem.

| Are you married/single? | **Er du gift/ugift?** | ær dew yift/ewyift |
| Do you have children? | **Har du barn?** | haar dew baa'n |
| What do you do? | **Hvilket yrke har du?** | vilkert ewrker haar dew |
| I'm a student. | **Jeg er student.** | yæi ær stewdehnt |
| What are you studying? | **Hva studerer du?** | vah stewdayrerr dew |
| I'm here on a business trip. | **Jeg er her på forretningsreise.** | yæi ær hær paw forrehtningsræisser |
| Do you travel a lot? | **Reiser du mye?** | ræisserr dew mewer |
| Do you play cards/chess? | **Spiller du kort/sjakk?** | spillerr dew ko't/shahk |

Nye venner

## The weather   *Været*

| What a lovely day! | **Hvilken herlig dag!** | vilkern hæ<sup>r</sup>li daag |
|---|---|---|

| What a lovely day! | **Hvilken herlig dag!** | vilkern hæ‍ᵣli daag |
| What awful weather! | **For et forferdelig vær!** | for eht forfærderli vær |
| Isn't it cold/hot today? | **Er det ikke kaldt/ varmt i dag?** | ær deh ikker kahlt/ vahrmt ee daag |
| Is it usually as rainy/warm as this? | **Pleier det å være så regnfullt/varmt?** | plæ‍ierr deh aw væ‍rer saw ræinfewlt/vahrmt |
| Do you think it's going to ... tomorrow? | **Tror du det kommer til å ... i morgen?** | tro‍or dew deh kommerr til aw ... ee mawer‍ᵣn |
| be a nice day | **bli pent vær** | blee pa‍ynt vær |
| rain | **regne** | ræiner |
| snow | **snø** | snur |
| What's the weather forecast? | **Hva er vær- utsiktene?** | vah ær væ‍rewtsikterner |

| cloud | **sky** | shew |
|---|---|---|
| fog | **tåke** | tawker |
| frost | **frost** | frost |
| hail | **hagl** | hahgl |
| ice | **is** | eess |
| lightning | **lyn** | lewn |
| midnight sun | **midnattssol** | midnahtsso‍ol |
| moon | **måne** | mawner |
| rain | **regn** | ræin |
| sky | **himmel** | himmerl |
| snow | **snø** | snur |
| star | **stjerne** | styæ‍ᵣner |
| sun | **sol** | so‍ol |
| thunder | **torden** | toordern |
| thunderstorm | **tordenvær** | toordernvær |
| wind | **vind** | vin |

## Invitations   *Innbydelser*

| Would you like to have dinner with us on ...? | **Vil du spise middag med oss på ...?** | vil dew speesser mid- dah(g) meh(d) oss paw |
|---|---|---|
| May I invite you to lunch? | **Får jeg by på lunsj?** | fawr yæi bew paw lurnsh |

DAYS OF THE WEEK, see page 150

| Can you come round for a drink this evening? | **Kan du komme til en drink i kveld?** | kahn dew **kom**mer til ehn dringk ee kvehl |
| We're having a party. Can you come? | **Vi skal ha fest. Kan du komme?** | vee skahl haa fehst. kahn dew **kom**mer |
| Great. I'd love to come. | **Mange takk. Jeg kommer gjerne.** | **mahng**er tahk. yæi **kom**merr yǣ<sup>r</sup>ner |
| What time shall I come? | **Når skal jeg komme?** | nor skahl yæi **kom**mer |
| May I bring a friend? | **Kan jeg ta med en venn?** | kahn yæi taa meh(d) ehn vehn |
| I'm afraid we've got to leave now. | **Vi må dessverre gå nå.** | vee maw **dehs**værer gaw naw |
| Next time you (pl.) must come to visit us. | **Neste gang må dere besøke oss.** | **neh**ster gahng maw **dāy**rer ber**sūr**ker oss |
| Thanks for the evening. | **Takk for i kveld.** | tahk for ee kvehl |
| It was great. | **Det var veldig hyggelig.** | det vaar **vehl**di **hew**gerli |

## Dating *Stevnemøte*

| Do you mind if I smoke? | **Har du noe imot at jeg røyker?** | haar dew **nōō**er ee**mōōt** aht yæi **roy**kerr |
| Would you like a cigarette? | **Vil du ha en sigarett?** | vil dew haa ehn sigga**reht** |
| Do you have a light, please? | **Har du fyr?** | haar dew fēwr |
| Why are you laughing? | **Hvorfor ler du?** | **voor**for lāyr dew |
| Is my Norwegian that bad? | **Snakker jeg så dårlig norsk?** | **snah**kerr yæi saw **daw**<sup>r</sup>li noshk |
| Do you mind if I sit down here? | **Har du noe imot at jeg setter meg her?** | haar dew **nōō**er ee**mōōt** aht yæi **seh**terr mæi hǣr |
| Would you like a drink? | **Har du lyst på en drink?** | haar dew lewst paw ehn dringk |
| Are you waiting for someone? | **Venter du på noen?** | **vehn**terr dew paw **nōō**ern |

| Are you free this evening? | **Er du ledig i kveld?** | ær dew lāydi ee kvehl |
| Would you like to go out with me tonight? | **Skal vi gå ut i kveld?** | skahl vee gaw ēwt ee kvehl |
| Would you like to go dancing? | **Har du lyst til å gå ut og danse?** | haar dew lewst til aw gaw ēwt o(g) dahnser |
| I know a good discotheque. | **Jeg vet om et bra diskotek.** | yæi vāyt om eht braa diskootāyk |
| Shall we go to the cinema (movies)? | **Skal vi gå på kino?** | skahl vee gaw paw **khee**noo |
| Would you like to go for a drive? | **Har du lyst til å kjøre en tur?** | haar dew lewst til aw **khur**rer ehn tēwr |
| Where shall we meet? | **Hvor skal vi møtes?** | voor skahl vee **mūr**terss |
| I'll pick you up at your hotel. | **Jeg henter deg på hotellet.** | yæi **hehn**terr dæi paw hoo**teh**ler |
| I'll call for you at 8. | **Jeg henter deg kl. 8.** | yæi **hehn**terr dæi **klok**kern 8 |
| May I take you home? | **Kan jeg få følge deg hjem?** | kahn yæi faw **furl**er dæi yehm |
| Can I see you again tomorrow? | **Skal vi ses igjen i morgen?** | skahl vee **sāy**ss ee**yehn** ee **maw**er'n |
| I hope we'll meet again. | **Jeg håper vi ses igjen.** | yæi **haw**perr vee **sāy**ss ee**yehn** |

... and you might answer:

| I'd love to, thank you. | **Takk, det vil jeg gjerne.** | tahk deh vil yæi **yæ**rner |
| That's very kind of you. | **Det er veldig snilt av deg.** | deh ær **vehl**di snilt ahv dæi |
| Thank you, but I'm busy. | **Takk, men jeg er dessverre opptatt.** | tahk mehn yæi ær dehs**væ**rer **op**taht |
| Leave me alone, please. | **Vær så snill å la meg være i fred.** | vær saw snill aw laa mæi **væ**rer ee frāy(d) |
| Thank you, it's been a wonderful evening. | **Takk, det har vært en veldig hyggelig kveld.** | tahk deh haar væ'rt ehn **vehl**di **hew**gerli kvehl |

# Shopping guide

This shopping guide is designed to help you find what you want with ease, accuracy and speed. It features:

1. A list of all major shops, stores and services (p. 98).
2. Some general expressions required when shopping to allow you to be specific and selective (p. 100).
3. Full details of the shops and services most likely to concern you. Here you'll find advice, alphabetical lists of items and conversion charts listed under the headings below.

|  |  | page |
|---|---|---|
| **Bookshop/ Stationer's** | books, magazines, newspapers, stationery | 104 |
| **Camping equipment** | all items required for camping | 106 |
| **Chemist's (Drugstore)** | medicine, first-aid, cosmetics, toilet articles | 108 |
| **Clothes** | clothes and accessories, shoes | 112 |
| **Electrical appliances** | hi-fi equipment, household appliances | 119 |
| **Grocer's/ Supermarket** | some general expressions, weights, measures and packaging | 120 |
| **Jeweller's Watchmaker's** | jewellery, watches, watch repairs | 121 |
| **Optician** | glasses, lenses, binoculars | 123 |
| **Photography** | cameras, films, developing, accessories | 124 |
| **Tobacconist's** | smoker's supplies | 126 |
| **Miscellaneous** | souvenirs, records, cassettes, toys | 127 |

LAUNDRY, see page 29/HAIRDRESSER, see page 30

**Shops, stores and services**   *Butikker og servicenæringer*

Hours vary, but most shops are open from 9 a.m. to 5 p.m.,
Monday to Friday, and from 9 a.m. to 2 p.m. on Saturdays.
Centrally located kiosks selling newspapers, tobacco and
sweets may stay open till 11 p.m. Fruit, vegetable and flower
markets normally open from 7 or 8 a.m. to 2 or 3 p.m., Monday to Saturday.

| Where can I find a/an ...? | **Hvor er det ...?** | voor ær deh |
|---|---|---|
| antique shop | **en antikvitets-forretning** | ehn ahntikvitt<del>ay</del>ts-forrehtning |
| art gallery | **et kunstgalleri** | eht kewnstgahlerree |
| baker's | **et bakeri** | eht baakerree |
| bank | **en bank** | ehn bahngk |
| barber's | **en herrefrisør** | ehn hærerfrissürr |
| beauty salon | **en skjønnhetssalong** | ehn shurnhehtssahlong |
| bookshop | **en bokhandel** | ehn b<del>oo</del>khahnderl |
| butcher's | **en slakter** | ehn shlahkterr |
| cake shop | **et konditori** | eht koondittooree |
| camera shop | **en fotoforretning** | ehn f<del>oo</del>tooforrehtning |
| candy store | **en godtebutikk** | ehn goterbewtik |
| cheese shop | **en osteforretning** | ehn oosterforrehtning |
| chemist's | **et apotek** | eht ahpoot<del>ay</del>k |
| china shop | **et glassmagasin** | eht glahsmahgahsseen |
| dairy | **en melkebutikk** | ehn mehlkerbewtik |
| delicatessen | **en delikatesse-forretning** | ehn dehlikkat**eh**sser-forrehtning |
| dentist | **en tannlege** | ehn tahnl<del>ay</del>ger |
| department store | **et stormagasin** | eht st<del>oo</del>rmahgahsseen |
| doctor | **en lege** | ehn l<del>ay</del>ger |
| drugstore | **et apotek** | eht ahpoot<del>ay</del>k |
| dry cleaner's | **et renseri** | eht rehnserree |
| electrical goods shop | **en elektrisitets-forretning** | ehn ehlehktrissit<del>ay</del>ts-forrehtning |
| fishmonger's | **en fiskebutikk** | ehn fiskerbewtik |
| flea market | **et loppemarked** | eht loppermahrkerd |
| florist's | **en blomsterbutikk** | ehn blomsterrbewtik |
| furrier's | **en pelsforretning** | ehn pehlsforrehtning |
| greengrocer's | **en grønnsakhandel** | ehn grurnsaakhahnderl |
| grocer's | **en matvarehandel** | ehn maatvaarerhahnderl |
| hairdresser (ladies/men) | **en frisør (dame-/herre-)** | ehn friss<del>ü</del>rr (daamer-/hærer-) |
| hardware store | **en jernvarehandel** | ehn yæ<sup>r</sup>nvaarerhahnderl |

| English | Norwegian | Pronunciation |
|---|---|---|
| health food shop | en helsekost-forretning | ehn **hehl**serkost-forrehtning |
| hospital | et sykehus | eht **sew**kerhewss |
| ironmonger's | en jernvarehandel | ehn yæ<sup>r</sup>nvaarerhahnderl |
| jeweller's | en gullsmed | ehn gewlsmāy(d) |
| launderette | et selvbetjenings-vaskeri | eht **sehl**bertyāynings-vahskerree |
| laundry | et vaskeri | eht vahskerree |
| library | et bibliotek | eht biblyootāyk |
| liquor store | et vinmonopol | eht **veen**moonoopōōl |
| market | en torghandel | ehn **torg**hahnderl |
| newsstand | en aviskiosk | ehn ah**vees**khyosk |
| optician | en optiker | ehn **op**tikkerr |
| pastry shop | et konditori | eht koondittooree |
| perfumery | et parfymeri | eht pahrfewmerree |
| pharmacy | et apotek | eht ahpootāyk |
| photographer | en fotograf | ehn footoograaf |
| police station | en politistasjon | ehn poolit**tee**stahshōōn |
| post office | et postkontor | eht **post**koontōōr |
| second-hand shop | en marsjandise-forretning | ehn mahshahn**dees**ser-forrehtning |
| shoemaker's (repairs) | en skomaker | ehn **skōō**maakerr |
| shoe shop | en skoforretning | ehn **skōō**forrehtning |
| shopping centre | et butikksenter | eht bew**tik**sehnterr |
| souvenir shop | en suvenirbutikk | ehn sewver**neer**bewtik |
| sporting goods shop | en sportsforretning | ehn **spo**<sup>r</sup>tsforrehtning |
| stationer's | en papirhandel | ehn pah**peer**hahnderl |
| supermarket | et supermarked | eht **sew**perrmahrkerd |
| sweet shop | en godtebutikk | ehn **go**terbewtik |
| tailor's | en skredder | ehn **skreh**derr |
| telegraph office | et telesenter | eht **tāy**lerssehnterr |
| tobacconist's | en tobakkshandel | ehn too**bahks**hahnderl |
| toy shop | en leketøysbutikk | ehn **lāy**kertoysbewtik |
| travel agency | et reisebyrå | eht **ræi**sserbewraw |
| vegetable store | en grønnsakhandel | ehn **grurn**saakhahnderl |
| veterinarian | en dyrlege | ehn **dewr**lāyger |
| watchmaker's | en urmaker | ehn **ēwr**maakerr |
| wine merchant | et vinmonopol | eht **veen**moonoopōōl |

| INNGANG | ENTRANCE |
|---|---|
| UTGANG | EXIT |
| NØDUTGANG | EMERGENCY EXIT |

## General expressions *Vanlige uttrykk*

### Where? *Hvor?*

| | | |
|---|---|---|
| Where's there a good ...? | **Hvor fins det en god ...?** | voor finss deh ehn goo(d) |
| Where can I find a ...? | **Hvor finner jeg en ...?** | voor finnerr yæi ehn |
| Where's the (main) shopping area? | **Hvor er (det største) handlestrøket?** | voor ær (deh sturshter) hahndlerstrürker |
| Is it far from here? | **Er det langt herfra?** | ær deh lahngt hærfrah |
| How do I get there? | **Hvordan kommer jeg dit?** | voorᵈdahn kommerr yæi deet |

| | |
|---|---|
| **(UT)SALG** | SALE |
| **TILBUDSVARE** | BARGAIN |

## Service *Betjening*

| | | |
|---|---|---|
| Can you help me? | **Kan du hjelpe meg?** | kahn dew yehlper mæi |
| I'm just looking. | **Jeg bare ser meg omkring.** | yæi baarer sāyr mæi omkring |
| Do you sell ...? | **Selger dere ...?** | sehlerr dāyrer |
| I'd like to buy ... | **Jeg vil gjerne kjøpe ...** | yæi vil yǣᵣner khürper |
| Can you show me ...? | **Kan du vise meg ...?** | kahn dew veesser mæi |
| this/that | **dette/det** | dehter/deh |
| the one in the window | **den i vinduet** | dehn ee vindewer |
| the one in the display case | **den i monteren** | dehn ee monterrern |
| Do you have any ...? | **Har du noen ...?** | har dew nōōern |
| Where's the ...? | **Hvor er ...?** | voor ær |
| ... department | **-avdelingen** | -ahvdāylingern |
| lift (elevator) | **heisen** | hæissern |
| escalator | **rulletrappen** | rewlertrahpern |
| Where do I pay? | **Hvor betaler man?** | voor bertaalerr mahn |

## Defining the article   *Varebeskrivelse*

| I'd like a ... one. | **Jeg vil gjerne ha en ...** | yæi vil yæ<sup>r</sup>ner haa ehn |
|---|---|---|

| big | **stor** | stoor |
| cheap | **rimelig** | reemerli |
| dark | **mørk** | murrk |
| good | **god** | goo(d) |
| heavy | **tung** | toong |
| large | **stor** | stoor |
| light (weight) | **lett** | leht |
| light (colour) | **lys** | lewss |
| oval | **oval** | oovaal |
| rectangular | **rektangulær** | rehktahngewlær |
| round | **rund** | rewn |
| small | **liten** | leetern |
| square | **firkantet** | firkahntert |
| sturdy | **robust/solid** | roobewst/sooleed |

| I don't want anything too expensive. | **Jeg vil ikke ha noe for dyrt.** | yæi vil ikker haa nooer for dew<sup>r</sup>t |

## Preference   *Jeg foretrekker ...*

| Can you show me some others? | **Kan du vise meg noen andre?** | kahn dew veesser mæi nooern ahndrer |
| Don't you have anything ...? | **Har du ikke noe ...?** | haar dew ikker nooer |

| cheaper/better | **rimeligere/bedre** | reemerleeyerrer/bāydrer |
| larger/smaller | **større/mindre** | sturrer/mindrer |

| It's too ... | **Den er for ...** | den ær for |

| big/small | **stor/liten** | stoor/leetern |
| dark/light | **mørk/lys** | murrk/lewss |

## How much?   *Hvor mye?*

| How much is this? | **Hvor mye koster dette?** | voor mēwer kosterr dehter |
| How much are they? | **Hvor mye koster de?** | voor mēwer kosterr dee |
| I don't understand. | **Jeg forstår ikke.** | yæi foshtawr ikker |
| Please write it down. | **Kan du skrive det?** | kahn dew skreever deh |
| I don't want to spend more than... kroner. | **Jeg vil ikke gi mer enn ... kroner.** | yæi vil ikker yee māyr ehn ... kroonerr |

COLOURS, see page 113

### Decision  *Avgjørelse*

| I'll take it. | **Jeg tar det.** | yæi taar deh |
| No, I don't like it. | **Nei, jeg liker det ikke.** | næi yæi leekerr deh ikker |
| It's not quite what I want. | **Det er ikke akkurat det jeg hadde tenkt meg.** | deh ær ikker ahkewraat deh yæi hahder tehngkt mæi |

### Ordering—Delivery  *Bestilling – Levering*

| Can you order it for me? | **Kan du bestille det til meg?** | kahn dew berstiller deh til mæi |
| How long will it take? | **Hvor lang tid tar det?** | voor lahng teed taar deh |
| I'll take it with me. | **Jeg tar det med meg.** | yæi taar deh meh(d) mæi |
| Deliver it to the ... Hotel. | **Kan du levere det til ... hotell?** | kahn dew lehvāyrer deh til ... hootehl |
| Please send it to this address. | **Kan du sende det til denne adressen?** | kahn dew sehner deh til dehner ahdrehssern |
| Will I have any difficulties with the customs? | **Kan jeg få problemer i tollen?** | kahn yæi faw prooblāymerr ee tollern |

### Paying  *Betaling*

| How much is it? | **Hvor mye blir det?** | voor mēwer bleer deh |
| Can I pay by traveller's cheque? | **Kan jeg betale med reisesjekk?** | kahn yæi bertaaler meh(d) ræissershehk |
| Do you accept dollars/pounds? | **Tar dere dollar/pund?** | taar dāyrer dollahr/pewn |
| Do you accept credit cards? | **Tar dere kreditt-kort?** | taar dāyrer krehditko<sup>r</sup>t |
| Can I get the VAT (sales tax) back? | **Får jeg tilbakebetalt momsen?** | fawr yæi tilbaakerbertaalt moomsern |
| Could I have a receipt? | **Kan jeg få kvittering?** | kahn yæi faw kvittāyring |
| I think there's a mistake in the bill. | **Jeg tror det er en feil på regningen.** | yæi trōor deh ær ehn fæil paw ræiningern |

Shopping

## Anything else?   *Noe annet?*

| No, thanks, that's all. | **Nei takk. Det var alt.** | næi tahk. deh vaar ahlt |
| Yes, I'd like ... | **Ja, jeg vil gjerne ha ...** | yaa yæi vil yæ<sup>r</sup>ner haa |
| May I have a bag, please? | **Kan jeg få en bærepose?** | kahn yæi faw ehn **bæ**rerpōosser |
| Could you wrap it up for me, please? | **Kan du pakke det inn for meg?** | kahn dew **pah**ker deh in for mæi |

## Dissatisfied?   *Misfornøyd?*

| Can you exchange this, please? | **Kan jeg få byttet dette?** | kahn yæi faw **bew**tert **deh**ter |
| I want to return this. | **Jeg vil gjerne levere tilbake dette.** | yæi vil yæ<sup>r</sup>ner leh**vāy**rer til**baa**ker **deh**ter |
| Could I have a refund? | **Kan jeg få pengene tilbake?** | kahn yæi faw **pehng**erner til**baa**ker. |
| Here's the receipt. | **Her er kvitteringen.** | hǣr ær kvit**tāy**ringern |

---

| 🖙 | 🖚 |
|---|---|
| **Kan jeg hjelpe deg?** | Can I help you? |
| **Hva skal det være?** | What would you like? |
| **Hvilken ... vil du ha?** | What ... would you like? |
| **farge/form** | colour/shape |
| **Jeg beklager. Det har vi ikke.** | I'm sorry, we don't have any. |
| **Det er vi utsolgt for.** | We're out of stock. |
| **Skal vi bestille det?** | Shall we order it for you? |
| **Tar du det med eller skal vi sende det?** | Will you take it with you or shall we send it? |
| **Skal det være noe annet?** | Anything else? |
| **Det blir ... kroner, takk.** | That comes to ... kroner. |
| **Kassen er der borte.** | The cash desk is over there. |

## Bookshop—Stationer's   *Bokhandel – Papirhandel*

In Norway, books and stationery are usually sold in the same shop. You'll find newspapers, magazines and paperbacks at newsstands and tobacconists.

| English | Norwegian | Pronunciation |
|---|---|---|
| Where's the nearest ...? | Hvor er nærmeste ...? | voor ær nærmehster |
| bookshop | bokhandel | bōokhahnderl |
| stationer's | papirhandel | pahpeerhahnderl |
| newsstand | aviskiosk | ahveeskhyosk |
| Where can I buy an English-language newspaper? | Hvor kan jeg få kjøpt en engelskspråklig avis? | voor kahn yæi faw khurpt ehn ehngerlsksprawkli ahveess |
| Where's the guidebook section? | Hvor står reisehåndbøkene? | voor stawr ræisserhonbūrkerner |
| Where are the English books? | Hvor står de engelske bøkene? | voor stawr dee ehngerlsker būrkerner |
| Do you have any of ...'s books in English? | Har dere noen av ...s bøker på engelsk? | haar dāyrer nōoern ahv ...s būrkerr paw ehngerlsk |
| I'd like a/an/some ... | Jeg vil gjerne ha ... | yæi vil yǣrner haa |
| address book | en adressebok | ehn ahdrehssserbōok |
| adhesive tape | limbånd | leembon |
| ball-point pen | en kulepenn | ehn kēwlerpehn |
| blotting paper | trekkpapir | trehkpahpeer |
| book | en bok | ehn bōok |
| calendar | en kalender | ehn kahlehnderr |
| carbon paper | blåpapir | blawpahpeer |
| chalk | kritt | krit |
| crayons | fargeblyanter | fahrggerblēwahnterr |
| dictionary | en ordbok | ehn ōorbōok |
|   pocket | lomme- | loommer- |
|   Norwegian-English | norsk-engelsk | noshk-ehngerlsk |
| drawing pad | en tegneblokk | ehn tæinerblok |
| drawing pins | tegnestifter | tæinerstifterr |
| envelopes | noen konvolutter | nōoern koonvoolewterr |
| eraser | et viskelær | eht viskerlǣr |
| exercise book | en skrivebok | ehn skreeverbōok |
| felt-tip pen | en tusjpenn | ehn tewshpehn |
| fountain pen | en fyllepenn | ehn fewlerpehn |
| gift wrapping paper | gavepapir | gaaverpahpeer |

| | | |
|---|---|---|
| glue | **lim** | leem |
| grammar book | **en grammatikk** | ehn grahmahtik |
| guidebook | **en reisehåndbok** | ehn ræisserhonbook |
| ink | **blekk** | blehk |
| (self-adhesive) labels | **noen (selvklebende) etiketter** | nooern (sehlklayberner) ehtikehterr |
| magazine | **et ukeblad** | eht ewkerblaa(d) |
| map | **et kart** | eht kahrt |
| street map of ... | **et kart over ...** | eht kahrt awverr |
| road map of ... | **et veikart over ...** | eht væikahrt awverr |
| mechanical pencil | **en skrublyant** | ehn skrewblewahnt |
| newspaper | **en avis** | ehn ahveess |
| American | **amerikansk** | ahm(eh)rikaansk |
| English | **engelsk** | ehngerlsk |
| notebook | **en notiskbok** | ehn nooteesbook |
| note paper | **brevpapir** | brayvpahpeer |
| phrase book | **en parlør** | ehn pahrlurr |
| paintbox | **et malerskrin** | eht maalerrskreen |
| paper | **papir** | pahpeer |
| paperback | **en pocketbok** | ehn pokkertbook |
| paperclips | **binders** | bindersh |
| paper napkins | **papirservietter** | pahpeersærvyehterr |
| pen | **penn** | pehn |
| pencil | **en blyant** | ehn blewahnt |
| pencil sharpener | **en blyantspisser** | ehn blewahntspisserr |
| picturebook | **en billedbok** | ehn billerdbook |
| playing cards | **spillkort** | spilkort |
| pocket calculator | **en lommekalkulator** | ehn lommerkahlkewlaatoor |
| postcard | **et postkort** | eht postkort |
| propelling pencil | **en skrublyant** | ehn skrewblewahnt |
| refill (for a pen) | **en refill** | ehn ''refill'' |
| rubber | **et viskelær** | eht viskerlær |
| rubber bands | **gummistrikker** | gewmistrikkerr |
| ruler | **en linjal** | ehn linyaal |
| stapler | **en heftemaskin** | ehn hehftermahsheen |
| staples | **heftestifter** | hehfterstifterr |
| string | **hyssing** | hewssing |
| thumbtacks | **tegnestifter** | tæinerstifterr |
| tissue paper | **silkepapir** | silkerpahpeer |
| travel guide | **en reisehåndbok** | ehn ræisserhonbook |
| typewriter ribbon | **et fargebånd (til skrivemaskin)** | eht fahrggerbon (til skreevermahsheen) |
| typing paper | **skrivemaskinpapir** | skreevermahsheenpahpeer |
| (box of) watercolors | **et malerskrin** | eht maalerrskreen |
| wrapping paper | **innpakningspapir** | inpahkningspahpeer |
| writing pad | **en skriveblokk** | ehn skreeverblok |
| writing paper | **skrivepapir** | skreeverpahpeer |

## Camping equipment *Campingutstyr*

I'd like a/an/ some ...

**Jeg vil gjerne ha ...** yæi vil yæ<sup>r</sup>ner haa

| | | |
|---|---|---|
| air bed (mattress) | en luftmadrass | ehn lewftmahdrahss |
| aluminum foil (Am.) | aluminiumsfolie | ahlewmeenyewmsfōolyer |
| backpack | en ryggsekk | ehn rewgsehk |
| bottle-opener | en flaskeåpner | ehn flahskerawpnerr |
| bucket | en bøtte | eht burter |
| butane gas | butangass | bewtaangahss |
| camp bed | en campingseng | ehn kæmpingsehng |
| candles | stearinlys | stehahreenlewss |
| can opener | en boksåpner | ehn boksawpnerr |
| charcoal briquets | trekullbriketter | trāykewlbrikkehterr |
| clothes pegs (pins) | klesklyper | klāysklēwperr |
| compass | et kompass | eht koompahss |
| cool bag | en kjøleboks | ehn khūrlerbokss |
| corkscrew | en korketrekker | ehn korkertrehkerr |
| crockery | et servise | eht særveesser |
| deck chair | en fluktstol | ehn flewktstōol |
| dish detergent | et oppvaskmiddel | eht opvahskmidderl |
| fire lighter | tennvæske | tehnvehsker |
| fishing tackle | fiskeutstyr | fiskerēwtstēwr |
| flashlight | en lommelykt | ehn loommerlewkt |
| folding chair | en klappstol | ehn klahpstōōl |
| folding table | et klappbord | eht klahpbōōr |
| food box | en matboks | ehn maatbokss |
| frying pan | en stekepanne | ehn stāykerpahner |
| groundsheet | et teltunderlag | eht tehltewnerrlaag |
| hammer | en hammer | ehn hahmerr |
| hammock | en hengekøye | ehn hehngerkoyer |
| ice chest | en kjøleboks | ehn khūrlerbokss |
| (cooler) ice packs | kjøleelementer | khurlerehlermehnterr |
| insect spray (killer) | en insektgift | ehn insehktyift |
| kerosene | parafin | pahrahfeen |
| (oil) lamp | en (olje)lampe | ehn (olyer)lahmper |
| lantern | en lykt | ehn lewkt |
| matches | fyrstikker | fewshtikkerr |
| (foam rubber) mattress | en (skumgummi-) madrass | ehn (skoomgewmmi-) mahdrahss |
| mosquito net | et myggnett | eht mewgneht |
| paper napkins | papirservietter | pahpeersærvyehterr |
| paper towel | husholdningspapir | hēwsholningspahpeer |
| paraffin | parafin | pahrahfeen |
| penknife | en lommekniv | ehn lommerkneev |
| picnic basket | en picnickurv | ehn piknikkewrv |

CAMPING, see page 32

| plastic bags | plastposer | plahstpōōsserr |
| pliers | en tang | ehn tahng |
| pocketknife | en lommekniv | ehn lommerkneev |
| pot holders | grytekluter | grēwterklewterr |
| primus stove | en primus | ehn preemewss |
| pump | en pumpe | ehn poomper |
| rope | et tau | eht tou |
| rucksack | en ryggsekk | ehn rewgsehk |
| saucepan | en kasserolle | ehn kahsserroller |
| scissors | en saks | ehn sahkss |
| screwdriver | en skrutrekker | ehn skrēwtrehkerr |
| sleeping bag | en sovepose | ehn sawverpōōsser |
| stew pot | en gryte | ehn grēwter |
| tent | et telt | eht tehlt |
| tent pegs | teltplugger | tehltplewgerr |
| tent pole | en teltstang | ehn tehltstahng |
| tinfoil | aluminiumsfolie | ahlewmeenyewmsfōōlyer |
| tin opener | en boksåpner | ehn boksawpnerr |
| torch | en lommelykt | ehn loommerlewkt |
| vacuum flask | en termosflaske | ehn tærmoosflahsker |
| washing powder | vaskepulver | vahskerpewlverr |
| water flask | en feltflaske | ehn fehltflahsker |

---

## Crockery   *Servise*

| cups | kopper | kopperr |
| mugs | krus | krēwss |
| dishes | fat | faat |
| bowls | skåler | skawlerr |
| plates | tallerkener | tahlærkernerr |
| saucers | skåler (til kopper) | skawlerr (til kopperr) |
| tumblers | drikkeglass | drikkerglahss |
| (made of) cardboard | (av) papp | (ahv) pahp |

## Cutlery (Flatware)   *Bestikk*

| forks | gafler | gahflerr |
| knives | kniver | kneeverr |
| spoons | skjeer | shayerr |
| teaspoons | teskjeer | tayshayerr |
| (made of) plastic | (av) plast | (ahv) plahst |
| (made of) stainless steel | (av) rustfritt stål | (ahv) rewstfrit stawl |

### Chemist's (Drugstore) *Apotek*

Norwegian pharmacies don't stock the wide range of goods that you'll find in Britain or the U.S. For example, they don't sell photographic equipment or toys. And for perfume, cosmetics, etc., you have to go to a *parfymeri* (pahrfewmer**ree**). You need a prescription for most medicine.

In the window you'll see a notice telling you where the nearest all-night pharmacy is.

This section is divided into two parts:

1. Pharmaceutical—medicine, first-aid, etc.
2. Toiletry—toilet articles, cosmetics

### General *Allment*

| | | |
|---|---|---|
| Where's the nearest (all-night) chemist's? | **Hvor er nærmeste (vakthavende) apotek?** | voor ær nærmehster (vahkthaaverner) ahpoot**ayk** |
| What time does the chemist's open/close? | **Når åpner/stenger apoteket?** | nor **awp**nerr/**stehng**err ahpoot**ay**ker |

### 1. Pharmaceutical *Medisiner*

| | | |
|---|---|---|
| I'd like something for ... | **Jeg vil gjerne ha noe mot ...** | yæi vil yæ͞ᵣner haa no͞oer mo͞ot |
| a cold | **forkjølelse** | forkhu͞rlerlser |
| a cough | **hoste** | hoo͞ster |
| a headache | **hodepine** | ho͞oderpeener |
| hay fever | **høysnue** | hoysne͞wer |
| insect bites | **insektstikk** | insehktstik |
| sunburn | **solforbrenning** | so͞olforbrehning |
| travel sickness | **reisesyke** | ræisserse͞wker |
| an upset stomach | **urolig mage** | ewro͞oli maager |
| Can you make up this prescription for me? | **Kan du gjøre i stand denne resepten for meg?** | kahn dew yu͞rrer ee stahn dehner rehssehptern for mæi |
| Can I get it without a prescription? | **Kan jeg få det uten resept?** | kahn yæi faw deh e͞wtern rehssehpt |
| Shall I wait? | **Skal jeg vente?** | skahl yæi **vehn**ter |

DOCTOR, see page 137

| Can I have a/an/some ...? | Kan jeg få ...? | kahn yæi faw |
|---|---|---|
| absorbent cotton | bomull | boomewl |
| analgesic | et analgetikum | eht ahnahlgāytikewm |
| antiseptic cream | en antiseptisk salve | ehn ahntissehptisk sahlver |
| aspirin | aspirin | ahspirreen |
| bandage | en bandasje | ehn bahndaasher |
| elastic bandage | et elastisk bind | eht ehlahstisk bin |
| Band-Aids | plaster | plahsterr |
| ... capsules | -kapsler | -kahpshlerr |
| charcoal tablets | kulltabletter | kewltahblehterr |
| condoms | kondomer | koondōōmerr |
| contraceptives | et preventivmiddel | eht prāyvahngteevmidderl |
| corn plasters | liktornplaster | leektōōᵣnplahsterr |
| cotton wool | bomull | boomewl |
| cough drops | halspastiller | hahlspahstillerr |
| cough syrup | hostesaft | hoostersahft |
| disinfectant | et desinfeksjons-middel | eht dehssinfehkshōōns-midderl |
| ear drops | øredråper | ūrrerdrawperr |
| Elastoplast | plaster | plahsterr |
| eye drops | øyendråper | oyerndrawperr |
| first-aid kit | et førstehjelpsskrin | eht furshteryehlpsskreen |
| (roll of) gauze | (en rull) gasbind | (ehn rewl) gahsbin |
| insect repellent | et insektmiddel | eht insehktmidderl |
| iodine | jod | yod |
| laxative | et laksermiddel | eht lahksāyrmidderl |
| mouthwash | et munnvann | eht mewnvahn |
| nose drops | nesedråper | nāysserdrawperr |
| ... ointment | -salve | -sahlver |
| painkiller | et smertestillende middel | eht smæᵣterstillerner midderl |
| sanitary towels (napkins) | sanitetsbind | sahnitāytsbin |
| suppositories | stikkpiller | stikpillerr |
| ... tablets | -tabletter | -tahblehterr |
| tampons | tamponger | tahmpongerr |
| thermometer | termometer | tærmoomāyterr |
| throat lozenges | halstabletter | hahlstahblehterr |
| vitamin pills | vitaminpiller | vittahmeenpillerr |

| GIFT | POISON |
|---|---|
| KUN TIL UTVENDIG BRUK | FOR EXTERNAL USE ONLY |

## 2. Toiletry   *Toalettartikler*

| I'd like a/an/ some ... | **Jeg vil gjerne ha ...** | yæi vil yǣᵣner haa |
|---|---|---|
| after-shave lotion | **et etterbarberings-vann** | eht ehterrbahrbāyrings-vahn |
| bath salts | **et badesalt** | eht baadersahlt |
| blusher | **en rouge** | ehn rōōsh |
| bubble bath | **et skumbad** | eht skoombaad |
| cosmetics | **noe kosmetikk** | nōōer koosmertik |
| cream | **en krem** | ehn krāym |
| cleansing cream | **en rensekrem** | ehn **rehn**serkrāym |
| foot cream | **en fotkrem** | ehn **fōōt**krāym |
| foundation cream | **en underlagskrem** | ehn **ewn**errlaagskrāym |
| hand cream | **en håndkrem** | ehn **hon**krāym |
| moisturizing cream | **en fuktighetskrem** | ehn **fookt**ihehtskrāym |
| night cream | **en nattkrem** | ehn **naht**krāym |
| sun-tan cream | **en solkrem** | ehn **sōōl**krāym |
| cuticle remover | **en neglebåndsfjerner** | ehn næilerbonsfyǣᵣnerr |
| deodorant | **en deodorant** | ehn dehoodoo**rahnt** |
| emery boards | **sandpapirfiler** | sahnpahpeerfeelerr |
| eyebrow pencil | **en øyenbrynsstift** | ehn oyernbrēwnsstift |
| eye liner | **en eyeliner** | ehn "eyeliner" |
| eye shadow | **en øyenskygge** | ehn oyernshewger |
| face flannel | **en ansiktsklut** | ehn ahnsiktsklēwt |
| face powder | **pudder** | pewderr |
| lipbrush | **en leppestiftpensel** | ehn lehperstiftpehnserl |
| lipsalve (balm) | **en leppepomade** | ehn lehperpoomaader |
| lipstick | **en leppestift** | ehn lehperstift |
| make-up bag | **en sminkepung** | ehn smingkerpoong |
| make-up remover pads | **bomullspads** | boomewls"pads" |
| mascara | **en øyensverte** | ehn oyernsvæᵣter |
| nail brush | **en neglebørste** | ehn næilerburshter |
| nail clippers | **en negleklipper** | ehn næilerklipperr |
| nail file | **en neglefil** | ehn næilerfeel |
| nail polish | **en neglelakk** | ehn næilerlahk |
| nail polish remover | **en neglelakkfjerner** | ehn næilerlahkfyǣᵣnerr |
| nail scissors | **en neglesaks** | ehn næilersahkss |
| perfume | **en parfyme** | ehn pahrfēwmer |
| powder | **pudder** | pewderr |
| powder puff | **en pudderkvast** | ehn pewderrkvahst |
| razor | **en barberhøvel** | ehn bahrbāyrhurverl |
| razor blades | **barberblader** | bahrbāyrblaaderr |
| safety pins | **sikkerhetsnåler** | sikkerrhehtsnawlerr |
| shaving brush | **en barberkost** | ehn bahrbāyrkoost |

| shaving cream | en barberkrem | ehn bahr$\overline{\text{bayr}}$krāym |
| soap | en såpe | ehn sawper |
| sponge | en svamp | ehn svahmp |
| sponge bag | en toalettmappe | ehn tooahlehtmahper |
| sun-tan oil | en sololje | ehn soōlolyer |
| talcum powder | en talkum | ehn tahlkewm |
| (facial) tissues | papirlommetørklær | pahpeerloommerturrklǣr |
| toilet paper | toalettpapir | tooahlehtpahpeer |
| toiletries bag | en toalettmappe | ehn tooahlehtmahper |
| toilet water | en eau de toilette | en aw deh tooahleht |
| toothbrush | en tannbørste | ehn tahnburshter |
| toothpaste | en tannpasta | ehn tahnpahstah |
| towel | et håndkle | eht hongkleh |
| tweezers | en pinsett | ehn pinseht |
| washcloth | en ansiktsklut | ehn ahnsiktsklēwt |

## For your hair   *For håret*

| barrette | en hårspenne | ehn hawshpehner |
| bobby pins | hårklemmer | hawrklehmerr |
| colour shampoo | en fargesjampo | ehn fahrggershahmpoo |
| comb | en kam | ehn kahm |
| curlers (rollers) | hårruller | hawrrewlerr |
| dry shampoo | tørrsjampo | turrshahmpoo |
| hairbrush | en hårbørste | ehn hawrburshter |
| hair dye | et hårfargingsmiddel | eht hawrfahrgingsmidderl |
| hair (styling) gel | en hårgelé | ehn hawrshehlāy |
| hairgrips | hårklemmer | hawrklehmerr |
| hair lotion | hårvann | hawrvahn |
| hair mousse | et hårskum | eht hawshkoom |
| hairpins | hårnåler | haw$^r$nawlerr |
| hair slide | en hårspenne | ehn hawshpehner |
| hair spray | hårlakk | haw$^r$lahk |
| setting lotion | et leggevann | eht lehgervahn |
| shampoo | en sjampo | ehn shahmpoo |
|   for dry/greasy | for tørt/fett hår | for tur$^r$t/feht hawr |
|   (oily) hair | | |
| tint | et hårtoningsmiddel | eht haw$^r$tōoningsmidderl |
| wig | en parykk | ehn pahrewk |

## For the baby   *For babyen*

| baby food | barnemat | baa$^r$nermaat |
| dummy (pacifier) | en narresmokk | ehn nahrersmook |
| feeding bottle | en tåteflaske | ehn tawterflahsker |
| nappies (diapers) | bleier | blæierr |

## Clothing  *Klær*

If you want to buy something specific, prepare yourself in advance. Look at the list of clothing on page 116. Get some idea of the colour, material and size you want. They're all listed on the next few pages.

### General  *Allment*

| | | |
|---|---|---|
| I'd like ... | **Jeg vil gjerne ha ...** | yæi vil y**ǣʳ**ner haa |
| I'm just looking. | **Jeg bare ser meg omkring.** | yæi **baarer s**ā̄**yr mæi omkring** |
| I'd like ... for a 10-year-old boy/girl. | **Jeg vil gjerne ha ... til en gutt/pike på 10 år.** | yæi vil y**ǣʳ**ner haa ... til ehn gewt/**pee**ker paw 10 awr |
| I'd like something like this. | **Jeg vil gjerne ha noe i denne stilen.** | yæi vil y**ǣʳ**ner haa n**ōō**er ee **dehner stee**lern |
| I like the one in the window. | **Jeg liker den i vinduet.** | yæi **lee**ker dehn ee **vind**ewer |
| How much is that per metre? | **Hvor mye koster det pr. meter?** | voor m**ēw**er kosterr deh pær m**ā̄y**terr |

| 1 centimetre (cm.) = 0.39 in. | 1 inch = 2.54 cm. |
|---|---|
| 1 metre (m.) = 39.37 in. | 1 foot = 30.5 cm. |
| 10 metres = 32.81 ft. | 1 yard = 0.91 m. |

### Colour  *Farge*

| | | |
|---|---|---|
| I'd like something in ... | **Jeg vil gjerne ha noe i ...** | yæi vil y**ǣʳ**ner haa n**ōō**er ee |
| I'd like a darker/lighter shade. | **Jeg vil gjerne ha en mørkere/lysere nyanse.** | yæi vil y**ǣʳ**ner haa en **murr**kerrer/**lēw**sserrer **new**ahngser |
| I'd like something to match this. | **Jeg vil gjerne ha noe som står til dette.** | yæi vil y**ǣʳ**ner haa n**ōō**er som stawr til **deh**ter |
| I don't like the colour/pattern. | **Jeg liker ikke fargen/mønstret.** | yæi **lee**kerr ikker **fahr**ggern⁄**murn**strer |

| beige | beige | bāysh |
| black | svart | svah$^r$t |
| blue | blå | blaw |
| brown | brun | brēwn |
| golden | gullfarget | gewlfahrggert |
| green | grønn | grurn |
| grey | grå | graw |
| mauve | lilla | lillah |
| orange | oransje | oorahngsh |
| pink | rosa | rōōssah |
| purple | fiolett | feeooleht |
| red | rød | rūr |
| scarlet | skarlagenrød | skah$^r$laagernrūr |
| silver | sølvfarget | surlfahrggert |
| turquoise | turkis | tewrkeess |
| white | hvit | veet |
| yellow | gul | gēwl |
| light ... | lyse- | lēwsser- |
| dark ... | mørke- | murrker- |

**ensfarget**
(āynsfahrggert)

**stripet**
(streepert)

**prikket**
(prikkert)

**rutet**
(rēwtert)

**mønstret**
(murnstrert)

## Fabric   *Tøystoff*

| Do you have anything in ...? | **Har du noe i ...?** | haar dew nōōer ee |
| Is that ...? | **Er det ...?** | ær deh |
| handmade | **håndlaget** | honlaagert |
| imported | **importert** | impo$^r$tāy$^r$t |
| made in Norway | **laget i Norge** | laagert ee norgger |
| What fabric/material is it? | **Hva slags stoff/ materiale er det?** | vah shlahkss stof/ maht(er)reeaaler ær deh |
| I'd like something thinner. | **Jeg vil gjerne ha noe tynnere.** | yæi vil yǣ$^r$ner haa nōōer tewnerrer |
| Do you have anything of better quality? | **Har du en bedre kvalitet?** | haar dew ehn bāydrer kvahlitāyt |

What's it made of? **Hva er det laget av?** vaa ær deh laagert ahv

| | | |
|---|---|---|
| cambric | **batist** | bahtist |
| camelhair | **kamelhår** | kahmaylhawr |
| chiffon | **chiffon** | shiffong |
| corduroy | **kordfløyel** | kaw'rdfloyerl |
| cotton | **bomull** | boomewl |
| crepe | **krepp** | krehp |
| denim | **denim** | dehneem |
| felt | **filt** | filt |
| flannel | **flanell** | flahnehl |
| gabardine | **gabardin** | gahbah'deen |
| lace | **knipling** | knipling |
| leather | **lær** | lær |
| linen | **lin** | leen |
| poplin | **poplin** | poplin |
| satin | **sateng** | sahtehng |
| silk | **silke** | silker |
| suede | **semsket skinn** | sehmskert shin |
| towelling | **frotté** | frootay |
| velvet | **fløyel** | floyerl |
| velveteen | **bomullsfløyel** | boomewlsfloyerl |
| wool | **ull** | ewl |
| worsted | **kamgarn** | kahmgaa'rn |

Is it ...? **Er det ...?** ær deh

| | | |
|---|---|---|
| pure cotton/wool | **ren bomull/ull** | rayn boomewl/ewl |
| synthetic | **syntetisk** | sewntaytisk |
| colourfast | **fargeekte** | fahrggerehkter |
| crease resistant (wrinkle-free) | **krøllfritt** | krurlfrit |

Is it hand washable/ machine washable? **Skal det vaskes for hånd/i maskin?** skahl deh vahskerss for hon/ee mahsheen

Will it shrink? **Krymper det?** krewmperr deh

### Size *Størrelse*

I take size 38. **Jeg bruker størrelse 38.** yæi brewkerr sturrerlser 38

Could you measure me? **Kan du ta mål av meg?** kahn dew taa mawl ahv mæi

I don't know the Norwegian sizes. **Jeg kjenner ikke de norske størrelsene.** yæi khehnerr ikker dee noshker sturrerlserner

Sizes vary from country to country and from one manufacturer to another, so be sure to try on the clothes before you buy.

**Women** *Kvinner*

| Dresses/Suits | | | | | | |
|---|---|---|---|---|---|---|
| American | 8 | 10 | 12 | 14 | 16 | 18 |
| British | 10 | 12 | 14 | 16 | 18 | 20 |
| Continental | 36 | 38 | 40 | 42 | 44 | 46 |

| Shoes | | | | |
|---|---|---|---|---|
| American } | 5½ | 6½ | 7½ | 8½ |
| British } | 4 | 5 | 6 | 7 |
| Continental | 37 | 38 | 39 | 40 |

**Men** *Menn*

| Suits/Overcoats | | | | | | | Shirts | | | |
|---|---|---|---|---|---|---|---|---|---|---|
| American } | 36 | 38 | 40 | 42 | 44 | 46 | 15 | 16 | 17 | 18 |
| British } | | | | | | | | | | |
| Continental | 46 | 48 | 50 | 52 | 54 | 56 | 38 | 40 | 42 | 44 |

| Shoes | | | | | | | | |
|---|---|---|---|---|---|---|---|---|
| American | 6½ | 7 | 7½ | 8 | 8½ | 9 | 10 | 11 |
| British | 5 | 6 | 7 | 8 | 9 | 10 | 11 | 12 |
| Continental | 38 | 39 | 40 | 41 | 42 | 43 | 44 | 45 |

**A good fit?** *Passer det?*

| | | |
|---|---|---|
| Can I try it on? | **Kan jeg få prøve den?** | kahn yæi faw prūrver dehn |
| Where's the changing room? | **Hvor er prøverommet?** | voor ær prūrverroommer |
| Is there a mirror? | **Fins det et speil her?** | finss deh eht spæil hær |
| It fits very well. | **Den passer meget bra.** | dehn pahsserr maȳgert braa |
| It doesn't fit. | **Den passer ikke.** | dehn pahsser ikker |

NUMBERS, see page 147

| It's too ... | Den er for ... | dehn ær for |
|---|---|---|
| short/long | kort/lang | ko$^r$t/lahng |
| tight/loose | trang/vid | trahng/vee(d) |
| How long will it take to alter it? | Hvor lang tid tar det å endre den? | voor lahng teed taar deh aw ehndrer dehn |

## Clothes and accessories  *Klær og tilbehør*

| I would like a/an/ some ... | Jeg vil gjerne ha ... | yæi vil yǣ$^r$ner haa |
|---|---|---|
| anorak | en anorakk | ehn ahnoorahk |
| bathing cap | en badehette | ehn baaderhehter |
| bathrobe | en badekåpe | ehn baaderkawper |
| blouse | en bluse | ehn blēwsser |
| bow tie | en flue | ehn flēwer |
| bra | en behå | ehn bāyhaw |
| braces | et par seler | eht pahr sāylerr |
| cap | en lue | ehn lēwer |
| cardigan | en golfjakke | ehn golfyahker |
| children's ... | barne- | baa$^r$ner- |
| coat (man's) | en frakk | ehn frahk |
| coat (woman's) | en kåpe | ehn kawper |
| dress | en kjole | ehn khooler |
|   with long sleeves |   med lange ermer |   meh(d) laanger ærmerr |
|   with short sleeves |   med korte ermer |   meh(d) ko$^r$ter ærmerr |
|   sleeveless |   uten ermer |   ēwtern ærmerr |
| dressing gown | en morgenkåpe | ehn mawer$^r$nkawper |
| evening dress (woman's) | en aftenkjole | ehn ahfternkhooler |
| fur coat | en pels | ehn pehlss |
| girdle | en hofteholder | ehn hofterhollerr |
| gloves | et par hansker | eht pahr hahnskerr |
| handbag | en håndveske | ehn honvehsker |
| handkerchief | et lommetørkle | eht loommerturrkler |
| hat | en hatt | ehn haht |
| jacket | en jakke | ehn yahker |
| jeans | et par jeans | eht pahr "jeans" |
| kneesocks | et par knestrømper | eht pahr knāystrurmperr |
| man's ... | herre- | hærer- |
| nightdress (night-gown) | en nattkjole | ehn nahtkhooler |
| overalls | en overall | ehn awverrol |
| pair of ... | et par ... | eht pahr |
| panties | et par truser | eht pahr trēwsserr |

| pants (Am.) | et par langbukser | eht pahr **lahng**bookserr |
| panty hose | en strømpebukse | ehn **strurm**perbooksser |
| parka | en anorakk | ehn ahnoo**rahk** |
| pullover | en genser | ehn **gehn**serr |
| crew-neck | med rund hals | meh(d) rewn hahlss |
| polo (turtle)-neck | høyhalset | **hoy**hahlsert |
| V-neck | V-genser | vāy-**gehn**serr |
| pyjamas | en pyjamas | ehn pew**shaa**mahss |
| raincoat | en regnfrakk | ehn **ræin**frahk |
| scarf | et skjerf | eht shærf |
| shirt | en skjorte | ehn **shoo**ʳter |
| shorts | et par shorts | eht pahr "shorts" |
| skirt | et skjørt | eht shurʳt |
| slip | en underkjole | ehn **ewnerrkhōō**ler |
| socks | et par sokker | eht pahr **sokk**err |
| sportswear | sportsklær | **spo**ʳts**klær** |
| stockings | et par strømper | eht pahr **strurm**perr |
| suit (man's) | en dress | ehn drehss |
| suit (woman's) | en drakt | ehn drahkt |
| suspenders (Am.) | et par seler | eht pahr **sāy**lerr |
| sweater | en genser | ehn **gehn**serr |
| sweat suit | en treningsdrakt | ehn **trāy**ningsdrahkt |
| swimming trunks | en badebukse | ehn **baa**derbooksser |
| swimsuit | en badedrakt | ehn **baa**derdrahkt |
| tie | et slips | eht shlipss |
| tights | en strømpebukse | ehn **strurm**perbooksser |
| tracksuit | en treningsdrakt | ehn **trāy**ningsdrahkt |
| trousers | et par langbukser | eht pahr **lahng**booksserr |
| T-shirt | en T-skjorte | ehn tāy-**shoo**ʳter |
| umbrella | en paraply | ehn pahrah**plēw** |
| underpants | en underbukse | ehn **ewnerr**booksser |
| undershirt | en trøye | ehn **troy**er |
| vest (Am.) | en vest | ehn vehst |
| vest (Br.) | en trøye | ehn **troy**er |
| waistcoat | en vest | ehn vehst |
| woman's ... | dame- | **daa**mer- |

| belt | et belte | eht **behl**ter |
| buckle | en spenne | ehn **speh**ner |
| button | en knapp | ehn knahp |
| collar | en krage | ehn **kraa**ger |
| pocket | en lomme | ehn **loom**mer |
| press stud (snap fastener) | en trykknapp | ehn **trewk**knahp |
| zip (zipper) | en glidelås | ehn **glee**derlawss |

## Shoes  *Sko*

| | | |
|---|---|---|
| I'd like a pair of ... | **Jeg vil gjerne ha et par ...** | yæi vil y**æ**ʳner haa eht pahr |
| athletic shoes | **turnsko** | tēwʳnskōō |
| boots | **støvler** | sturvlerr |
| lined/unlined | **forede/uforede** | fōōrerder/**ēw**fōōrerder |
| moccasins | **mokkasiner** | mookah**ssee**nerr |
| plimsolls | **turnsko** | tēwʳnskōō |
| sandals | **sandaler** | sahndaalerr |
| shoes | **sko** | skōō |
| flat | **lavhælte** | laavh**āy**lter |
| with a heel | **med hæl** | meh(d) h**āy**l |
| with leather soles | **med lærsåler** | meh(d) l**ǣ**ʳsawlerr |
| with rubber soles | **med gummisåler** | meh(d) **gew**missawlerr |
| slippers | **tøfler** | turflerr |
| These are too ... | **Disse er for ...** | disser ær for |
| narrow/wide | **smale/vide** | smaaler/**vee**(d)er |
| big/small | **store/små** | stōōrer/smaw |
| Do you have a smaller/larger size? | **Har du et nummer mindre/større?** | haar dew eht **noom**merr **min**drer/**stur**rer |
| Do you have the same in black? | **Har du de samme i svart?** | haar dew dee **sah**mer ee svahʳt |
| cloth/leather/rubber/ suede | **tøy/lær/gummi/ semsket skinn** | toy/lær/**gew**mi/ **sehm**skert shin |
| Is it real leather? | **Er det ekte lær?** | ær deh **ehk**ter lær |
| I need some ... | **Jeg trenger ...** | yæi **treh**ngerr |
| insoles | **innleggssåler** | **in**lehgssawlerr |
| shoe polish | **skokrem** | **skōō**krāym |
| shoelaces | **skolisser** | **skōō**lisserr |

## Shoe repairs  *Skoreparasjon*

| | | |
|---|---|---|
| Can you repair these shoes? | **Kan du reparere disse skoene?** | kahn dew rehpahr**āy**rer disser sk**ōō**erner |
| Can you stitch this? | **Kan du sy sammen dette?** | kahn dew sēw **sah**mern dehter |
| I want new soles and heels. | **Jeg vil ha nye såler og hæler.** | yæi vil haa **nēw**er sawler o(g) h**āy**lerr |
| When will they be ready? | **Når blir de ferdig?** | nor bleer dee f**ǣ**ʳdi |

COLOURS, see page 113

**Electrical appliances**   *Elektrisk utstyr*

Standard voltage (*strømstyrke*) is 220 volts, 50 cycles A.C.

| | | |
|---|---|---|
| Do you have a battery for this? | **Har du et batteri til denne?** | haar dew eht bahter**ree** til **deh**ner |
| This is broken. Can you repair it? | **Denne er gått i stykker. Kan du reparere den?** | **deh**ner ær got ee **stew**kerr. kahn dew rehpah**ray**rer dehn |
| Can you show me how it works? | **Kan du vise meg hvordan den fungerer?** | kahn dew **vee**sser mæi voo<sup>r</sup>dahn dehn fewng**ay**rerr |
| How do I switch it on? | **Hvordan setter man den i gang?** | voo<sup>r</sup>dahn **seh**terr mahn dehn ee gahng |
| I'd like to hire (rent) a video cassette. | **Jeg vil gjerne leie en videokassett.** | yæi vil **yæ**<sup>r</sup>ner **læ**ier ehn **vee**dyookahsseht |
| I'd like a/an/ some ... | **Jeg vil gjerne ha ...** | yæi vil **yæ**<sup>r</sup>ner haa |
| adaptor | **en adapter** | ehn ah**dahp**terr |
| amplifier | **en forsterker** | ehn fo**shtær**kerr |
| bulb | **en lyspære** | ehn **lew**spærer |
| cassette player | **en kassettspiller** | ehn kahs**seht**spillerr |
| (radio) cassette recorder | **en (radio)kassett- opptaker** | ehn (**raa**dyoo)kahs**seht**- optaakerr |
| clock-radio | **en klokkeradio** | ehn **klok**kerraadyoo |
| electric toothbrush | **en elektrisk tannbørste** | ehn eh**lehk**trisk **tahn**burshter |
| extension lead (cord) | **en skjøteledning** | ehn **shur**terlay̆dning |
| hair dryer | **en hårføner** | ehn **hawr**furnerr |
| headphones | **et par høre- telefoner** | eht pahr **hur**rer- tehler**foo**nerr |
| (travelling) iron | **et (reise)strykejern** | eht (**ræi**sser)**strew**keryæ<sup>r</sup>n |
| lamp | **en lampe** | ehn **lahm**per |
| personal stereo (pocket radio) | **en lommeradio** | ehn **loom**merraadyoo |
| portable ... | **bærbar ...** | **bær**baar |
| radio | **en radio** | ehn **raa**dyoo |
| record player | **en platespiller** | ehn **plaa**terspillerr |
| shaver | **en barbermaskin** | ehn bahr**bay**rmahsheen |
| speakers | **høyttalere** | **hoy**ttaalererr |
| (colour) television | **en (farge)TV** | ehn (**fahr**gger)**tay**veh |
| transformer | **en transformator** | ehn trahnsfor**maa**toor |
| video recorder | **en videokassett- opptaker** | ehn **vee**dyookahsseht- optaakerr |

## Grocer's   *Matvarehandel*

| I'd like some bread, please. | **Jeg vil gjerne ha litt brød.** | yæi vil yǣ<sup>r</sup>ner haa lit brūr |
|---|---|---|

I'd like some bread, please. — **Jeg vil gjerne ha litt brød.** — yæi vil yǣ<sup>r</sup>ner haa lit brūr

crispbread — **knekkebrød** — knehkerbrūr
sliced bread — **oppskåret brød** — opskawrert brūr
white bread — **loff** — loof

What sort of cheese do you have? — **Hva slags ostesorter har du?** — vaa shlakss oosterso<sup>r</sup>terr haar dew

A piece of that one, please. — **Et stykke av den, takk.** — eht stewker ahv dehn tahk

I'll have one of those, please. — **Kan jeg få en av dem?** — kahn yæi faw ehn ahv dehm

May I help myself? — **Kan jeg ta selv?** — kahn yæi taa sehl

I'd like ... — **Jeg vil gjerne ha ...** — yæi vil yǣ<sup>r</sup>ner haa

a kilo of apples — **1 kg epler** — ehn kheeloo ehplerr
half a kilo of tomatoes — **½ kg tomater** — ehn hahl kheeloo toomaaterr
250 grams of coffee — **¼ kg kaffe** — ehn kvah<sup>r</sup>t kheeloo kahfer
3 hg. (300 g.) of salami — **3 h salami** — trāy hehktoo sahlaami
a litre of milk — **1 l melk** — ehn leeterr mehlk
4 slices of ham — **4 skiver skinke** — feerer sheeverr shingker
a packet of tea — **en pakke te** — ehn pahker tāy
a jar of jam — **et glass syltetøy** — eht glahss sewltertoy
a tin (can) of peaches — **en boks fersken** — ehn bokss fæshkern
a tube of mustard — **en tube sennep** — ehn tēwber sehnerp
a box of chocolates — **en eske sjokolade** — ehn ehsker shookoolaader

---

### Weights and measures

1 kilogram or kilo (kg.) = 1,000 grams (g.)

| | |
|---|---|
| 100 g. = 3.5 oz. | ½ kg. = 1.1 lb. |
| 200 g. = 7.0 oz. | 1 kg. = 2.2 lb. |

1 oz. =  28.35 g.
1 lb. = 453.60 g.

---

1 litre (l.) = 0.88 imp. qt. or 1.6 U.S. qt.

| | |
|---|---|
| 1 imp. qt. = 1.14 l. | 1 U.S. qt. = 0.95 l. |
| 1 imp. gal. = 4.55 l. | 1 U.S. gal. = 3.80 l. |

FOOD, see also page 64

### Jeweller's—Watchmaker's  *Gullsmed − Urmaker*

| | | |
|---|---|---|
| Can you show me some jewellery, please? | **Kan jeg få se på noen smykker?** | kahn yæi faw sāy paw nōōern **smewk**err |
| I want a present for ... | **Jeg vil gjerne ha en presang til ...** | yæi vil yǣ<sup>r</sup>ner haa ehn preh**ssahng** til |
| Could I see that, please? | **Kan jeg få se på det?** | kahn yæi faw sāy paw dāy |
| Do you have anything in gold? | **Har du noe i gull?** | haar dew nōōer ee gewl |
| How many carats is this? | **Hvor mange karat har dette?** | voor **mahng**er kah**raat** haar **deh**ter |
| Is this real silver? | **Er dette ekte sølv?** | ær **deh**ter **ehk**ter surl |
| Can you engrave these initials on it? | **Kan du gravere disse initialene?** | kahn dew grah**vāy**rer **diss**er ini(t)see**aal**erner |
| Can you repair this watch? | **Kan du reparere denne klokken?** | kahn dew rehpah**rāy**rer **deh**ner **klok**kern |
| I'd like a/an/ some ... | **Jeg vil gjerne ha ...** | yæi vil yǣ<sup>r</sup>ner haa |

| | | |
|---|---|---|
| alarm clock | **en vekkeklokke** | ehn **vehk**erklokker |
| bangle | **en armring** | ehn **ahrm**ring |
| battery | **et batteri** | eht bah**ter**ree |
| bracelet | **et armbånd** | eht **ahrm**bon |
|   chain bracelet | **en armlenke** | ehn **ahrm**lehngker |
|   charm bracelet | **et berlokkarmbånd** | eht **bær**lok**ahrm**bon |
| brooch | **en brosje** | ehn **brō**sher |
| chain | **et kjede** | eht **khā**yder |
| charm | **en berlokk** | ehn **bær**lok |
| clock | **en klokke** | ehn **klok**ker |
| cross | **et kors** | eht kosh |
| cuff links | **et par mansjett-knapper** | eht pahr mahn**sheht**-knahperr |
| earrings | **et par øreringer** | eht pahr **ūr**rerringerr |
| gem | **en edelsten** | ehn **āy**derlstāyn |
| jewel box | **et smykkeskrin** | eht **smewk**erskreen |
| mechanical pencil | **en skrublyant** | ehn skrēw**ble**wahnt |
| music box | **en spilledåse** | ehn **spil**lerdawsser |
| necklace | **et halskjede** | eht **hahls**khāyder |
| pendant | **et hengesmykke** | eht **hehng**ersmewker |
| pocket watch | **et lommeur** | eht **loom**merēwr |
| powder compact | **en pudderdåse** | ehn **pew**derrdawsser |
| propelling pencil | **en skrublyant** | ehn skrēw**ble**wahnt |

| ring | en ring | ehn ring |
|---|---|---|
| engagement ring | en forlovelsesring | ehn forlawverlsersring |
| signet ring | en signetring | ehn singnāytring |
| wedding ring | en giftering | ehn yifterring |
| silverware | noe sølvtøy | nōōer surltoy |
| string (strand) | et perlekjede | eht pæ<sup>r</sup>lerkhāyder |
| of pearls | | |
| tie clip | en slipsklype | ehn shlipsklewper |
| tie pin | en slipsnål | ehn shlipsnawl |
| watch | en klokke | ehn klokker |
| automatic | automatisk | outoomaatisk |
| digital/analogue | digital/analog | diggitaal/ahnahlawg |
| quartz | kvarts | kvah<sup>r</sup>tss |
| with a second | med sekundviser | meh(d) sehkewn- |
| hand | | veesserr |
| waterproof | vanntett | vahnteht |
| watchstrap | en klokkerem | ehn klokkerrehm |
| wristwatch | et armbåndsur | eht ahrmbonsēwr |

| amber | rav | raav |
|---|---|---|
| amethyst | ametyst | ahmertewst |
| brass | messing | mehssing |
| bronze | bronse | brongser |
| chromium | krom | kroom |
| copper | kopper | kopperr |
| coral | korall | koorahl |
| crystal | krystall | krewstahl |
| cut glass | slepet glass | shlāypert glahss |
| diamond | diamant | deeahmahnt |
| emerald | smaragd | smahrahgd |
| enamel | emalje | ehmahlyer |
| gold | gull | gewl |
| gold plate | gullbelagt | gewlberlahkt |
| jade | jade | yaader |
| mother-of-pearl | perlemor | pæ<sup>r</sup>lermōōr |
| onyx | onyks | oonewkss |
| pearl | perle | pæ<sup>r</sup>ler |
| pewter | tinn | tin |
| platinum | platina | plaateenah |
| ruby | rubin | rewbeen |
| sapphire | safir | sahfeer |
| silver | sølv | surl |
| silver plate | sølvplett | surlpleht |
| topaz | topas | toopaass |
| turquoise | turkis | tewrkeess |

## Optician   *Optiker*

| I've broken my glasses. | Brillene mine er gått i stykker. | brillerner meener ær got ee stawkerr |
|---|---|---|
| Can you repair them for me? | Kan du reparere dem for meg? | kahn dew rehpahrāyrer dehm for mæi |
| When will they be ready? | Når blir de ferdig? | nor bleer dee fæʳdi |
| Can you change the lenses? | Kan du skifte ut glassene? | kahn dew shifter ēwt glahsserner |
| I'd like tinted lenses. | Jeg vil gjerne ha fargede glass. | yæi vil yǣʳner haa fahrggerder glahss |
| The frame is broken. | Innfatningen er brukket. | infahtningern ær brookkert |
| I'd like a glasses case. | Jeg vil gjerne ha et brillefutteral. | yæi vil yǣʳner haa eht brillerfewterraal |
| I'd like to have my eyesight checked. | Jeg vil gjerne få kontrollert synet. | yæi vil yǣʳner faw koontroolāyʳt sēwner |
| I'm ... | Jeg er ... | yæi ær |
| short-sighted long-sighted | nærsynt langsynt | nǣʳsēwnt lahngsēwnt |
| I'd like some contact lenses. | Jeg vil gjerne ha kontaktlinser. | yæi vil yǣʳner haa koontahktlinserr |
| I've lost one of my contact lenses. | Jeg har mistet en kontaktlinse. | yæi haar mistert ehn koontahktlinser |
| Could you give me another one? | Kan jeg få en ny? | kahn yæi faw ehn nēw |
| I have hard/soft lenses. | Jeg har harde/ myke linser. | yæi haar haarer/ mēwker linserr |
| Do you have any contact-lens fluid? | Har du en kontakt-linsevæske? | haar dew ehn koontahkt-linservehsker |
| I'd like to buy a pair of sunglasses. | Jeg vil gjerne kjøpe et par solbriller. | yæi vil yǣʳner khūrper eht pahr soolbrillerr |
| May I look in the mirror? | Kan jeg få se meg i speilet? | kahn yæi faw sāy mæi ee spæiler |
| I'd like to buy a pair of binoculars. | Jeg vil gjerne kjøpe en kikkert. | yæi vil yǣʳner khūrper ehn khikkeʳt |

## Photography *Fotografering*

| | | |
|---|---|---|
| I'd like a(n) ... camera. | **Jeg vil gjerne ha et ... fotoapparat.** | yæi vil yǣᵣner haa eht ... fōōtooahpahraat |
| automatic | **helautomatisk** | hāyloutoomaatisk |
| compact | **kompakt** | koompahkt |
| simple | **enkelt** | ehngkehrlt |
| Can you show me some video cameras, please? | **Kan jeg få se på noen video-kameraer?** | kahn yæi faw sāy paw nōōern veedyoo-kaamerraherr |
| I'd like to have some passport photos. | **Jeg vil gjerne få tatt noen passfoto.** | yæi vil yǣᵣner faw taht nōōern pahsfōōtoo |

## Film *Film*

| | | |
|---|---|---|
| I'd like a film (for this camera). | **Jeg vil gjerne ha en film (til dette apparatet).** | yæi vil yǣᵣner haa ehn film (til dehter ahpahraater) |
| black and white | **svart-hvitt** | svahᵣt-vit |
| colour | **farge** | fahrgger |
| colour negative | **fargenegativ** | fahrggernāygahteev |
| cartridge | **en kassett** | ehn kahsseht |
| disc film | **en disc** | ehn disk |
| roll film | **en rullefilm** | ehn rewlerfilm |
| slide film | **film for lysbilder** | film for lēwsbilderr |
| video cassette | **en videokassett** | ehn veedyookahsseht |
| 24/36 exposures | **24/36 bilder** | khēwerfeerer/trehtisehkss bilderr |
| this size | **dette formatet** | dehter formaater |
| this ASA/DIN number | **dette ASA-/DIN-nummeret** | dehter aassah-/din-noommerrer |
| artificial light type | **for kunstig belysning** | for kewnsti berlēwsning |
| daylight type | **for dagslys** | for dahkslēwss |
| fast (high-speed) | **hurtig** | hewᵣti |
| fine grain | **finkornet** | feenkōōᵣnert |

## Processing *Fremkalling*

| | | |
|---|---|---|
| Does the price include processing? | **Er fremkalling inkludert i prisen?** | ær frehmkahling inklewdāyᵣt ee preessern |
| How much do you charge for processing? | **Hvor mye koster fremkallingen?** | voor mēwer kosterr frehmkahlingern |

| I'd like ... prints of each negative. | **Jeg vil gjerne ha ... kopier av hvert negativ.** | yæi vil yǣ<sup>r</sup>ner haa ... koopeeyerr ahv væ<sup>r</sup>t nāygahteev |
| with a mat finish | **med matt overflate** | meh(d) maht awwverflaater |
| with a glossy finish | **med blank overflate** | meh(d) blahngk awwver-flaater |
| Will you enlarge this, please? | **Kan du forstørre dette?** | kahn dew foshturrer dehter |
| When will the photos be ready? | **Når blir bildene ferdig?** | nor bleer bilderner fæ<sup>r</sup>di |

## Accessories and repairs   *Tilbehør og reparasjon*

| I'd like a/an/some ... | **Jeg vil gjerne ha ...** | yæi vil yǣ<sup>r</sup>ner haa |
| battery | **et batteri** | eht bahterree |
| cable release | **en snorutløser** | ehn snōōrewtlursserr |
| camera case | **en kameraveske** | ehn kaamerrahvehsker |
| (electronic) flash | **en (elektronisk) blitz** | ehn (ehlehktrōōnisk) blitss |
| filter | **et filter** | eht filterr |
|   for black and white |   **for svart-hvitt** |   for svah<sup>r</sup>t-vit |
|   for colour |   **for farge** |   for fahrgger |
| lens | **et objektiv** | eht obyehkteev |
|   telephoto lens |   **et teleobjektiv** |   eht tāylerobyehkteev |
|   wide-angle lens |   **et vidvinkel-objektiv** |   eht vee(d)vinkler-obyehkteev |
| lens cap | **en linsebeskytter** | ehn linserbershewterr |
| slide projector | **et lysbildeapparat** | eht lēwsbilderahpahraat |
| Can you repair this camera? | **Kan du reparere dette apparatet?** | kahn dew rehpahrāyrer dehter ahpahraater |
| The film is jammed. | **Filmen sitter fast.** | filmern sitter fahst |
| There's something wrong with the ... | **Det er noe i veien med ...** | deh ær nōōer ee væiern meh(d) |
| exposure counter | **telleverket** | tehlervǣrker |
| film winder | **fremtrekkeren** | frehmtrehkerrern |
| flash attachment | **blitzaggregatet** | blitsahgrergaater |
| lens | **objektivet** | obyehkteever |
| light meter | **lysmåleren** | lēwsmawlerrern |
| rangefinder | **avstandsmåleren** | aavstahnsmawlerrern |
| self-timing release | **selvutløseren** | sehlewtlursserrern |
| shutter | **lukkeren** | lookkerrern |

NUMBERS, see page 147

## Tobacconist's  *Tobakkshandel*

Virtually all international brands of cigarettes, cigars and tobacco are available at tobacconists, in kiosks and supermarkets. Local cigarettes are quite good, and Norwegian pipe tobacco is noted for its quality.

| | | |
|---|---|---|
| A packet of cigarettes, please. | En pakke sigaretter, takk. | ehn pahker siggahrehterr tahk |
| How much are they per ...? | Hvor mye koster de pr. ...? | voor mewer kosterr dee pær |
| packet/carton | pakke/kartong | pahker/kahᵣtong |
| Could I have a carton, please? | Kan jeg få en kartong? | kahn yæi faw ehn kahᵣtong |
| I'd like a/some ... | Jeg vil gjerne ha ... | yæi vil yæᵣner haa |
| candy | noen godter | nooern goterr |
| chewing gum | en pakke tyggegummi | ehn pahker tewgergewmi |
| chewing tobacco | litt skråtobakk | lit skrawtoobahk |
| chocolate bar | en sjokoladeplate | ehn shookoolaaderplaater |
| cigarette case | et sigarettetui | eht siggahrehtehtewee |
| cigarette holder | et sigarettmunnstykke | eht siggahrehtmewnstewker |
| cigarettes | sigaretter | siggahrehterr |
| filter-tipped | med filter | meh(d) filterr |
| without filter | uten filter | ewtern filterr |
| light/dark tobacco | lys/mørk tobakk | lewss/murrk toobahk |
| mild/strong | milde/sterke | miller/stærker |
| menthol | mentol- | mehntool- |
| king-size | king-size | "king-size" |
| cigars | noen sigarer | nooern siggaarerr |
| lighter | en lighter | ehn "lighter" |
| lighter fluid | lighterbensin | "lighter"behnseen |
| lighter gas | lightergass | "lighter"gahss |
| matches | fyrstikker | fewshtikkerr |
| pipe | en pipe | ehn peeper |
| pipe cleaners | piperensere | peeperrehnserrer |
| pipe tobacco | pipetobakk | peepertoobahk |
| postcards | noen postkort | nooern postkoᵣt |
| snuff | en eske snus | ehn ehsker snewss |
| stamps | noen frimerker | nooern freemærkerr |
| sweets | noen godter | nooern goterr |
| tobacco | tobakk | toobahk |
| wick | en veke | ehn vayker |

**Miscellaneous**  *Forskjellig*

**Souvenirs**  *Suvenirer*

The most attractive Norwegian souvenirs to look for are products of home craftsmen, like handmade knitwear—pullovers (sweaters), cardigans, mittens, scarves and ski caps—painted wooden figurines, trolls, sealskin slippers and "rose-painted" wooden articles, such as small boxes, egg cups, plates and miniature bellows; the rococo floral designs are typically Norwegian. Other popular souvenirs include miniature Viking ships of wood, pewter, enamel or silver, dolls in native costume, reindeer-skin rugs, woven runners, table cloths and wall hangings.

| | | |
|---|---|---|
| I'd like a souvenir from ... | **Jeg vil gjerne ha en suvenir fra ...** | yæi vil yǣ<sup>r</sup>ner haa ehn sewverneer fraa |
| Something typically Norwegian, please. | **Noe typisk norsk.** | nōoer tēwpisk noshk |
| cardigan (with Norwegian design) | **en lusekofte** | ehn lēwsserkofter |
| doll in native costume | **en dukke med bunad** | ehn dewker meh(d) bēwnahd |
| drinking horn | **et drikkehorn** | eht drikkerhōo<sup>r</sup>n |
| hunting knife | **en jaktkniv** | ehn yahktkneev |
| reindeer skin | **et reinsdyrskinn** | eht ræinsdēwrshin |
| sealskin slippers | **et par selskinnstøfler** | eht pahr sāylshinsturflerr |
| troll | **et troll** | eht trol |
| Viking ship | **et vikingskip** | eht vēekingsheep |
| wooden figurine | **en trefigur** | ehn trāyfiggēwr |
| woven runner | **en rye** | ehn rēwer |
| A "rose-painted" ... | **En rosemalt ...** | ehn rōossermaalt |
| bowl | **bolle** | boller |
| candlestick | **lysestake** | lewsserstaaker |
| plate | **asjett** | ahsheht |

**Records—Cassettes**  *Plater – Kassetter*

| | | |
|---|---|---|
| I'd like a ... | **Jeg vil gjerne ha ...** | yæi vil yǣ<sup>r</sup>ner haa |
| cassette | **en kassett** | ehn kahsseht |
| video cassette | **en videokassett** | ehn veedyookahsseht |
| compact disc | **en CD-plate** | ehn sāy-dāy-plaater |

| Do you have any records by ...? | Har du noen plater av ...? | haar dew nooern plaaterr ahv |
| Can I listen to this record? | Kan jeg få høre på denne platen? | kahn yæi faw hūrrer paw dehner plaatern |
| chamber music | kammermusikk | kahmerrmewssik |
| classical music | klassisk musikk | klahssisk mewssik |
| folk music | folkemusikk | folkermewssik |
| folk songs | folkesanger | folkersahngerr |
| instrumental music | instrumentalmusikk | instrewmehntaalmewssik |
| jazz | jazz | yahss |
| light music | underholdnings-musikk | ewnerrholdnings-mewssik |
| orchestral music | orkestermusikk | orkehsterrmewssik |
| pop music | pop | pop |

## Toys and games   *Leker og spill*

| I'd like a toy/game. | Jeg vil gjerne ha en leke/et spill. | yæi vil yæ'ner haa ehn lāyker/eht spil |
| (beach) ball | en (bade)ball | ehn (baader)bahl |
| board/card game | et brettspill/kortspill | eht brehtspil/ko'tspil |
| bucket and spade (pail and shovel) | spann og spade | spahn o(g) spaader |
| building blocks (bricks) | noen byggeklosser | nooern bewgerklosserr |
| building set | et byggesett | eht bewgersseht |
| chess set | et sjakkspill | eht shahkspil |
| doll | en dukke | ehn dewker |
| electronic game | et elektronisk spill | eht ehlehktrōonisk spil |
| flippers | et par svømme-føtter | eht pahr svurmer-furterr |
| roller skates | et par rulleskøyter | eht pahr rewlershoyter |
| snorkel | en snorkel | ehn snorkerl |
| stuffed animal | et stoffdyr | eht stofdewr |
| toy car | en lekebil | ehn lāykerbeel |
| battery-powered | batteridrevet | bahterreedrāyvert |
| remote-controlled | ledningstyrt | lāydningstew't |

# Your money: banks—currency

At most banks there's sure to be someone who speaks English. You'll find small currency exchange offices in most tourist centres, especially during the summer season. Remember to take your passport along with you, as you may need it for identification.

Traveller's cheques and credit cards are widely accepted in tourist-oriented shops, hotels, restaurants, etc. However, if you're exploring way off the beaten track, you'll probably come across stores where they are not taken. The same goes for garages and filling stations—generally, only major agency garages will accept payment in traveller's cheques or by credit card.

**Opening hours**. Banks are generally open from 8.15 a.m. to 3.30 p.m., Monday to Wednesday and Fridays, until 5 or 6 p.m. on Thursdays. Between June 1 and August 31, however, they close at 3 p.m. (5 or 5.30 p.m. on Thursdays). At Oslo airport and central railway station, the currency exchange offices have longer hours.

**Monetary unit**. The Norwegian krone (meaning "crown", pronounced **kroo**ner, plural kroner—**kroo**nerr, abbreviated kr/kr.) is divided into 100 øre (**ur**rer).

Coins: 50 øre, kr 1, 5, 10, and 20.
Banknotes: kr 50, 100, 200, 500, and 1,000.

| Where's the nearest bank? | **Hvor er nærmeste bank?** | voor ær nærmehster bahngk |
| Where's the nearest currency exchange office? | **Hvor er nærmeste vekslingskontor?** | voor ær nærmehster vehkshlingskoontoor |
| When is the bank open? | **Når er banken åpen?** | nor ær bahngkern awpern |
| When is the currency exchange office open? | **Når er vekslings-kontoret åpent?** | nor ær vehkshlings-koontoorer awpernt |

## At the bank  *I banken*

| I'd like to change some dollars/pounds. | **Jeg vil gjerne veksle noen dollar/pund.** | yæi vil **yæᵣ**ner **vehk**shler nōōern dollahr/pewn |
| I'd like to cash a traveller's cheque. | **Jeg vil gjerne løse inn en reisesjekk.** | yæi vil **yæᵣ**ner **lūr**sser in ehn **ræis**sershehk |
| What's the exchange rate? | **Hva er vekslingskursen?** | vaa ær **vehk**shlingskēwshern |
| How much commission do you charge? | **Hvor mye tar dere i kommisjon?** | voor **mēw**er taar **dāy**rer ee koomi**shōōn** |
| Can you cash this cheque? | **Kan du løse inn denne sjekken?** | kahn dew **lūr**sser in **dehn**er **shehk**ern |
| Can you telex my bank in London? | **Kan du sende en telex til min bank i London?** | kahn dew **seh**ner ehn **tāy**lekss til meen bahngk ee **lon**don |
| I have a/an/some ... | **Jeg har ...** | yæi haar |
| credit card | **kredittkort** | kreh**dit**koᵣt |
| Eurocheques | **eurosjekker** | **yēw**rooshehkerr |
| letter of credit | **et kredittbrev** | eht kreh**dit**brāyv |
| I'm expecting some money from New York. Has it arrived? | **Jeg venter penger fra New York. Har de kommet?** | yæi **vehn**terr **pehn**gerr fraa new york. haar dee **kom**met |
| Please give me ... in notes (bills) and some small change. | **Gi meg ... i sedler og litt småpenger.** | yee mæi ... ee **sehd**lerr o(g) litt **smaw**pehngerr |
| Give me ... in large notes and the rest in small notes. | **Gi meg ... i store sedler og resten i små sedler.** | yee mæi ... ee **stōō**rer **sehd**lerr o(g) **rehs**tern ee smaw **sehd**lerr |

## Deposit—Withdrawal  *Innskudd – Uttak*

| I'd like to ... | **Jeg vil gjerne ...** | yæi vil **yæᵣ**ner |
| open an account | **åpne en konto** | **awp**ner ehn **kon**too |
| withdraw ... kroner | **ta ut ... kroner** | taa **ēwt** ... **krōō**nerr |
| Where should I sign? | **Hvor skal jeg undertegne?** | voor skahl yæi **ewn**errtæiner |
| I'd like to pay this into my account. | **Jeg vil gjerne sette dette inn på kontoen min.** | yæi vil **yæᵣ**ner **seh**terr **deh**ter in paw **kon**tooern meen |

NUMBERS, see page 147

## Business terms    *Forretningsuttrykk*

| My name is ... | **Mitt navn er ...** | mit nahvn ær |
| Here's my card. | **Her er mitt kort.** | hǣr ær mit ko'rt |
| I have an appointment with ... | **Jeg har avtalt et møte med ...** | yæi haar aavtahlt eht mūrter meh(d) |
| Can you give me an estimate of the cost? | **Kan du gi meg et overslag over kostnadene?** | kahn dew yee mæi eht awvershlaag awverr kostnahderner |
| What's the rate of inflation? | **Hvor høy er inflasjonsraten?** | voor hoy ær inflahshōōnsraatern |
| Can you provide me with a/an ... | **Kan du skaffe meg en ...** | kahn dew skahfer mæi ehn |
| interpreter | **tolk** | tolk |
| secretary | **sekretær** | sehkrertǣr |
| translation | **oversettelse** | awvershehterlser |
| translator | **oversetter** | awvershehterr |
| Where can I make photocopies? | **Hvor kan jeg ta fotokopier?** | voor kahn yæi taa fōōtookoopeeyerr |

| amount | **et beløp** | eht berlūrp |
| balance | **en balanse** | ehn bahlahngser |
| capital | **en kapital** | ehn kahpitaal |
| contract | **en kontrakt** | ehn koontrahkt |
| credit | **en kreditt** | ehn krehdit |
| discount | **en rabatt** | ehn rahbaht |
| expenses | **utgifter** | ēwtyifterr |
| interest | **en rente** | ehn rehnter |
| investment | **en investering** | ehn investāyring |
| invoice | **en faktura** | ehn fahktēwrah |
| loan | **et lån** | eht lawn |
| loss | **et tap** | eht taap |
| mortgage | **et hypotek** | eht hewpootāyk |
| payment | **en betaling** | ehn bertaaling |
| percentage | **en prosentsats** | ehn proosehntsahtss |
| profit | **et utbytte** | eht ēwtbewter |
| purchase | **et kjøp** | eht khūrp |
| sale | **et salg** | eht sahlg |
| share | **en aksje** | ehn ahksher |
| tax | **en skatt** | ehn skaht |
| transfer | **en overføring** | ehn awverfūrring |
| value | **en verdi** | ehn vær'dee |

# At the post office

The post office only handles mail; for fax, telephone and telegram or telex services you have to go to a *telesenter* office.

Business hours are generally from 8 a.m. to 5 or 5.30 p.m., Monday to Friday (4 or 4.30 p.m. in summer), and from 9 a.m. to 1 p.m. on Saturdays.

Letter (mail) boxes are painted red.

| | | |
|---|---|---|
| Where's the nearest post office? | **Hvor er nærmeste postkontor?** | voor ær **nær**mehster postkoontōōr |
| What time does the post office open/close? | **Når åpner/stenger postkontoret** | nor **awp**nerr/**stehng**err postkoontōōrer |
| A stamp for this letter/postcard, please. | **Et frimerke til dette brevet/kortet, takk.** | eht **free**mærker til **deh**ter brāȳver/**ko**ᶠter tahk |
| A ... -kroner stamp, please. | **Et ... -kroners frimerke, takk.** | eht ... -**krōō**nersh **free**mærker tahk |
| What's the postage for a letter to England? | **Hva er portoen for et brev til England?** | vah ær **poo**ᶠtooern for eht brāȳv til **ehng**lahn |
| What's the postage for a postcard to the U.S.? | **Hva er portoen for et postkort til USA?** | vah ær **poo**ᶠtooern for eht **pos**tko't til **ēw**-ehss-aa |
| Where's the letter box (mailbox)? | **Hvor er postkassen?** | voor ær **pos**tkahssern |
| I want to send this parcel. | **Jeg vil gjerne sende denne pakken.** | yæi vil **yǣ**ᶠner **seh**ner **deh**ner **pah**kern |
| I'd like to register this parcel. | **Jeg vil gjerne rekommandere denne pakken.** | yæi vil **yǣ**ᶠner rehkoomahn**dāȳ**rer **deh**ner **pah**kern |
| I'd like to send this by ... | **Jeg vil gjerne sende dette ...** | yæi vil **yǣ**ᶠner **seh**ner **deh**ter |
| airmail | **med fly** | meh(d) flēw |
| express mail | **ekspress** | ehk**sprehss** |
| registered mail | **rekommandert** | rehkoomahn**dāȳ**ᶠt |

| I'd like some ..., please. | Jeg vil gjerne ha noen ... | yæi vil yæ\`ner haa nōōern |
| aerogrammes | aerogrammer | ehroograhmerr |
| airmail labels | luftpostetiketter | lewftpostehtikehterr |
| At which counter can I cash an international money order? | I hvilken luke kan jeg løse inn en internasjonal postanvisning? | ee vilkern lēwker kahn yæi lūrsser in ehn inter\`nahshoonaal postahnveesning |
| Where's the poste restante (general delivery)? | Hvor er poste-restanteluken? | voor ær post-rehstahngtlēwkern |
| Is there any post (mail) for me? | Har det kommet noe post til meg? | haar deh kommert nōōer post til mæi |
| My name is ... | Mitt navn er ... | mit nahvn ær |

| FRIMERKER | STAMPS |
| PAKKER | PARCELS |
| POSTANVISNINGER | MONEY ORDERS |

## Telegrams—Telex—Fax   *Telegrammer – Telex – Telefax*

| Where's the nearest telegraph office? | Hvor er nærmeste telesenter? | voor ær nærmehster tāylerssehnterr |
| I'd like to send a ... | Jeg vil gjerne sende ... | yæi vil yæ\`ner sehner |
| fax | en telefax | ehn tāylerfahkss |
| telegram | et telegram | eht tehlergrahm |
| telex | en telex | ehn tāylehkss |
| May I have a form, please? | Kan jeg få en blankett? | kahn yæi faw ehn blahngkeht |
| How much is it per word? | Hva koster det pr. ord? | vaa kosterr deh pær ōōr |
| How long will a telegram to Boston take? | Hvor lang tid tar et telegram til Boston? | voor lahng teed taar eht tehlergrahm til boston |
| How much will this telex cost? | Hvor mye vil denne telexen komme på? | voor mēwer vil dehner tāylehksern kommer paw |

## Telephone   *Telefon*

International and long-distance calls can be made from phone booths, but if you need help in making a call, go to a telegraph office. Dialling instructions in English are posted inside the booth and can be found at the front of the telephone directory.

For direct calls abroad, dial 00, then the country code (Britain, 44, U.S.A. and Canada, 1), the national dialing (area) code (minus the initial "0") and the local telephone number.

| | | |
|---|---|---|
| Where's the telephone? | **Hvor er telefonen?** | voor ær tehler**foo**nern |
| Where's the nearest telephone booth? | **Hvor er nærmeste telefonkiosk?** | voor ær **nær**mehster tehler**foo**nkhyosk |
| May I use your phone? | **Kan jeg få låne telefonen?** | kahn yæi faw **law**ner tehler**foo**nern |
| Do you have a telephone directory for Bergen? | **Har du en telefon- katalog for Bergen?** | haar dew ehn tehler**foo**n- kahtahlawg for **bær**gern |
| I'd like to call some- one in England. | **Jeg vil gjerne ringe til England.** | yæi vil yæ͞r ner **ring**er til **ehng**lahn |
| What's the dialling (area) code for …? | **Hva er retnings- nummeret til …?** | vah ær **reht**nings- noommerer til |
| How do I get the international operator? | **På hvilket nummer kan jeg få hjelp med fjernvalg til ut- landet?** | paw **vil**kert **noom**merr kahn yæi faw yehlp meh(d) **fyæ͞r**nvahlg til **ew**tlahner |

## Operator   *Telefonist*

| | | |
|---|---|---|
| Could you give me the number of …? | **Kan du gi meg nummeret til …?** | kahn dew yee mæi **noom**merrer til |
| Can you help me get this number? | **Kan du hjelpe meg å komme til dette nummeret?** | kahn dew **yehl**per mæi aw **kom**mer til **deh**ter **noom**merrer |
| I'd like to place a personal (person-to- person) call. | **Jeg vil gjerne bestille en personlig samtale.** | yæi vil **yæ͞r**ner ber**stil**ler ehn pæ**shoo**nli **sahm**taaler |

NUMBERS, see page 147

| I'd like to reverse the charges (call collect). | **Jeg vil gjerne bestille en note-ringsoverføring.** | yæi vil yǣ<sup>r</sup>ner berstiller ehn nootāy-ringsawverrfūrring |
|---|---|---|

**Telephone alphabet** *Bokstavering*

| | | | | | |
|---|---|---|---|---|---|
| A | **Anna** | ahnah | P | **Petter** | pehterr |
| B | **Bernhard** | bǣ<sup>r</sup>nah<sup>r</sup>t | Q | **Quintus** | kvintewss |
| C | **Cæsar** | sāyssahr | R | **Rikard** | rikah<sup>r</sup>t |
| D | **David** | daaveed | S | **Sigrid** | sigree |
| E | **Edith** | āydit | T | **Teodor** | tāyoodōōr |
| F | **Fredrik** | frehdrik | U | **Ulrik** | ewlrik |
| G | **Gustav** | gewstahv | V | **enkelt-V** | ehngkerlt-vāy |
| H | **Harald** | hahrahl | W | **dobbelt-V** | dobberlt-vāy |
| I | **Ivar** | eevahr | X | **Xerxes** | ksærksehss |
| J | **Johan** | yoohahn | Y | **Yngling** | ewngling |
| K | **Karin** | kaareen | Z | **Zakarias** | sahkahreeahss |
| L | **Ludvig** | lewdvik | Æ | **Ærlig** | ǣ<sup>r</sup>li |
| M | **Martin** | mah<sup>r</sup>tin | Ø | **Ørn** | ūr<sup>r</sup>n |
| N | **Nils** | nilss | Å | **Åse** | awsser |
| O | **Olivia** | ooleeveeah | | | |

**Speaking** *Samtale*

| Hello. This is ... | **Hallo. Dette er ...** | hahlōō. dehter ær |
|---|---|---|
| I'd like to speak to ... | **Kan jeg få snakke med ...?** | kahn yæi faw snahker meh(d) |
| Is ... there? | **Er ... til stede?** | ær ... til stāyder |
| Extension ... | **Linje ...** | linyer |
| Who's speaking? | **Hvem er det jeg snakker med?** | vehm ær deh yæi snahkerr meh(d) |
| Pardon? | **Unnskyld?** | ewnshewl |
| Can you speak louder/more slowly, please. | **Kan du snakke litt høyere/litt lang-sommere?** | kahn dew snahker lit hoyerrer/lit lahng-sommerrer |

**Bad luck** *Uheldig*

| Operator, you gave me the wrong number. | **Jeg tror du ga meg feil nummer.** | yæi trōōr dew gaa mæi fæil noommerr |
|---|---|---|
| We were cut off. | **Vi ble avbrutt.** | vee bleh aavbrewt |

### Not there  *Ikke til stede*

| When will he/she be back? | **Når kommer han/ hun tilbake?** | nor **kommerr** hahn/ hewn tilbaaker |
| Will you tell him I called? | **Kan du si til ham at jeg har ringt?** | kahn dew see til hahm aht yæi haar ringt |
| My name is ... | **Mitt navn er ...** | mit nahvn ær |
| Would you ask her to phone me? | **Kan du be henne om å ringe meg?** | kahn dew bāy **heh**ner om aw **ring**er mæi |
| My number is ... | **Mitt nummer er ...** | mit **noom**merr ær |
| Would you take a message? | **Kan du ta imot en beskjed?** | kahn dew taa ee**moot** ehn ber**shāy** |
| I'll call back later. | **Jeg ringer senere.** | yæi **ring**err **sāy**nerrer |

### Charges  *Gebyr*

| How much did the call cost? | **Hvor mye kostet samtalen?** | voor **mēw**er kostert **sahm**taalern |
| I'd like to pay for the call. | **Jeg vil gjerne betale samtalen.** | yæi vil **yāᵣ**ner ber**taal**er **sahm**taalern |

| 👉 | 👈 |
|---|---|
| **Det er telefon til deg.** | There's a telephone call for you. |
| **Hvilket nummer ringer du?** | What number are you calling? |
| **Linjen er opptatt.** | The line's engaged. |
| **Det svarer ikke.** | There's no answer. |
| **Du har ringt feil.** | You've got the wrong number. |
| **Telefonen er i uorden.** | The phone is out of order. |
| **Et øyeblikk.** | Hold on, please/Just a moment. |
| **Han/Hun er ute for øyeblikket.** | He's/She's out at the moment. |
| **Han/Hun er tilbake klokken ...** | He'll/She'll be back at ... |
| **Kan du prøve igjen litt senere?** | Would you try again later? |

# Doctor

British subjects are covered by a British-Norwegian health insurance agreement. For nationals of other countries it is advisable to take out health insurance covering the cost of illness or accident while on holiday.

## General  *Allment*

| | | |
|---|---|---|
| Can you get me a doctor? | **Kan du skaffe meg en lege?** | kahn dew **skah**fer mæi ehn **lay**ger |
| Is there a doctor here? | **Fins det en lege her?** | finss deh ehn **lay**ger hǣr |
| I need a doctor, quickly. | **Jeg trenger lege øyeblikkelig.** | yæi **treh**ngerr **lay**ger oyerblikkerli |
| Where can I find a doctor who speaks English? | **Hvor kan jeg få tak i en lege som snakker engelsk?** | voor kahn yæi faw taak ee ehn **lay**ger som **snah**kerr **ehng**erlsk |
| Where's the surgery (doctor's office)? | **Hvor er lege-kontoret?** | voor ær **lay**ger-koont**ōō**rer |
| What are the surgery (office) hours? | **Når har legen kontortid?** | nor haar **lay**gern koont**ōō**rteed |
| Could the doctor come to see me here? | **Kan legen komme hit å undersøke meg?** | kahn **lay**gern **kom**mer heet aw **ew**nershurker mæi |
| What time can the doctor come? | **Når kan legen komme?** | nor kahn **lay**gern **kom**mer |
| Can you recommend a/an ...? | **Kan du anbefale en ...?** | kahn dew **ahn**berfaaler ehn |
| general practitioner | **allmennpraktiker** | **ahl**mehnprahktikkerr |
| children's doctor | **barnelege** | baarnerlayger |
| eye specialist | **øyenlege** | oyern**lay**ger |
| gynaecologist | **gynekolog** | gewnerkoo**lawg** |
| Can I have an appointment ...? | **Kan jeg få time ...?** | kahn yæi faw **tee**mer |
| immediately | **med én gang** | meh(d) **ayn** gahng |
| tomorrow | **i morgen** | ee **maw**ern |
| as soon as possible | **så snart som mulig** | saw snaart som **mew**li |

CHEMIST'S (DRUGSTORE), see page 108

## Parts of the body  *Kroppsdeler*

| English | Norwegian | Pronunciation |
|---|---|---|
| appendix | **blindtarmen** | blintahrmern |
| arm | **armen** | ahrmern |
| artery | **pulsåren** | pewlsawrern |
| back | **ryggen** | rewgern |
| bladder | **urinblæren** | ewreenblǣrern |
| bone | **benet (i kroppen)** | bāyner (ee kroppern) |
| bowel | **tarmen** | tahrmern |
| breast | **brystet** | brewster |
| chest | **brystkassen** | brewstkahssern |
| ear | **øret** | ūrrer |
| face | **ansiktet** | ahnsikter |
| finger | **fingeren** | fingerrern |
| foot | **foten** | fōōtern |
| genitals | **kjønnsorganene** | khurnsorgaanerner |
| gland | **kjertelen** | khæ<sup>r</sup>terlern |
| hand | **hånden** | honern |
| head | **hodet** | hōōder |
| heart | **hjertet** | yæ<sup>r</sup>ter |
| jaw | **kjeven** | khāyvern |
| joint | **leddet** | lehder |
| kidney | **nyren** | nēwrern |
| knee | **kneet** | knāyer |
| leg | **benet** | bāyner |
| lip | **leppen** | lehpern |
| liver | **leveren** | lehverrern |
| lung | **lungen** | loongern |
| mouth | **munnen** | mewnern |
| muscle | **muskelen** | mewskerlern |
| neck | **nakken** | nahkern |
| nerve | **nerven** | nærvern |
| nervous system | **nervesystemet** | nærversewstāymer |
| nose | **nesen** | nāyssern |
| rib | **ribbenet** | ribbāyner |
| shoulder | **skulderen** | skewlderrern |
| skin | **huden** | hewdern |
| spine | **ryggraden** | rewgraadern |
| stomach | **magen** | maagern |
| tendon | **senen** | sāynern |
| thigh | **låret** | lawrer |
| throat | **halsen** | hahlsern |
| thumb | **tommelen** | tommerlern |
| toe | **tåen** | tawern |
| tongue | **tungen** | toongern |
| tonsils | **mandlene** | mahndlerner |
| vein | **venen/åren** | vāynern/awrern |

139

## Accident—Injury  *Ulykke – Skade*

| There's been an accident. | Det har skjedd en ulykke. | deh haar shehd ehn ō͞wlewker |
|---|---|---|
| My child has had a fall. | Barnet mitt har falt og slått seg. | baaʳner mit haar fahlt o(g) shlot sæi |
| He/She has hurt his/her head. | Han/Hun har slått seg i hodet. | hahn/hewn haar shlot sæi ee hō͞oder |
| He's/She's unconscious. | Han/Hun er bevisstløs. | hahn/hewn ær bervistlū͞rss |
| He's/She's bleeding (heavily). | Han/Hun blør (kraftig). | hahn/hewn blū͞rr (krahfti) |
| He's/She's (seriously) injured. | Han/Hun er (alvorlig) skadet. | hahn/hewn ær (ahlvawʳli) skaadert |
| His/Her ankle is swollen. | Han/Hun har en hoven ankel. | hahn/huhn haar ehn hawvern ahngkerl |
| I've broken my arm. | Jeg har brukket armen. | yæi haar brookkert ahrmern |
| I've been stung. | Jeg er blitt bitt. | yæi ær blit bit |
| I've got something in my eye. | Jeg har fått noe i øyet. | yæi haar fawt nō͞oer ee oyer |
| I've been bitten by a dog. | Jeg er blitt bitt av en hund. | yæi ær blit bit ahv ehn hewn |
| I've got a/an ... | Jeg har fått ... | yæi haar fot |
| blister | en blemme | ehn blehmer |
| boil | en byll | ehn bewl |
| bruise | et blått merke | eht blot mærker |
| bump | en kul | ehn kē͞wl |
| burn | et brannsår | eht brahnsawr |
| cut | et kutt | eht kewt |
| graze | et skrubbsår | eht skrewbsawr |
| rash | et utslett | eht ē͞wtshleht |
| sting | et stikk | eht stik |
| swelling | en hevelse | ehn hā͞yverlser |
| wound | et sår | eht sawr |
| Could you have a look at it? | Kan du undersøke det? | kahn dew ewnershū͞rker deh |
| I can't move my ... | Jeg kan ikke bevege ... | yæi kahn ikker bervā͞yger |
| It hurts. | Det gjør vondt. | deh yū͞rr voont |

| Hvor gjør det vondt? | Where does it hurt? |
|---|---|
| Hva slags smerte er det? | What kind of pain is it? |
| dump/skarp | dull/sharp |
| pulserende/konstant | throbbing/constant |
| kommer og går | on and off |
| Det er ... | It's ... |
| brukket/vrikket/ute av ledd | broken/sprained/dislocated |
| Du har et avslitt leddbånd. | You have a torn ligament. |
| Det bør røntgenfotograferes. | I'd like you to have an X-ray. |
| Det må gipses. | We'll have to put it in plaster. |
| Det er infisert. | It's infected. |
| Er du vaksinert mot stivkrampe? | Have you been vaccinated against tetanus? |
| Jeg skal gi deg noe smertestillende. | I'll give you a painkiller. |
| Har du noen allergier? | Do you have any allergies? |

## Illness  *Sykdom*

| | | |
|---|---|---|
| I'm not feeling well. | Jeg føler meg ikke bra. | yæi fūrlerr mæi ikker braa |
| I'm ill. | Jeg er syk. | yæi ær sēwk |
| I feel ... | Jeg føler meg ... | yæi fūrler mæi |
| dizzy/nauseous/ weak | svimmel/kvalm/ svak | svimmerl/kvahlm/ svaak |
| I feel shivery. | Jeg har kulde-gysninger. | yæi haar kewler-yēwsningerr |
| I have a temperature (fever). | Jeg har feber. | yæi haar fāyberr |
| I've been vomiting. | Jeg har kastet opp. | yæi haar kahstert op |
| I'm constipated. | Jeg har forstoppelse. | yæi haar foshtopperlser |
| I've got diarrhoea. | Jeg har diarré. | yæi haar deeahrāy |
| My ... hurt(s). | Jeg har vondt i ... | yæi haar voont ee |

| I've got (a/an) ... | Jeg har ... | yæi haar |
|---|---|---|
| asthma | astma | ahstmah |
| backache | ryggsmerter | rewgsmaᵉrterr |
| cough | hoste | hooster |
| cramps | krampe | krahmper |
| earache | øreverk | ūrrerværk |
| hay fever | høysnue | hoysnēwer |
| headache | hodepine | hōōderpeener |
| indigestion | fordøyelsesbesvær | foᵉdoyerlsersbersvær |
| nosebleed | neseblødning | nāÿsserblūrdning |
| palpitations | hjerteklapp | yæᵉterklahp |
| rheumatism | reumatisme | rehvmahtismer |
| sore throat | sår hals | sawr hahlss |
| stiff neck | stiv nakke | steev nahker |
| stomach ache | magesmerter | maagersmæᵉterr |
| sunburn | solforbrenning | sōōlforbrehning |

| I've got a cold. | Jeg er forkjølet. | yæi ær foᵉkhūrlert |
| I have difficulties breathing. | Jeg har vanskeligheter med å puste. | yæi haar vahnskerlihehter meh(d) aw pewster |
| I have chest pains. | Jeg har vondt i brystet. | yæi haar voont ee brewster |
| I had a heart attack ... years ago. | Jeg hadde et hjerteslag for ... år siden. | yæi hahder eht yæᵉtershlaag for ... awr seedern |
| My blood pressure is too high/too low. | Jeg har for høyt/ for lavt blodtrykk. | yæi haar for hoyt/ for laavt blōōtrewk |
| I'm allergic to ... | Jeg er allergisk mot ... | yæi ær ahlærgisk mōōt |
| I'm diabetic. | Jeg er diabetiker. | yæi ær deeahbāÿtikkerr |

## At the gynaecologist's  *Hos gynekologen*

| I have period (menstrual) pains. | Jeg har menstruasjonssmerter. | yæi haar mehnstrewahshōōnssmæᵉterr |
| I have a vaginal infection. | Jeg har underlivsbetennelse. | yæi haar ewnerrleevsbertehnerlser |
| I'm on the pill. | Jeg tar p-piller. | yæi taar pāÿ-pillerr |
| I haven't had a period for 2 months. | Jeg har ikke hatt menstruasjon på 2 måneder. | yæi haar ikker haht mehnstrewahshōōn paw 2 mawnerderr |
| I'm pregnant. | Jeg er gravid. | yæi ær grahveed |

| Hvor lenge har du følt deg slik? | How long have you been feeling like this? |
| Har du hatt dette før? | Have you had this before? |
| Jeg skal ta temperaturen/ måle blodtrykket. | I'll take your temperature/ blood pressure. |
| Vær snill å rulle opp ermet. | Roll up your sleeve, please. |
| Vær snill å ta av deg ... | Take off your ..., please. |
| Vær snill å kle av deg (på overkroppen). | Please undress (down to the waist). |
| Sett/Legg deg ned der borte. | Please sit/lie down over there. |
| Gap opp. | Open your mouth. |
| Pust dypt/Host. | Breathe deeply/Cough. |
| Hvor gjør det vondt? | Where does it hurt? |
| Du har ... | You've got (a/an) ... |
| en allergi | allergy |
| en betennelse i ... | inflammation of ... |
| blindtarmbetennelse | appendicitis |
| blærekatarr | cystitis |
| gulsott | jaundice |
| influensa | flu |
| en kjønnssykdom | venereal disease |
| lungebetennelse | pneumonia |
| magekatarr | gastritis |
| en matforgiftning | food poisoning |
| meslinger | measles |
| Det er (ikke) smittsomt. | It's (not) contagious. |
| Jeg skal gi deg en sprøyte. | I'll give you an injection. |
| Jeg vil ha en blodprøve/ avføringsprøve/urinprøve. | I want a specimen of your blood/stools/urine. |
| Du bør holde sengen i ... dager. | You must stay in bed for ... days. |
| Du bør oppsøke en spesialist. | I want you to see a specialist. |
| Du bør få foretatt en allmenn undersøkelse på sykehuset. | I want you to go to the hospital for a general check-up. |

## Prescription—Treatment  *Resept — Behandling*

| | | |
|---|---|---|
| This is my usual medicine. | **Dette er min vanlige medisin.** | dehter ær meen vaanleeyer mehdisseen |
| Can you give me a prescription for this? | **Kan du gi meg en resept på dette?** | kahn dew yee mæi ehn rehsehpt paw dehter |
| Can you prescribe a/an/some ...? | **Kan du skrive ut ...?** | kahn dew skreever ēwt |
| antidepressant | **et middel mot depresjoner** | eht midderl mōōt dehprershōōnerr |
| sleeping pills | **noen sovetabletter** | nōōern sawvertahblehterr |
| tranquillizer | **et beroligende middel** | eht berrōōleeyerner midderl |
| I'm allergic to certain antibiotics/ penicillin. | **Jeg er allergisk mot visse antibiotika/ penicillin.** | yæi ær ahlærgisk mōōt visser ahntibeeōōtikkah/ pehnissileen |
| I don't want anything too strong. | **Jeg vil ikke ha noe som er for sterkt.** | yæi vil ikker haa nōōer som ær for stærkt |
| How many times a day should I take it? | **Hvor mange ganger om dagen skal jeg ta det?** | voor mahnger gahngerr om daagern skahl yæi taa deh |
| Must I swallow the tablets whole? | **Må jeg svelge tablettene hele?** | maw yæi svehlger tahblehterner hāyler |

---

| | |
|---|---|
| **Hva slags behandling får du?** | What treatment are you having? |
| **Hvilken medisin tar du?** | What medicine are you taking? |
| **Tar du noen andre medisiner?** | Are you taking any other medicines? |
| **Intravenøst eller oralt?** | By injection or orally? |
| **Ta 2 teskjeer/1 tablett ...** | Take 2 teaspoons/1 tablet ... |
| **hver ... time** | every ... hour(s) |
| **... ganger om dagen** | ... times a day |
| **før/etter hvert måltid** | before/after every meal |
| **om morgenen/om kvelden** | in the morning/at night |
| **i ... dager** | for ... days |
| **ved smerter** | if there is any pain |

CHEMIST'S (DRUGSTORE), see page 108

## Fee   *Honorar*

| How much do I owe you? | **Hvor mye skylder jeg?** | voor **mew**er **shew**lerr yæi |
| May I have a receipt for my health insurance? | **Kan jeg få en kvittering for syke-forsikringen?** | kahn yæi faw ehn kvitt**ay**ring for **sew**ker-foshikringern |
| Can I have a medical certificate? | **Kan jeg få en legeattest?** | kahn yæi faw ehn **lay**gerahtehst |
| Would you fill in this health insurance form, please? | **Kan du fylle ut dette sykeforsik-ringsskjemaet?** | kahn dew **few**ler **ewt** dehter **sew**kerfoshik-ringss**hay**maher |

## Hospital   *Sykehus*

| Please notify my family. | **Vær snill å under-rette familien min.** | vær snil aw **ew**nerr-rehter fah**meel**yern meen |
| What are the visiting hours? | **Når er det besøks-tid?** | nor ær deh ber**surks**-teed |
| How long do I have to stay in bed? | **Hvor lenge må jeg ligge til sengs?** | voor **lehng**er maw yæi **lig**ger til **sehng**ss |
| When can I get up? | **Når kan jeg stå opp?** | nor kahn yæi staw op |
| When will the doctor come? | **Når kommer legen?** | nor **kom**merr **lay**gern |
| I am in pain. | **Jeg har smerter.** | yæi haar smæ**r**terr |
| I can't eat. | **Jeg kan ikke spise.** | yæi kahn **ik**ker **spee**sser |
| I can't sleep. | **Jeg får ikke sove.** | yæi fawr **ik**ker **saw**ver |
| Where is the bell? | **Hvor er ringe-klokken?** | voor ær **ring**erklokkern |

| nurse | **en sykepleier** | ehn **sew**kerplæierr |
| patient | **en pasient** | ehn pahssee**yehnt** |
| anaesthetic | **en narkose** | ehn nahr**koo**sser |
| blood transfusion | **en blodoverføring** | ehn **bloo(d)**awverrf**ur**ring |
| injection | **en sprøyte** | ehn **sprøy**ter |
| operation | **en operasjon** | ehn operrah**shoon** |
| bed | **en seng** | ehn sehng |
| bedpan | **et stikkbekken** | eht **stik**behkern |
| thermometer | **et termometer** | eht tærmoo**may**terr |

## Dentist  *Tannlege*

| English | Norwegian | Pronunciation |
|---|---|---|
| Can you recommend a good dentist? | Kan du anbefale en god tannlege? | kahn dew ahnberfaaler ehn goo(d) tahnlāyger |
| Can I make an (urgent) appointment to see Dr. ...? | Kan jeg få time (så snart som mulig) hos dr. ... | kahn yæi faw teemer (saw snaaᴿt som mēwli) hooss doktoor |
| Couldn't you make it earlier? | Er det ikke mulig å få time tidligere? | ær deh ikker mēwli aw faw teemer teeleeyerrer |
| I have a broken tooth. | Jeg har brukket en tann. | yæi haar brookkert ehn tahn |
| I have a loose tooth. | Jeg har en løs tann. | yæi har ehn lūrss tahn |
| I have toothache. | Jeg har tannpine. | yæi haar tahnpeener |
| Is it an abscess? | Er det en byll? | ær deh ehn bewl |
| This tooth hurts. | Denne tannen verker. | dehner tahnern værkerr |
| at the top | her oppe | hǣr opper |
| at the bottom | her nede | hǣr nāyder |
| at the front | her foran | hǣr forahn |
| at the back | her bak | hǣr baak |
| Can you fix it temporarily? | Kan du foreta en provisorisk behandling? | kahn dew fawrertah ehn prooveessōōrisk berhahndling |
| I don't want it taken out. | Jeg vil ikke ha den trukket. | yæi vil ikker haa dehn trookkert |
| Could you give me an anaesthetic? | Kan jeg få bedøvelse? | kahn yæi faw berdūrverlser |
| I've lost a filling. | Jeg har mistet en plombe. | yæi haar mistert ehn ploomber |
| My gums are bleeding/sore. | Tannkjøttet blør/er sårt. | tahnkhurter blūrr/ær sawᴿt |
| I've broken my dentures. | Jeg har brukket gebisset. | yæi haar brookkert gerbisser |
| Can you repair my dentures? | Kan du reparere gebisset? | kahn dew rehpahrāyrer gerbisser |
| When will they be ready? | Når blir det ferdig? | nor bleer deh fǣᴿdi |

# Reference section

## Where do you come from?   *Hvor kommer du fra?*

| I'm from ... | Jeg er fra ... | yæi ær fraa |
|---|---|---|
| Africa | **Afrika** | aafreekah |
| Asia | **Asia** | aasseeah |
| Australia | **Australia** | oustraaleeah |
| Europe | **Europa** | ourōōpah |
| North America | **Nord-Amerika** | nōōr-ahmāyreekah |
| South America | **Sør-Amerika** | sūrr-ahmāyreekah |
| Austria | **Østerrike** | ursterreeker |
| Belgium | **Belgia** | behlgeeah |
| Canada | **Kanada** | kahnahdah |
| China | **Kina** | kheenah |
| Croatia | **Kroatia** | krōōahteeah |
| Denmark | **Danmark** | dahnmahrk |
| England | **England** | ehnglahn |
| Finland | **Finland** | finlahn |
| France | **Frankrike** | frahngkreeker |
| Germany | **Tyskland** | tewsklahn |
| Great Britain | **Storbritannia** | stoorbrittahneeah |
| Greece | **Hellas** | hehlahss |
| Hungary | **Ungarn** | oonggah'n |
| Iceland | **Island** | eeslahn |
| India | **India** | indeeah |
| Ireland | **Irland** | eerlahn |
| Israel | **Israel** | eesrahehl |
| Italy | **Italia** | eetaaleeah |
| Japan | **Japan** | yaapahn |
| Luxembourg | **Luxembourg** | lewksermbewrg |
| Netherlands | **Nederland** | nāyderlahn |
| New Zealand | **Ny-Zealand** | nēw-sāylahn |
| Norway | **Norge** | norgger |
| Poland | **Polen** | pōōlern |
| Portugal | **Portugal** | poo'tewgahl |
| Russia | **Russland** | rēwslahn |
| Scotland | **Skottland** | skotlahn |
| South Africa | **Sør-Afrika** | sūrr-aafreekah |
| Spain | **Spania** | spaaneeah |
| Sweden | **Sverige** | sværyer |
| Switzerland | **Sveits** | svæitss |
| Turkey | **Tyrkia** | tewrkeeah |
| United States | **USA** | ēw-ehss-aa |
| Wales | **Wales** | væilss |

## Numbers *Tall*

| | | |
|---|---|---|
| 0 | **null** | newl |
| 1 | **en** | āyn |
| 2 | **to** | tōō |
| 3 | **tre** | trāy |
| 4 | **fire** | feerer |
| 5 | **fem** | fehm |
| 6 | **seks** | sehkss |
| 7 | **sju** | shēw |
| 8 | **åtte** | otter |
| 9 | **ni** | nee |
| 10 | **ti** | tee |
| 11 | **elleve** | ehlver |
| 12 | **tolv** | tol |
| 13 | **tretten** | trehtern |
| 14 | **fjorten** | fyoo<sup>r</sup>tern |
| 15 | **femten** | fehmtern |
| 16 | **seksten** | sæistern |
| 17 | **sytten** | surtern |
| 18 | **atten** | ahtern |
| 19 | **nitten** | nittern |
| 20 | **tjue** | khēwer |
| 21 | **tjueen** | khēwerāyn |
| 22 | **tjueto** | khēwertōō |
| 23 | **tjuetre** | khēwertrāy |
| 24 | **tjuefire** | khēwerfeerer |
| 25 | **tjuefem** | khēwerfehm |
| 26 | **tjueseks** | khēwersehkss |
| 27 | **tjuesju** | khēwershēw |
| 28 | **tjueåtte** | khēwerotter |
| 29 | **tjueni** | khēwernee |
| 30 | **tretti** | trehti |
| 31 | **trettien** | trehtiāyn |
| 32 | **trettito** | trehtitōō |
| 33 | **trettitre** | trehtitrāy |
| 40 | **førti** | fur<sup>r</sup>ti |
| 50 | **femti** | fehmti |
| 60 | **seksti** | sehksti |
| 70 | **sytti** | surti |
| 80 | **åtti** | otti |
| 90 | **nitti** | nitti |
| 100 | **hundre** | hewndrer |
| 101 | **hundreogen** | hewndrero(g)āyn |
| 102 | **hundreogto** | hewndrero(g)tōō |
| 110 | **hundreogti** | hewndrero(g)tee |
| 120 | **hundreogtjue** | hewndrero(g)khēwer |

| | | |
|---|---|---|
| 200 | **to hundre** | tōō **hewndrer** |
| 300 | **tre hundre** | trāy **hewndrer** |
| 400 | **fire hundre** | feerer **hewndrer** |
| 500 | **fem hundre** | fehm **hewndrer** |
| 600 | **seks hundre** | sehkss **hewndrer** |
| 700 | **sju hundre** | shēw **hewndrer** |
| 800 | **åtte hundre** | otter **hewndrer** |
| 900 | **ni hundre** | nee **hewndrer** |
| 1,000 | **tusen** | tēwssern |
| 1,100 | **et tusen et hundre** | eht tēwssern eht hewndrer |
| 1,200 | **et tusen to hundre** | eht tēwssern tōō hewndrer |
| 2,000 | **to tusen** | tōō tēwssern |
| 10,000 | **ti tusen** | tee tēwssern |
| 50,000 | **femti tusen** | fehmti tēwssern |
| 100,000 | **hundre tusen** | hewndrer tēwssern |
| 1,000,000 | **en million** | ehn milyōōn |
| 1,000,000,000 | **en milliard** | ehn milyahrd |

| | | |
|---|---|---|
| first | **første** | furshter |
| second | **annen/andre** | aaern/ahndrer |
| third | **tredje** | trāydyer |
| fourth | **fjerde** | fyǣrer |
| fifth | **femte** | fehmter |
| sixth | **sjette** | shehter |
| seventh | **sjuende** | shewerner |
| eighth | **åttende** | otterner |
| ninth | **niende** | neeerner |
| tenth | **tiende** | teeerner |

| | | |
|---|---|---|
| once/twice | **en gang/to ganger** | ehn gahng/tōō gahngerr |
| three times | **tre ganger** | trāy **gahngerr** |
| a half | **en halv** | ehn hahl |
| half a ... | **en halv ...** | ehn hahl |
| half of ... | **halvparten av ...** | hahlpahʳtern ahv |
| half (adj.) | **halv** | hahl |
| a quarter | **en fjerdedel** | ehn fyǣrerdāyl |
| three quarters | **tre fjerdedeler** | trāy fyǣrerdāylerr |
| a third | **en tredjedel** | ehn trāydyerdāyl |
| two thirds | **to tredjedeler** | tōō trāydyerdāylerr |
| a pair of | **et par** | eht pahr |
| a dozen | **et dusin** | eht dewsseen |
| 3.4% | **3,4%** | trāy **kommah** feerer prōōssehnt |

| | | |
|---|---|---|
| 1981 | **nitten åttien** | nittern ottiāyn |
| 1992 | **nitten nittito** | nittern nittitōō |
| 2003 | **to tusen og tre** | tōō tēwssern o(g) trāy |

## Year and age  *År og alder*

| year | et år | eht awr |
|------|-------|---------|
| leap year | et skuddår | eht skewdawr |
| decade | et tiår | eht teeawr |
| century | et århundre | eht awrhewndrer |

| this year | i år | ee awr |
|-----------|------|--------|
| last year | i fjor | ee fyōor |
| next year | neste år | nehster awr |
| each year | hvert år | væ^rt awr |

| 2 years ago | for 2 år siden | for 2 awr seedern |
|-------------|----------------|-------------------|
| in one year | om et år | om eht awr |
| in the eighties | på 80-tallet/ i 80-årene | paw ottitahler/ ee ottiawrerner |
| the 17th century | 17. århundre/ 1600-tallet | surterner awrhewndrer/ sæistern-hewndrertahler |
| in the 20th century | i 20. århundre | ee khēwerner awrhewndrer |
| in the 21st century | i 21. århundre | ee khēwerfurshter awrhewndrer |

| old/young | gammel/ung | gahmerl/oong |
|-----------|------------|--------------|
| old/new | gammel/ny | gahmerl/nēw |
| How old are you? | Hvor gammel er du? | voor gahmerl ær dew |
| I'm 30 years old. | Jeg er 30 år. | yæi ær 30 awr |
| At my age ... | I min alder ... | ee meen ahlderr |
| He/She was born in 1980. | Han/Hun ble født i 1980. | hahn/hewn bleh furt ee nittern otti |
| He/She is under 4. | Han/Hun er under 4 år. | hahn/hewn ær ewnerr feerer awr |

## Seasons  *Årstider*

| spring | vår | vawr |
|--------|-----|------|
| summer | sommer | sommerr |
| autumn | høst | hurst |
| winter | vinter | vinterr |

| in spring | om våren | om vawrern |
|-----------|----------|-----------|
| during the summer | i løpet av sommeren | ee lūrper(t) ahv sommerrern |
| in autumn | om høsten | om hurstern |
| during the winter | i løpet av vinteren | ee lūrper(t) ahv vinterrern |

| high season | høysesong | hoysehssong |
|-------------|-----------|------------|
| low season | lavsesong | laavsehssong |

## Months   *Måneder*

| January | **januar** * | yahnewaar |
|---|---|---|
| February | **februar** | fehbrewaar |
| March | **mars** | mahsh |
| April | **april** | ahpreel |
| May | **mai** | maay |
| June | **juni** | yēwnee |
| July | **juli** | yēwlee |
| August | **august** | ougewst |
| September | **september** | sehptehmberr |
| October | **oktober** | oktawberr |
| November | **november** | noovehmberr |
| December | **desember** | dehssehmberr |

| after June | **etter juni** | ehterr jēwnee |
|---|---|---|
| before July | **før juli** | furr yēwlee |
| during the month of August | **i løpet av august** | ee lūrper(t) ahv ougewst |
| in September | **i september** | ee sehptehmberr |
| until October | **til oktober** | til oktawberr |
| not until November | **ikke før november** | ikker fūrr noovehmberr |
| since December | **siden desember** | seedern dehssehmberr |
| last month | **forrige måned** | foryer mawnerd |
| next month | **neste måned** | nehster mawnerd |
| the month before | **måneden før** | mawnerdern fūrr |
| the month after | **måneden etter** | mawnerdern ehterr |
| the beginning of January | **begynnelsen av januar** | beryewnerlsern ahv yahnewaar |
| the middle of February | **midten av februar** | mittern ahv fehbrewaar |
| the end of March | **slutten av mars** | shlewtern ahv mahsh |

## Days and date   *Dager og dato*

| What day is it today? | **Hvilken dag er det i dag?** | vilkern daag ær deh ee daag |
|---|---|---|
| Monday | **mandag** * | mahndah(g) |
| Tuesday | **tirsdag** | teeshdah(g) |
| Wednesday | **onsdag** | oonsdah(g) |
| Thursday | **torsdag** | tawshdah(g) |
| Friday | **fredag** | frāydah(g) |
| Saturday | **lørdag** | lūrʳdah(g) |
| Sunday | **søndag** | surndah(g) |

---

* The names of months and days aren't capitalized in Norwegian.

Aliment

| What's the date today? | Hvilken dato er det i dag? | vilkern daatoo ær deh ee daag |
| It's ... | Det er ... | deh ær |
| July 1 | 1. juli | furshter yewlee |
| March 31 | 31. mars | trehtifurshter mahsh |
| When's your birthday? | Når har du fødsels-dag? | nor haar dew furtserls-daag |
| May 17th. | 17. mai. | surterner maay |
| in the morning | om morgenen | om maw‵nern |
| during the day | om dagen/i løpet av dagen | om daagern/ee lūrper(t) ahv daagern |
| in the afternoon | om ettermiddagen | om ehterrmiddaagern |
| in the evening | om kvelden | om kvehlern |
| at night | om natten | om nahtern |
| the day before yesterday | i forgårs | ee forgosh |
| yesterday | i går | ee gawr |
| today | i dag | ee daag |
| tomorrow | i morgen | ee mawer‵n |
| the day after tomorrow | i overmorgen | ee awverrmawer‵n |
| the day before | dagen før | daagern fūrr |
| the next day | neste dag | nehster daag |
| two days ago | for to dager siden | for tōō daagerr seedern |
| in a few days | om et par dager | om eht pahr daagerr |
| in three days' time | om tre dager | om trāy daagerr |
| the other day | forleden dag | fo‵laydern daag |
| all day long | hele dagen | hāyler daagern |
| day by day | dag for dag | daag for daag |
| Monday to (through) Friday | mandag til fredag | mahndah(g) til frāydah(g) |
| nowadays | i våre dager | ee vawrer daagerr |
| day off | fridag | freedaag |
| holiday | helligdag | hehlidaag |
| holidays/vacation | ferie | fāyryer |
| school holidays | skoleferie | skōōlerfāyryer |
| week | uke | ēwker |
| last week | forrige uke | foryer ēwker |
| next week | neste uke | nehster ēwker |
| for a fortnight (two weeks) | i fjorten dager | ee fyoo‵tern daagerr |
| weekday | hverdag | væ‵daag |
| weekend | weekend | veekehnd |
| working day | arbeidsdag | ahrbæidsdaag |

## Greetings and wishes  *Hilsener og gratulasjoner*

| Merry Christmas! | **God jul!** | goo(d) yewl |
| Happy New Year! | **Godt nytt år!** | got newt awr |
| Happy Easter! | **God påske!** | goo(d) pawsker |
| Happy birthday! | **Gratulerer med dagen!** | grahtewlāyrerr meh(d) daagern |
| Best wishes for a Happy New Year! | **De beste ønsker om et godt nytt år!** | dee behster urnskerr om eht got newt awr |
| Many happy returns of the day! | **Til lykke med dagen!** | til lewker meh(d) daagern |
| Congratulations! | **Gratulerer!** | grahtewlāyrerr |
| Good luck/All the best! | **Lykke til!** | lewker til |
| Have a good trip! | **God reise!** | goo(d) ræisser |
| Have a good holiday (vacation)! | **God ferie!** | goo(d) fāyryer |
| Regards from ... | **Jeg skal hilse fra ...** | yæi skahl hilser fraa |
| My regards to ... | **Hils til ...** | hilss til |

## Public (Legal) holidays  *Offentlige høytidsdager*

Offices, banks, post offices and shops close early on Christmas Eve and New Year's Eve.

| January 1 | **Første nyttårsdag** | New Year's Day |
| May 1 | **Første mai** | May Day (Labor Day) |
| May 17 | **Grunnlovsdagen** | Constitution Day |
| December 25 | **Første juledag** | Christmas Day |
| December 26 | **Annen juledag** | Boxing Day |
| Movable Dates: | **Skjærtorsdag** | Maundy Thursday |
| | **Langfredag** | Good Friday |
| | **Annen påskedag** | Easter Monday |
| | **Kristi himmelfartsdag** | Ascension Day |
| | **Annen pinsedag** | Whit Monday |

## What time is it?   *Hvor mange er klokken?*

| Excuse me. Can you tell me the time? | **Unnskyld, men kan du si meg hvor mange klokken er?** | ewnshewl mehn kahn dew see mæi voor mahnger klokkern ær |
|---|---|---|
| It's ... | **Den er ...** | dehn ær |
| five past one | **fem over ett** * | fehm **aw**verr eht |
| ten past two | **ti over to** | tee **aw**verr tōō |
| a quarter past three | **kvart over tre** | kvah'rt **aw**verr trāȳ |
| twenty past four | **tjue over fire/ ti på halv fem** | khēwer **aw**verr feerer/ tee paw hahl fehm |
| twenty-five past five | **fem på halv seks** | fehm paw hahl sehkss |
| half past six | **halv sju** | hahl shēw |
| twenty-five to seven | **fem over halv sju** | fehm **aw**verr hahl shēw |
| twenty to eight | **ti over halv åtte/ tjue på åtte** | tee **aw**ver hahl otter/ khewer paw otter |
| a quarter to nine | **kvart på ni** | kvah'rt paw nee |
| ten to ten | **ti på ti** | tee paw tee |
| five to eleven | **fem på elleve** | fehm paw **ehl**ver |
| twelve o'clock | **tolv** | tol |
| noon | **klokken tolv (om dagen)** | klokkern tol (om daagern) |
| midnight | **midnatt** | midnaht |
| in the morning | **om morgenen** | om maw'nern |
| in the afternoon | **om ettermiddagen** | om ehtermiddaagern |
| in the evening | **om kvelden** | om kvehlern |
| What time does the train leave? | **Når går toget?** | nor gawr tawger |
| It leaves at ... | **Det går kl. ...** | deh gawr klokkern |
| 13.04 (1.04 p.m.) | **13.04** | trehtern newl feerer |
| 00.40 (00.40 a.m.) | **00.40** | newl fur'ti |
| in five minutes | **om fem minutter** | om fehm minnewterr |
| in a quarter of an hour | **om et kvarter** | om eht kvah'tāȳr |
| half an hour ago | **for en halvtime siden** | for ehn hahlteemer seedern |
| about two hours | **ca. to timer** | sirrkah tōō teemerr |
| a few seconds | **et par sekunder** | eht pahr sehkewnerr |
| The clock is fast/ slow. | **Klokken går for fort/sakte.** | klokkern gawr for foo't/sahkter |

---

* In everyday conversation, time is expressed as shown here. However, official time uses a 24-hour clock, which means that after noon hours are counted from 13 to 24.

Allment

## Common abbreviations  *Vanlige forkortelser*

| | | |
|---|---|---|
| A/S | aksjeselskap | Ltd./Inc. |
| ca. | cirka | around |
| e.Kr. | etter Kristus | A.D. |
| EM | europamesterskap | European Championship |
| ent. | entall | singular |
| et. | etasje | floor |
| f.Kr. | før Kristus | B.C. |
| fl. | flertall | plural |
| f.m. | forrige måned | last month |
| FN | De forente nasjoner | United Nations |
| g | gram | gram |
| gt. | gate | street |
| hg | hekto(gram) | hectogram |
| hk | hestekrefter | horsepower |
| H.M. | Hans Majestet | His Majesty |
| kg | kilo(gram) | kilogram |
| kl. | klokken | o'clock |
| km | kilometer | kilometre |
| KNA | Kongelig Norsk Auto-mobilklub | Royal Norwegian Automobile Club |
| kr/kr. | kroner | kroner |
| l | liter | litre |
| md. | måned(er) | month(s) |
| moms | merverdiavgift | VAT/sales tax |
| NAF | Norges Automobil-Forbund | Norwegian Automobile Association |
| nr. | nummer | number |
| NRK | Norsk rikskringkasting | Norwegian Broadcasting System |
| NSB | Norges Statsbaner | Norwegian State Railways |
| NTB | Norsk Telegrambyrå | Norwegian News Agency |
| NTH | Norges tekniske høgskole | Norwegian Technical University |
| osv. | og så videre | etc. |
| pk. | pakke | packet, parcel |
| pr. stk. | per stykk | per item |
| str. | størrelse | size |
| s.u. | svar utbes | R.S.V.P. |
| tlf. | telefon | telephone |
| t.v. | til venstre | to the left |
| UD | Utenriksdepartementet | Ministry for Foreign Affairs |
| veil. pris | veiledende pris | recommended price |
| VM | verdensmesterskap | World Championship |

## Signs and notices *Skilt og oppslag*

| | |
|---|---|
| **Adgang forbudt (for uvedkommende)** | No trespassing, No entrance |
| **Damer** | Ladies |
| **Fare** | Danger |
| **Forsiktig** | Caution |
| **Forsiktig, trapp** | Mind the step |
| **Gangbro/Gangbru** | Footbridge |
| **Gratis adgang** | Admission free |
| **Gågate** | Pedestrian zone |
| **Heis** | Lift (Elevator) |
| **Herrer** | Gentlemen |
| **Høgspenning** | High voltage |
| **Inngang** | Entrance |
| **I uorden** | Out of order |
| **Kaldt** | Cold |
| **Kasse** | Cash desk (Cashier) |
| **Ledig** | Free/Vacant |
| **Livsfare** | Danger of death |
| **Ned** | Down |
| **Nymalt** | Wet paint |
| **Nødutgang** | Emergency exit |
| **Opp** | Up |
| **Opptatt** | Occupied |
| **Privat** | Private |
| **Privat vei/veg** | Private road |
| **Reservert** | Reserved |
| **Røyking forbudt** | No smoking |
| **Røyking (ikke) tillatt** | (Non)Smoker |
| **Stengt** | Closed |
| **Skyv** | Push |
| **Til leie** | For hire (rent), To let |
| **Til salgs** | For sale |
| **Trekk** | Pull |
| **Trykk** | Press |
| **Tråkk ikke på gresset** | Keep of the grass |
| **Underetasje** | Lower ground floor |
| **Utgang** | Exit |
| **Utsalg** | Sales |
| **Utsolgt** | Sold out |
| **Vareheis** | Goods lift (Freight elevator) |
| **Varmt** | Hot |
| **Vokt deg/Dem for hunden** | Beware of the dog |
| **Åpent** | Open |
| **Åpningstider** | Opening hours |

Allment

## Emergency   *Nødsfall*

| Call the police | **Ring til politiet** | ring til poolitteeyer |
|---|---|---|
| Consulate | **Konsulat** | koonsewlaat |
| DANGER | **FARE** | faarer |
| Embassy | **Ambassade** | ahmbahssaader |
| FIRE | **BRANN** | brahn |
| Gas | **Gass** | gahss |
| Get a doctor | **Hent en lege** | hehnt ehn lāyger |
| Go away | **Gå vekk** | gaw vehk |
| HELP | **HJELP** | yehlp |
| Get help quickly | **Hent hjelp øyeblikkelig** | hehnt yehlp oyerblikkerli |
| I'm ill | **Jeg er syk** | yæi ær sēwk |
| I'm lost | **Jeg har gått meg bort** | yæi haar got mæi booʳt |
| Leave me alone | **La meg være i fred** | lah mæi vǣrer ee frāy(d) |
| LOOK OUT | **SE OPP** | sāy op |
| Poison | **Gift** | yift |
| POLICE | **POLITI** | poolittee |
| Stop that man/ woman | **Stopp den mannen/ kvinnen** | stop dehn mahnern/ kvinnern |
| STOP THIEF | **STOPP TYVEN** | stop tēwvern |

## Emergency telephone numbers   *Nødnummere*

| In Oslo or Bergen: | Fire | 110 |
|---|---|---|
| | Police | 112 |
| | Ambulance | 113 |

## Lost property—Theft   *Hittegods – Tyveri*

| Where's the ... | **Hvor er ...** | voor ær |
|---|---|---|
| lost property (lost and found) office | **hittegodskontoret** | hittergoodskoontōōrer |
| police station | **politistasjonen** | poolitteestahshōōnern |
| I want to report a theft. | **Jeg vil anmelde et tyveri.** | yæi vil ahnmehler eht tewverree |
| My ... has been stolen. | **... er blitt stjålet.** | ... ær blit styawlert |
| I've lost my ... | **Jeg har mistet ...** | yæi haar mistert |
| handbag/passport/ wallet | **håndvesken/passet lommeboken** | honvehskern/pahsser/ loommerbōōkern |

CAR ACCIDENTS, see page 78

157

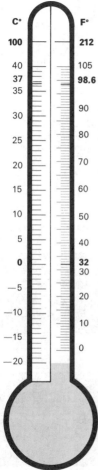

## Conversion tables

### Centimetres and inches

To change centimetres into inches, multiply by .39.
To change inches into centimetres, multiply by 2.54.

|        | in.   | feet  | yards |
|--------|-------|-------|-------|
| 1 mm.  | 0.039 | 0.003 | 0.001 |
| 1 cm.  | 0.39  | 0.03  | 0.01  |
| 1 dm.  | 3.94  | 0.32  | 0.10  |
| 1 m.   | 39.40 | 3.28  | 1.09  |

|        | mm.   | cm.   | m.    |
|--------|-------|-------|-------|
| 1 in.  | 25.4  | 2.54  | 0.025 |
| 1 ft.  | 304.8 | 30.48 | 0.305 |
| 1 yd.  | 914.4 | 91.44 | 0.914 |

(32 metres = 35 yards)

### Temperature

To convert centigrade into degrees Fahrenheit, multiply centigrade by 1.8 and add 32.
To convert degrees Fahrenheit into centigrade, subtract 32 from Fahrenheit and divide by 1.8.

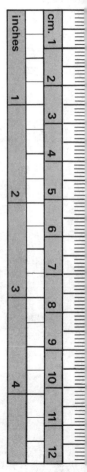

## Kilometres into miles

1 kilometre (km.) = 0.62 miles

| km. | 10 | 20 | 30 | 40 | 50 | 60 | 70 | 80 | 90 | 100 | 110 | 120 | 130 |
|-------|----|----|----|----|----|----|----|----|----|-----|-----|-----|-----|
| miles | 6 | 12 | 19 | 25 | 31 | 37 | 44 | 50 | 56 | 62 | 68 | 75 | 81 |

## Miles into kilometres

1 mile = 1.609 kilometres (km.)

| miles | 10 | 20 | 30 | 40 | 50 | 60 | 70 | 80 | 90 | 100 |
|-------|----|----|----|----|----|----|-----|-----|-----|-----|
| km. | 16 | 32 | 48 | 64 | 80 | 97 | 113 | 129 | 145 | 161 |

## Fluid measures

1 litre (l.) = 0.88 imp. quart or = 1.06 U.S. quart

| 1 imp. quart = 1.14 l. | 1 U.S. quart = 0.95 l. |
|---|---|
| 1 imp. gallon = 4.55 l. | 1 U.S. gallon = 3.8 l. |

| litres | 5 | 10 | 15 | 20 | 25 | 30 | 35 | 40 | 45 | 50 |
|-----------|-----|-----|-----|-----|-----|-----|-----|------|------|------|
| imp. gal. | 1.1 | 2.2 | 3.3 | 4.4 | 5.5 | 6.6 | 7.7 | 8.8 | 9.9 | 11.0 |
| U.S. gal. | 1.3 | 2.6 | 3.9 | 5.2 | 6.5 | 7.8 | 9.1 | 10.4 | 11.7 | 13.0 |

## Weights and measures

1 kilogram or kilo (kg.) = 1000 grams (g.)

| 100 g. = 3.5 oz. | ½ kg. = 1.1 lb. |
|---|---|
| 200 g. = 7.0 oz. | 1 kg. = 2.2 lb. |

| 1 oz. = 28.35 g. |
| 1 lb. = 453.60 g. |

CLOTHING SIZES, see page 115/YARDS AND INCHES, see page 112

# Basic grammar

Norway has two official written, mutually comprehensible languages, *bokmål* and *nynorsk*. A traveller in Norway must expect to see and hear both, but *bokmål*—the most common—is used throughout this book.

### Articles

The article shows the gender of Norwegian nouns, that are either common (masculine), feminine or neuter. The majority of feminine\* nouns also have a common form, so we have chosen to simplify matters by using only the two most frequently met genders: the common and the neuter.

1. Indefinite article (a/an)

| | | |
|---|---|---|
| common: | *en* **bil** | *a* car |
| neuter: | *et* **eple** | *an* apple |

2. Definite article (the)

Where we, in English say "the house", Norwegians tag the definite article onto the end of the noun and say "house-the". In common nouns "the" is **-(e)n**, in neuter nouns **-(e)t**.

| | | |
|---|---|---|
| common: | **bilen** | *the* car |
| neuter: | **eplet** | *the* apple |

### Nouns

1. There are no easy rules for determining the gender. Learn each new word with its accompanying article.

2. The plural of most nouns is formed by an **-(e)r** ending (indefinite plural) and an **-(e)ne** ending (definite plural).

| | | | | |
|---|---|---|---|---|
| common: | **biler** | cars | **bilene** | *the* cars |
| neuter: | **epler** | apples | **eplene** | *the* apples |

---

\* In the feminine form "a night, the night" would be *ei* natt, natt*a*; the common form is *en* natt, natt*en*.

Many monosyllabic nouns have irregular plurals.

| en mann | a man | **menn** | men | **mennene** | the men |
|---------|-------|----------|-----|-------------|---------|
| en sko | a shoe | **sko** | shoes | **skoene** | the shoes |
| et hus | a house | **hus** | houses | **husene** | the houses |
| et barn | a child | **barn** | children | **barna** | the children |

3. Possession is shown by adding **-s** (singular and plural). Note that there is no apostrophe.

| **Johns bror** | John's brother |
|----------------|----------------|
| **hotellets eier** | the owner of the hotel |
| **barnas far** | the children's father |

### Adjectives

1. Adjectives agree with the noun in gender and number. For the indefinite form, the neuter is generally formed by adding **-t**, the plural by adding **-e**.

| **(en) stor hund** | (a) big dog | **store hunder** | big dogs |
|--------------------|-------------|------------------|----------|
| **(et) stort hus** | (a) big house | **store hus** | big houses |

2. For the definite declension of the adjective, add the ending **-e** (common, neuter and plural). This form is used when the adjective is preceded by **den, det, de** (the definite article used with adjectives) or by a demonstrative or a possessive adjective.

| **den store hunden** | the big dog |
|----------------------|-------------|
| **de store hundene** | the big dogs |
| **det store huset** | the big house |
| **de store husene** | the big houses |

3. Comparative and superlative

The comparative and superlative are normally formed either by adding the endings **-(e)re** and **-(e)st**, respectively, to the adjective or by putting **mer** (more) and **mest** (most) before the adjective.

| **stor/større/størst** | big/bigger/biggest |
|------------------------|---------------------|
| **lett/lettere/lettest** | easy/easier/easiest |
| **imponerende/ *mer* imponerende/ *mest* imponerende** | impressive/more impressive/ the most impressive |

4. Demonstrative adjectives:

|  | common | neuter | plural |
|---|---|---|---|
| this/these | **denne** | **dette** | **disse** |
| that/those | **den** | **det** | **de** |

5. Possessive adjectives agree in number and gender with the noun they modify, i.e. with the thing possessed and not the possessor.

|  | common | neuter | plural |
|---|---|---|---|
| my | **min** | **mitt** | **mine** |
| your | **din** | **ditt** | **dine** |
| his | **sin, hans** | **sitt, hans** | **sine, hans** |
| her | **sin, hennes** | **sitt, hennes** | **sine, hennes** |
| its | **sin, dens/dets\*** | **sitt, dens/dets** | **sine, dens/dets** |
| our | **vår** | **vårt** | **våre** |
| their | **sin, deres** | **sitt, deres** | **sine, deres** |

The forms **sin**, **sitt**, **sine** always refer back to the subject, but cannot be used to modify a subject.

**Han har mistet broken sin.**    He has lost his (own) book.
**De har mistet bøkene sine.**    They have lost their (own) books.

but:

**Boken hans er blitt borte.**    His book has disappeared.

The forms **hans**, **hennes**, **dens/dets**, **deres** are actually the genitive of the personal pronouns (see page 162). These forms can qualify the subject, as shown above, as well as the object. However, qualifying the latter, they indicate that the subject and the possessor of the object are two different people.

**Han har misted boken hans.**    He has lost his (John's) book.
**De har mistet bøkene deres.**    They have lost their (John and Mary's) books.

---

\* Use **dens** if "it" is of common gender and **dets** if "it" is neuter.

### Adverbs

Adverbs are often formed by adding **-t** to the corresponding adjective.

| | |
|---|---|
| **rask/raskt** | quick/quickly |
| **langsom/langsomt** | slow/slowly |

### Personal pronouns

| | subject | object | genitive |
|---|---|---|---|
| I | **jeg** | **meg** | – |
| you | **du** | **deg** | – |
| he | **han** | **ham/han** | hans |
| she | **hun** | **henne** | hennes |
| it | **den/det** | **den/det** | dens/dets |
| we | **vi** | **oss** | – |
| you (plural) | **dere** | **dere** | – |
| they | **de** | **dem** | deres |

Norwegian has two forms for "you", an informal one (**du**) and a formal one (**De**). However, today the use of the formal **De** has practically disappeared from the language.

### Verbs

Here we are concerned only with the infinitive, imperative and present tense. The present tense is simple, because it has the same form for all persons. The infinitive of most Norwegian verbs ends in **-e** (some compound and monosyllabic end in other vowels). Here are three useful auxiliary verbs:

| | to be | to have | to be able to |
|---|---|---|---|
| Infinitive | **å være** | **å ha** | **å kunne** |
| Present tense (same form for all persons) | **er** | **har** | **kan** |
| Imperative | **vær** | **ha** | – |

The present tense of most Norwegian verbs ends in **-r**:

|  | to ask | to buy | to go | to do |
|---|---|---|---|---|
| Infinitive | **å spørre** | **å kjøpe** | **å gå** | **å gjøre** |
| Present tense (same form for all persons) | **spør** | **kjøper** | **går** | **gjør** |
| Imperative | **spør** | **kjøp** | **gå** | **gjør** |

There is no equivalent to the English present continuous tense. Thus:

**Jeg reiser.**                    I travel/I am travelling.

## Negatives

Negation is expressed by using the adverb **ikke** (not). It is usually placed immediately after the verb in a main clause. In compound tenses, **ikke** appears between the auxiliary and the main verb.

**Jeg snakker norsk.**              I speak Norwegian.
**Jeg snakker ikke norsk.**         I do not speak Norwegian.

## Questions

Questions are formed by reversing the order of the subject and the verb:

**Bussen stanser her.**             The bus stops here.
**Stanser bussen her?**             Does the bus stop here?

**Jeg kommer i kveld.**             I am coming tonight.
**Kommer du i kveld?**              Are you coming tonight?

a     164     apple juice

# Dictionary
and alphabetical index

# English–Norwegian

| c common | nt neuter | pl plural |
| --- | --- | --- |

**a** en 159; et 159
**abbreviation** forkortelse c 154
**able, to be** kunne 162
**about** *(approximately)* ca./cirka 79, 153
**above** ovenfor 62; over 15
**abscess** byll c 145
**absorbent cotton** bomull c 109
**accept, to** *(take)* ta 61, 102
**accessories** tilbehør nt 116, 125
**accident** ulykke c 79, 139
**accommodation service** inn-kvarteringsservice c 22
**account** konto c 130
**adaptor** adapter c 119
**address** adresse c 21, 31, 76, 79, 102
**adhesive tape** limbånd nt 104
**admission** adgang c 82, 155; *(fee)* inngangsbillett c 89
**adult** voksen c 82
**aerogramme** aerogram nt 133
**Africa** Afrika 146
**after** etter 15, 77, 150
**afternoon** ettermiddag c 151, 153
**after-shave lotion** etter-barberingsvann nt 110
**age** alder c 149
**ago** for ... siden 149, 153
**air bed** luftmadrass c 106
**airmail** med fly 132
**airmail label** luftpostetikett c 133
**air mattress** luftmadrass c 106
**airplane** fly nt 65
**airport** flyplass c 16, 21, 65
**alarm clock** vekkeklokke c 121
**alcohol** alkohol c 37, 59
**alcoholic** alkoholholdig 58
**all** alt 103
**allergic** allergisk 141, 143
**allergy** allergi c 140

**allowed** tillatt 155
**almond** mandel c 54
**alphabet** alfabet nt 9, 135
**also** også 15
**alter, to** endre 116
**amazing** praktfull 84
**ambulance** sykebil c 79, 156
**American** amerikansk 105
**American** amerikaner c 93
**American plan** helpensjon c 24
**amount** beløp nt 61, 131
**amplifier** forsterker c 119
**amusement park** fornøyelsespark c 81
**anaesthetic** bedøvelse c 145; narkose c 144
**analgesic** analgetikum nt 109
**analogue** analog 122
**and** og 15
**animal** dyr nt 85
**ankle** ankel c 139
**anorak** anorakk c 116
**answer, to** svare 136
**antibiotic** antibiotikum nt 143
**antidepressant** middel mot depresjoner nt 143
**antique** antikvitet c 83
**antique shop** antikvitetsforretning c 98
**antiseptic** antiseptisk 109
**any** noe 15
**anyone** noen 12
**anything** noe 17, 101, 103, 113, 143
**anywhere** noe sted 89
**aperitif** aperitiff c 58
**appendicitis** blindtarmbetennelse c 142
**appendix** blindtarm c 138
**appetizer** forrett c 43
**apple** eple nt 54, 64
**apple juice** eplesaft c 59

**apple pie** eplekake *c* 55, 63
**appointment** avtalt møte *nt* 131; time *c* 30, 137, 145
**April** april *(c)* 150
**aquarium** akvarium *nt* 81
**aquavit** akevitt *c* 56
**archaeology** arkeologi *c* 83
**architect** arkitekt *c* 83
**area** *(of town)* strøk *nt* 81
**area code** retningsnummer *nt* 134
**arm** arm *c* 138, 139
**around** *(approximately)* ca./cirka 154; *(nearby)* i nærheten 35
**arrival** ankomst *c* 16, 25, 65
**arrive, to** være fremme 65, 68
**art** kunst *c* 83
**artery** pulsåre *c* 138
**art gallery** kunstgalleri *nt* 98
**artificial** kunstig 124
**artificial sweetener** søtnings-middel *nt* 37
**artist** kunstner *c* 83
**art museum** kunstmuseum *nt* 81
**ashtray** askebeger *nt* 36
**Asia** Asia 146
**ask, to** spørre 76, 163; *(beg)* be 136
**ask for, to** be om 25, 60
**asparagus** asparges *c* 51
**aspirin** aspirin *c* 109
**asthma** astma *c* 141
**at** ved 15
**athletics meeting** friidrettsstevne *nt* 89
**athletic shoe** turnsko *c* 118
**at least** minst 24
**at once** med én gang 31
**August** august *(c)* 150
**aunt** tante *c* 93
**Australia** Australia 146
**automatic** automatisk 122, 124; *(car)* med automatgir 20
**auto repair shop** bilverksted *nt* 78
**autumn** høst *c* 149
**average** middels(god) 91
**awful** forferdelig 84, 94

**B**
**baby** baby *c* 24, 111
**baby food** barnemat *c* 111
**babysitter** barnevakt *c* 27
**back** rygg *c* 138
**backache** ryggsmerte *c* 141
**backpack** ryggsekk *c* 106
**bacon** bacon *nt* 38
**bacon and eggs** egg og bacon 38

**bad** dårlig 14, 95
**bag** bag *c* 17, 18; *(carrier)* bærepose *c* 103
**baggage** bagasje *c* 18, 26, 31, 71
**baggage cart** bagasjetralle *c* 18, 71
**baggage checking** reisegods-ekspedisjon *c* 71
**baggage locker** oppbevaringsboks *c* 18, 67, 71
**baked** bakt 52
**baker's** bakeri *nt* 98
**balance** *(finance)* balanse *c* 131
**balcony** balkong *c* 23
**ball** *(inflated)* ball *c* 128
**ballet** ballett *c* 88
**ball-point pen** kulepenn *c* 104
**banana** banan *c* 54, 64
**bandage** bandasje *c* 109
**Band-Aid** plaster *nt* 109
**bangle** armring *c* 121
**bank** *(finance)* bank *c* 98, 129, 130
**banknote** seddel *c* 130
**bar** *(room)* bar *c* 33; *(chocolate)* plate *c* 64
**barber's** herrefrisør *c* 30, 98
**barrette** hårspenne *c* 111
**bath** bad *nt* 23, 25, 27
**bathing cap** badehette *c* 116
**bathing hut** badehus *nt* 91
**bathrobe** badekåpe *c* 116
**bathroom** bad *nt* 27
**bath salts** badesalt *c* 110
**bath towel** badehåndkle *nt* 27
**battery** batteri *nt* 75, 78, 119, 125
**battery-powered** batteridrevet 128
**be, to** være 162
**beach** strand *c* 90
**beach ball** badeball *c* 128
**bean** bønne *c* 51
**beard** skjegg *nt* 31
**beautiful** pen 14; vakker 84
**beauty salon** skjønnhetssalong *c* 30, 98
**bed** seng *c* 24, 144
**bed and breakfast** rom med frokost 24
**bedpan** stikkbekken *nt* 144
**beef** oksekjøtt *nt* 47; okse- 48
**beefsteak** biff *c* 47, 49
**beer** øl *nt* 56, 64
**before** før 15, 143, 150
**begin, to** begynne 87, 88
**beginner** begynner *c* 91
**beginning** begynnelse *c* 150
**behind** bak 15, 77

**bell** *(electric)* ringeklokke *c* 144
**bell captain** portier *c* 26
**bellman** bærer *c* 26
**below** nedenfor 62; under 15
**belt** belte *nt* 117
**berth** køye *c* 69, 71
**better** bedre 14, 25, 101
**between** mellom 15
**bicycle** sykkel *c* 74
**bicycle racing** sykkelløp *nt* 89
**bidet** bidet *nt* 28
**big** stor 14, 25, 101, 118
**bilberry** blåbær *nt* 54
**bill** regning *c* 31, 61, 102;
*(banknote)* seddel *c* 130
**billion** *(Am.)* milliard *c* 148
**binoculars** kikkert *c* 123
**bird** fugl *c* 85
**birthday** fødselsdag *c* 151
**biscuit** *(Br.)* småkake *c* 63
**bite, to** bite 139
**bitter** besk 60
**black** svart 113
**black and white** svart-hvitt 124, 125
**blackberry** bjørnebær *nt* 54
**blackcurrant** solbær *nt* 54
**bladder** urinblære *c* 138
**blanket** ullteppe *nt* 27
**bleed, to** blø 139, 145
**blind** *(window shade)* rullegardin *c* 29
**blister** blemme *c* 139
**blood** blod *nt* 141, 142
**blood pressure** blodtrykk *nt* 141, 142
**blood transfusion** blodoverføring *c* 144
**blotting paper** trekkpapir *nt* 104
**blouse** bluse *c* 116
**blow-dry, to** føne 30
**blue** blå 113
**blueberry** blåbær *nt* 54
**blusher** rouge *c* 110
**boat** båt *c* 73, 74
**bobby pin** hårklemme *c* 111
**body** kropp *c* 138
**boil** byll *c* 139
**boiled** kokt 49, 51, 52
**bone** ben *nt* 138
**book** bok *c* 12, 104
**booking office** billettkontor *c* 19, 67
**booklet of tickets** billetthefte *nt* 72
**bookshop** bokhandel *c* 98, 104

**boot** støvel *c* 118
**born** født 149
**botanical gardens** botanisk hage *c* 81
**botany** botanikk *c* 83
**bottle** flaske *c* 17, 56, 57
**bottle-opener** flaskeåpner *c* 106
**bowel** tarm *c* 138
**bowl** *(container)* bolle *c* 127; skål *c* 107
**bow tie** flue *c* 116
**box** eske *c* 120
**boy** gutt *c* 112
**boyfriend** venn *c* 93
**bra** behå *c* 116
**bracelet** armbånd *nt* 121
**braces** *(suspenders)* (bukse)seler *c/pl* 116
**braised** braisert 49
**brake** brems *c* 78
**brake fluid** bremsevæske *c* 75
**brandy** brandy *c* 58
**brass** messing *c* 122
**bread** brød *nt* 36, 38, 64, 120
**break, to** brekke 139
**break down, to** få motorstopp 78
**breakdown** motorstopp *c* 78
**breakdown van** kranbil *c* 78
**breakfast** frokost *c* 24, 34, 38
**breast** bryst *nt* 138
**breathe, to** puste 141, 142
**bridge** bro *c* 81
**bring, to** gi 13; ta med 95
**bring down, to** bære ned 31
**British** brite *c* 93
**broiled** *(Am.)* grillstekt 49
**broken** brukket 140; gått i stykker 29, 119, 123
**bronze** bronse *c* 122
**brooch** brosje *c* 121
**brother** bror *c* 93
**brown** brun 113
**bruise** blått merke *nt* 139
**brush** børste *c* 111
**Brussels sprouts** rosenkål *c/pl* 51
**bubble bath** skumbad *nt* 110
**bucket** bøtte *c* 106; spann *nt* 128
**buckle** spenne *c* 117
**buffet car** kafeteriavogn *c* 70
**build, to** bygge 83
**building** bygning *c* 81, 83
**building blocks/bricks** bygge-klosser *c/pl* 128
**bulb** *(light)* lyspære *c* 28, 75, 119
**bump** *(lump)* kul *c* 139

**bun** bolle *c* 63
**burn** brannsår *nt* 139
**burned out** *(bulb)* gått 28
**bus** buss *c* 18, 19, 65, 66, 72, 80
**business** forretning *c* 16, 131
**business district** forretningskvarter
*nt* 81
**business trip** forretningsreise *c* 93
**bus stop** bussholdeplass *c* 72
**busy** opptatt 96
**but** men 15
**butane gas** butangass *c* 32, 106
**butcher's** slakter *c* 98
**butter** smør *nt* 36, 38, 64
**button** knapp *c* 29, 117
**buy, to** kjøpe 100, 104, 123, 163

**C**

**cabana** badehus *nt* 91
**cabbage** kål *c* 51
**cabin** *(camping)* hytte *c* 32; *(ship)*
lugar *c* 74
**cabin luggage** håndbagasje *c* 65
**cable car** taubane *c* 74
**cable release** snorutløser *c* 125
**café** kafé *c* 33
**cafeteria** kafeteria *c* 32, 33, 67
**cake** kake *c* 55, 63, 64
**cake shop** konditori *nt* 98
**calculator** kalkulator *c* 105
**calendar** kalender *c* 104
**call** *(phone)* samtale *c* 134, 135,
136
**call, to** *(give name)* hete 11;
*(phone)* ringe 79, 134, 136, 156
**camera case** kameraveske *c* 125
**camera shop** fotoforretning *c* 98
**camp, to** campe 32
**camp bed** campingseng *c* 106
**camping** camping *c* 32
**camping equipment** camping-
utstyr *nt* 106
**camp site** campingplass *c* 32
**can** *(container)* boks *c* 120
**can** *(be able to)* kunne 12, 162
**Canada** Kanada 146
**Canadian** kanadier *c* 93
**cancel, to** annullere 65
**candle** stearinlys *nt* 106
**candlestick** lysestake *c* 127
**candy** godter *nt/pl* 126
**candy store** godtebutikk *c* 98
**canoe** kano *c* 74
**can opener** boksåpner *c* 106

**cap** lue *c* 116
**capital** *(finance)* kapital *c* 131
**capsule** *(medical)* kapsel *c* 109
**car** bil *c* 19, 20, 32, 75, 76, 78;
*(train)* vogn *c* 70, 71
**carafe** karaffel *c* 57
**carat** karat *c* 121
**caraway seed** karve *c* 53
**carbon paper** blåpapir *nt* 104
**carburettor** forgasser *c* 78
**card** kort *nt* 93, 131
**cardboard** papp *c* 107
**card game** kortspill *nt* 128
**cardigan** golfjakke *c* 116; lusekofte
*c* 127
**car ferry** bilterge *c* 74
**car hire** bilutleie *c* 20
**car park** parkeringsplass *c* 77;
*(multistorey)* parkeringshus *nt*
77
**car racing** billøp *nt* 89
**car rental** bilutleie *c* 20
**carrot** gulrot *c* 51
**carry, to** bære 21
**cart** tralle *c* 18, 71
**carton** kartong *c* 17, 126
**cartridge** *(camera)* kassett *c* 124
**car wash** bilvask *c* 76
**case** futteral *nt* 123; veske *c* 125;
*(cigarette)* etui *nt* 121, 126
**cash, to** løse inn 130, 133
**cash desk** kasse *c* 103, 155
**cassette** kassett *c* 127
**cassette player** kassettspiller *c* 119
**cassette recorder** kassettopptaker
*c* 119
**castle** slott *nt* 81
**catalogue** katalog *c* 82
**cathedral** domkirke *c* 81
**Catholic** katolsk 84
**cauliflower** blomkål *c* 51
**caution** forsiktig 155
**cave** hule *c* 81
**celery** selleri *c* 51
**cemetery** gravlund *c* 81
**centimetre** centimeter *c* 112
**centre** sentrum *nt* 19, 21, 76, 81
**century** århundre *nt* 149
**ceramics** keramikk *c* 83
**cereal** frokostblanding *c* 38
**chain** *(jewellery)* kjede *nt* 121
**chain bracelet** armlenke *c* 121
**chair** stol *c* 36
**chalk** kritt *c* 104

change *(money)* småpenger *c/pl* 130; vekslepenger *c/pl* 61, 77
change, to endre 65; *(replace)* bytte 60; skifte ut 123; *(money)* veksle 18, 130; *(trains)* bytte 68, 69, 73
changing room prøverom *nt* 115
chapel kapell *nt* 81
charcoal briquet trekullbrikett *c* 106
charcoal tablet kulltablett *c* 109
charge gebyr *nt* 136
charge, to koste 77
charm *(trinket)* berlokk *c* 121
charm bracelet berlokkarmbånd *nt* 121
cheap billig 14; *(inexpensive)* rimelig 24, 25, 101
check sjekk *c* 130; *(restaurant)* regning *c* 61
check, to kontrollere 75
check in, to *(airport)* sjekke inn 65
check out, to reise 31
checkroom *(railway)* bagasje-oppbevaring *c* 67, 71
check-up *(medical)* undersøkelse *c* 142
cheers! skål! 58
cheese ost *c* 38, 53, 62, 64
cheese shop osteforretning *c* 98
chef kjøkkensjef *c* 40
chemist's apotek *nt* 98, 108
cheque sjekk *c* 130
cherry kirsebær *nt* 54
chess sjakk *c* 93
chess set sjakkspill *nt* 128
chest bryst *nt* 141; brystkasse *c* 138
chewing gum tyggegummi *c* 126
chewing tobacco skråtobakk *c* 126
chicken kylling *c* 50
child barn *nt* 24, 60, 82, 90, 93, 139
children's ... barne- 116
children's doctor barnelege *c* 137
chilled avkjølt 58
China Kina 146
china shop glassmagasin *nt* 98
chips pommes frites *c/pl* 52, 62; *(Am.)* potetgull *nt* 52, 64
chives gressløk *c* 53
chocolate sjokolade *c* 38, 55, 59, 62
chocolate bar sjokoladeplate *c* 64, 126
cholesterol kolesterol *c* 37
chop *(meat)* kotelett *c* 48

Christmas jul *c* 152
chromium krom *c* 122
church kirke *c* 81, 84
cigar sigar *c* 126
cigarette sigarett *c* 17, 95, 126
cigarette case sigarettetui *nt* 126
cigarette holder sigarett-munnstykke *nt* 126
cigarette lighter lighter *c* 126
cinema kino *c* 86, 96
circle *(theatre)* balkong *c* 87
citadel festning *c* 81
city by *c* 81, 88
city centre sentrum *nt* 81
city hall rådhus *nt* 82
classical klassisk 128
clean ren 61
clean, to vaske 76
cleansing cream rensekrem *c* 110
cliff klippe *c* 85
cloakroom garderobe *c* 87
clock klokke *c* 121, 153
clock-radio klokkeradio *c* 119
close, to stenge 11, 82, 108, 132
closed stengt 155
cloth tøy *nt* 118
clothes klær *pl* 29, 116
clothes peg (pin) klesklype *c* 106
clothing klær *pl* 112
cloud sky *c* 94
coach *(bus)* ekspressbuss *c* 66; rutebil *c* 66
coach station busstasjon *c* 67
coast kyst *c* 85
coat *(man's)* frakk *c* 116; *(woman's)* kåpe *c* 116
coffee kaffe *c* 38, 59, 64
coffee shop konditori *nt* 33
cognac konjakk *c* 58
coin mynt *c* 83
cold kald 14, 25, 38, 60, 94, 155
cold *(illness)* forkjølelse *c* 108, 141
collar krage *c* 117
collect call noteringsoverføring *c* 135
colour farge *c* 112, 113, 124, 125
colour chart fargekart *nt* 30
colourfast fargeekte 114
colour rinse fargeskylling *c* 30
colour shampoo fargesjampo *c* 111
comb kam *c* 111
come, to komme 35, 92, 95 137
comedy komedie *c* 86
commission *(fee)* kommisjon *c* 130

DICTIONARY

**compact disc** CD-plate *c* 127
**compartment** *(train)* kupé *c* 71
**compass** kompass *nt* 106
**complaint** klage *c* 60
**concert** konsert *c* 88
**concert hall** konserthus *nt* 81, 88
**condom** kondom *nt* 109
**conductor** *(orchestra)* dirigent *c* 88
**conference room** konferanserom *nt* 23
**confirm, to** bekrefte 65
**confirmation** bekreftelse *c* 23
**congratulation** gratulasjon *c* 152
**congress hall** kongresshall *c* 81
**connection** *(transport)* forbindelse *c* 65, 68
**consommé** buljong *c* 44
**constipation** forstoppelse *c* 140
**consulate** konsulat *nt* 156
**contact lens** kontaktlinse *c* 123
**contagious** smittsom 142
**contain, to** inneholde 37
**contraceptive** prevensjonsmiddel *nt* 109
**contract** kontrakt *c* 131
**control** kontroll *c* 16
**cookie** småkake *c* 63
**cool box** kjøleboks *c* 106
**cooler ice pack** kjøleelement *nt* 106
**copper** kopper *nt* 122
**corkscrew** korketrekker *c* 106
**corn** *(Am.)* mais *c* 51; *(foot)* liktorn *c* 109
**corner** hjørne *nt* 21, 36
**corn plaster** liktornplaster *nt* 109
**cosmetics** kosmetikk *c* 110
**cost** kostnad *c* 131
**cost, to** koste 11, 24, 80, 136
**cot** barneseng *c* 24
**cotton** bomull *c* 114
**cotton wool** bomull *c* 109
**couchette** køye i liggevogn *c* 69
**cough** hoste *c* 108, 141
**cough, to** hoste 142
**cough drops** halspastiller *c/pl* 109
**cough syrup** hostesaft *c* 109
**counter** luke *c* 133
**country** land *nt* 92, 146
**countryside** land *nt* 85
**court house** tinghus *nt* 81
**cousin** *(male)* fetter *c* 93; *(female)* kusine *c* 93
**crab** krabbe *c* 43, 46
**cramp** krampe *c* 141
**cranberry** tyttebær *nt* 54

**crayfish** *(river)* kreps *c* 46
**crayon** fargeblyant *c* 104
**cream** fløte *c* 38, 55, 59; *(toiletry)* krem *c* 110; *(pharmaceutical)* salve *c* 109
**crease resistant** krøllfri 114
**credit** kreditt *c* 131
**credit card** kredittkort *nt* 20, 31, 61, 102, 130
**crew-neck** med rund hals 117
**crispbread** knekkebrød *nt* 120
**crisps** potetgull *nt* 52, 64
**crockery** servise *nt* 106, 107
**cross** kors *nt* 121
**cross-country skiing** langrenn *nt* 91
**crossing** *(maritime)* overfart *c* 73
**crossroads** (vei)kryss *nt* 77
**cruise** cruise *nt* 74
**crystal** krystall *nt* 122
**cucumber** agurk *c* 51
**cuff link** mansjettknapp *c* 121
**cuisine** kjøkken *nt* 34
**cup** kopp *c* 36, 59, 107
**curler** hårrull *c* 111
**currant** korint *c* 54
**currency** valuta *c* 18, 129
**currency exchange office** vekslingskontor *c* 18, 67, 129
**current** strøm *c* 90
**curry** *(seasoning)* karri *c* 53
**curtain** gardin *c* 28
**customs** toll *c* 16, 79, 102
**cut** *(wound)* kutt *nt* 139
**cut, to** *(with scissors)* klippe 30
**cut off, to** avbryte 135
**cut glass** slepet glass *nt* 122
**cuticle remover** neglebåndsfjerner *c* 110
**cutlery** (spise)bestikk *nt* 107
**cycling** sykling *c* 90

**D**
**dairy** melkebutikk *c* 98
**dance, to** danse 88, 96
**danger** fare *c* 155, 156
**dangerous** farlig 90
**Danish pastry** wienerbrød *nt* 63
**dark** mørk 25, 101, 112, 113
**date** *(day)* dato *c* 25, 151; *(appointment)* stevnemøte *nt* 95; *(fruit)* daddel *c* 54
**daughter** datter *c* 93
**day** dag *c* 20, 24, 32, 80, 150, 151
**daylight** dagslys *nt* 124

Ordliste

**day off** fridag *c* 151
**decade** tiår *nt* 149
**decaffeinated** koffeinfri 38, 59
**December** desember *(c)* 150
**decision** avgjørelse *c* 102;
  beslutning *c* 25
**deck** *(ship)* dekk *nt* 74
**deck chair** fluktstol *c* 106
**declare, to** *(customs)* fortolle 17
**deep** dyp 90, 142
**deep fried** frityrstekt 46
**deer** hjort *c* 50
**delicatessen** delikatesseforretning
  *c* 98
**delicious** utsøkt 61
**deliver, to** levere 102
**delivery** levering *c* 102
**Denmark** Danmark 146
**dentist** tannlege *c* 98, 145
**denture** gebiss *nt* 145
**deodorant** deodorant *c* 110
**department** avdeling *c* 83, 100
**department store** stormagasin *nt*
  98
**departure** avgang *c* 65
**deposit** *(down payment)*
  depositum *nt* 20; *(in bank)*
  innskudd *nt* 130
**dessert** dessert *c* 37, 55
**detour** *(traffic)* omkjøring *c* 79
**diabetic** diabetiker *c* 37, 141
**dialling code** retningsnummer *nt*
  134
**diamond** diamant *c* 122
**diaper** bleie *c* 111
**diarrhoea** diarré *c* 140
**dictionary** ordbok *c* 104
**diesel** diesel *c* 75
**diet** diett *c* 37
**difficult** vanskelig 14
**difficulty** problem *nt* 102;
  vanskelighet *c* 28
**dill** dill *c* 53
**dining car** spisevogn *c* 68, 70
**dining room** spisesal *c* 27
**dinner** middag *c* 27, 34, 94
**direct** direkte 65
**direct, to** vise vei 13
**direction** retning *c* 76
**directory** *(phone)* telefonkatalog *c*
  134
**disabled** bevegelseshemmet *c* 82
**disc** plate *c* 127
**discotheque** diskotek *nt* 88, 96
**discount** rabatt *c* 131

**disease** sykdom *c* 142
**dish** asjett *c* 127; fat *nt* 107; *(food)*
  rett *c* 37
**dish detergent** oppvaskmiddel *nt*
  106
**dish of the day** dagens rett *c* 39, 40
**disinfectant** desinfeksjonsmiddel
  *nt* 109
**dislocated** ute av ledd 140
**display case** monter *c* 100
**dissatisfied** misfornøyd 103
**district** *(of town)* kvarter *nt* 81
**dive, to** dykke 90
**diversion** *(traffic)* omkjøring *c* 79
**dizzy** svimmel 140
**do, to** gjøre 163
**doctor** lege *c* 79, 98. 137, 144, 156;
  *(title)* dr./doktor 145
**doctor's office** legekontor *nt* 137
**dog** hund *c* 139, 155
**doll** dukke *c* 127, 128
**dollar** dollar *c* 18, 102, 130
**double** dobbel 74
**double bed** dobbeltseng *c* 23
**double room** dobbeltrom *nt* 19, 23
**doughnut** smultring *c* 63
**down** ned 15, 155
**downhill skiing** utforkjøring *c* 91
**downstairs** nede 15
**downtown area** sentrum *nt* 81
**dozen** dusin *nt* 148
**draught beer** fatøl *nt* 56
**drawing pad** tegneblokk *c* 104
**drawing pin** tegnestift *c* 104
**dress** kjole *c* 116
**dressing gown** morgenkåpe *c* 116
**drink** drikk *c* 58, 59; drikkevare *c*
  56; drink *c* 60, 95
**drink, to** drikke 35, 36, 59
**drinking water** drikkevann *nt* 32
**drip, to** dryppe 28
**drive, to** kjøre 21, 76, 79
**driving licence** førerkort *nt* 20, 79
**drop** *(liquid)* dråpe *c* 109
**drugstore** apotek *nt* 98, 108
**dry** tørr 30, 58, 111
**dry cleaner's** rens *c* 29; renseri *nt*
  98
**dry shampoo** tørrsjampo *c* 111
**duck** and *c* 50
**dummy** *(baby's)* narresmokk *c* 111
**during** i løpet av 15, 149, 151
**duty** *(customs)* toll *c* 17
**duty-free shop** tax-free-butikk *c* 19
**dye, to** farge 30

**E**

**each** hver 125, 149
**ear** øre *nt* 138
**earache** øreverk *c* 141
**ear drops** øredråper *c/pl* 109
**early** tidlig 14, 31
**earring** ørering *c* 121
**east** øst 77
**Easter** påske *c* 152
**easy** lett 14
**eat, to** spise 36, 37, 62, 144
**eel** ål *c* 43, 46
**egg** egg *nt* 38, 45, 62, 64
**eight** åtte 147
**eighteen** atten 147
**eighty** åtti 147
**elastic** elastisk 109
**Elastoplast** plaster *nt* 109
**electric(al)** elektrisk 119
**electrical appliance** elektrisk utstyr *nt* 119
**electrical goods shop** elektrisitetsforretning *c* 98
**electricity** elektrisitet *c* 32
**electronic** elektronisk 125, 128
**elevator** heis *c* 27, 100, 155
**eleven** elleve 147
**elk** elg *c* 50
**embarkation point** kai *c* 73
**embassy** ambassade *c* 156
**emergency** nødsfall *nt* 156
**emergency exit** nødutgang *c* 27, 99, 155
**emery board** sandpapirfil *c* 110
**empty** tom 14
**enamel** emalje *c* 122
**end** slutt *c* 150
**engaged** *(phone)* opptatt 136
**engagement ring** forlovelsesring *c* 122
**engine** *(car)* motor *c* 78
**England** England 146
**English** engelsk 12, 82, 84, 104
**English** englender *c* 93
**engrave, to** gravere 121
**enjoyable** hyggelig 31
**enlarge, to** forstørre 125
**enough** nok 15
**enquiry** forespørsel *c* 68
**entrance** inngang *c* 67, 99, 155; innkjørsel *c* 79
**entrance fee** inngangsbillett *c* 82
**entree** *(meal)* hovedrett *c* 40
**envelope** konvolutt *c* 104
**equipment** utstyr *nt* 91, 106

**eraser** viskelær *nt* 104
**escalator** rulletrapp *c* 100
**estimate** *(cost)* overslag *nt* 131
**Europe** Europa 146
**evening** kveld *c* 87, 95, 96, 151, 153
**evening dress** *(woman's)* aftenkjole *c* 116
**event** begivenhet *c* 80; *(sport)* stevne *nt* 89
**everything** alt 61
**examine, to** undersøke 137
**exchange, to** bytte 103
**exchange rate** vekslingskurs *c* 18, 130
**excursion** utflukt *c* 80
**excuse, to** unnskylde 10
**exercise book** skrivebok *c* 104
**exhaust pipe** eksosrør *nt* 78
**exhibition** utstilling *c* 81
**exit** utgang *c* 67, 99, 155; utkjørsel *c* 79
**expect, to** vente 130
**expenses** utgift *c* 131
**expensive** dyr 14, 19, 24, 101
**exposure** *(photography)* bilde *nt* 124
**exposure counter** telleverk *nt* 125
**express** ekspress 132
**expressway** motorvei *c* 76
**extension** *(phone)* linje *c* 135
**extension cord/lead** skjøteledning *c* 119
**extra** ekstra 27, 36
**eye** øye *nt* 139
**eyebrow pencil** øyenbrynsstift *c* 110
**eye drops** øyendråper *c/pl* 109
**eye liner** eyeliner *c* 110
**eye shadow** øyenskygge *c* 110
**eyesight** syn *nt* 123
**eye specialist** øyenlege *c* 137

**F**

**fabric** *(cloth)* (tøy)stoff *nt* 113
**face** ansikt *nt* 138
**face flannel** ansiktsklut *c* 110
**face pack** ansiktsmaske *c* 30
**face powder** pudder *nt* 110
**facial tissue** papirlommetørkle *nt* 111
**factory** fabrikk *c* 81
**fair** messe *c* 81
**fall** *(autumn)* høst *c* 149
**fall, to** falle 139
**family** familie *c* 93, 144

**fan belt** vifterem *c* 75
**fantastic** fantastisk 84
**far** fjern 14; langt 11, 100
**fare** takst *c* 69
**farm** bondegård *c* 85
**fast** hurtig 124
**fat** *(meat)* fett *nt* 37
**father** far *c* 93
**faucet** kran *c* 28
**fax** telefax *c* 133
**February** februar (*c*) 150
**fee** *(doctor's)* honorar *nt* 144
**feeding bottle** tåteflaske *c* 111
**feel, to** *(physical state)* føle seg
  140, 142
**felt** filt *c* 114
**felt-tip pen** tusjpenn *c* 104
**ferry** ferge *c* 74; ferje *c* 74
**fever** feber *c* 140
**few** få 14; *(a few)* noen få 14
**field** jorde *nt* 85
**fifteen** femten 147
**fifty** femti 147
**file** *(tool)* fil *c* 110
**fill in, to** fylle ut 26, 144
**filling** *(tooth)* plombe *c* 145
**filling station** bensinstasjon *c* 75
**film** film *c* 86, 124, 125
**film winder** fremtrekker *c* 125
**filter** filter *nt* 125
**filter-tipped** med filter 126
**find, to** finne 11, 12, 100
**fine** *(OK)* bra 11, 25
**finger** finger *c* 138
**finish, to** slutte 87
**Finland** Finland 146
**fire** brann *c* 156
**fire lighter** tennvæske *c* 106
**first** første 68, 69, 148
**first-aid kit** førstehjelpsskrin *nt* 109
**first class** første klasse *c* 69
**first name** fornavn *nt* 25
**fish** fisk *c* 45
**fish, to** fiske 91
**fishing** fiske *nt* 90
**fishing permit** fiskekort *nt* 90
**fishing tackle** fiskeutstyr *nt* 106
**fishmonger's** fiskebutikk *c* 98
**fit, to** passe 115
**five** fem 147
**fix, to** reparere 75, 145
**fizzy** *(mineral water)* med kullsyre
  59
**fjord** fjord *c* 85
**flash** *(photography)* blitz *c* 125

**flashlight** lommelykt *c* 106
**flat** *(shoe)* lavhælt 118
**flat** *(apartment)* leilighet *c* 19
**flat tyre** punktering *c* 75, 78
**flatware** (spise)bestikk *nt* 107
**flea market** loppemarked *nt* 81, 98
**flight** fly *nt* 65
**flippers** svømmeføtter *c/pl* 128
**floor** etasje *c* 23, 27, 154
**floor show** show *nt* 88
**florist's** blomsterbutikk *c* 98
**flounder** flyndre *c* 45
**flour** mel *nt* 37
**flower** blomst *c* 85
**flu** influensa *c* 142
**fluid** væske *c* 75, 123
**foam rubber** skumgummi *c* 106
**fog** tåke *c* 94
**folding chair** klappstol *c* 106
**folding table** klappbord *nt* 106
**folk art** folkekunst *c* 83
**folk music** folkemusikk *c* 128
**follow, to** følge 77
**food** mat *c* 37, 60, 111
**food poisoning** matforgiftning *c*
  142
**foot** fot *c* 138
**football** fotball *c* 89
**footbridge** gangbro *c* 155
**foot cream** fotkrem *c* 110
**footpath** sti *c* 85
**for** for 15; *(time)* i 143, 151
**forbid, to** forby 155
**forest** skog *c* 85
**forget, to** glemme 60
**fork** gaffel *c* 36, 60, 107
**form** *(document)* blankett *c* 133;
  skjema *nt* 25, 26, 144
**fortnight** fjorten dager *c/pl* 151
**fortress** borg *c* 81
**forty** førti 147
**foundation cream** underlagskrem
  *c* 110
**fountain** fontene *c* 81
**fountain pen** fyllepenn *c* 104
**four** fire 147
**fourteen** fjorten 147
**fowl** fugl *c* 50
**frame** *(for glasses)* innfatning *c*
  123
**France** Frankrike 146
**free** *(of charge)* gratis 155; *(vacant)*
  ledig 14, 71, 96, 155
**French bean** brekkbønne *c* 51
**French fries** pommes frites *c/pl* 52

**fresh** fersk 60; frisk 54
**Friday** fredag *c* 150
**fried** stekt 46, 49
**fried egg** speilegg *nt* 38, 45
**friend** venn *c* 93, 95
**from** fra 15
**frost** frost *c* 94
**fruit** frukt *c* 54, 55
**fruit juice** (frukt)juice *c* 37, 38
**fruit salad** fruktsalat *c* 54
**frying pan** stekepanne *c* 106
**full** full 14
**full board** helpensjon *c* 24
**full insurance** full forsikring *c* 20
**fur coat** pels *c* 116
**furniture** møbler *nt/pl* 83
**furrier's** pelsforretning *c* 98

## G

**gallery** galleri *nt* 98
**game** spill *nt* 128; (food) vilt *nt* 50
**gangway** landgang *c* 74
**garage** (parking) garasje *c* 26; (repairs) bilverksted *nt* 78
**garden(s)** hage *c* 81, 85
**garlic** hvitløk *c* 52, 53
**gas** gass *c* 126, 156
**gasoline** bensin *c* 75
**gastritis** magekatarr *c* 142
**gauze** gasbind *nt* 109
**gem** edelsten *c* 121
**general** allmenn 27; vanlig 100
**general delivery** poste restante 133
**general practitioner** allmenn-praktiker *c* 137
**genitals** kjønnsorgan *nt* 138
**gentleman** herre *c* 155
**genuine** (real) ekte 118, 121
**geology** geologi *c* 83
**Germany** Tyskland 146
**get, to** (obtain) få 108; (fetch) skaffe 21, 31, 137; (find) få tak i 11, 19, 21, 32
**get off, to** gå av 72
**get to, to** komme til 11, 19, 70, 76
**get up, to** stå opp 144
**gherkin** sylteagurk *c* 51, 64
**gift** gave *c* 17
**gin and tonic** gin tonic *c* 58
**girdle** hofteholder *c* 116
**girl** pike *c* 112
**girlfriend** venninne *c* 93
**give, to** gi 13, 131, 135
**gland** kjertel *c* 138
**glass** glass *nt* 36, 57, 59, 60

**glasses** briller *c/pl* 123
**glasses case** brillefutteral *nt* 123
**gloomy** dyster 84
**glove** hanske *c* 116
**glue** lim *c* 105
**go, to** gå 96, 163
**go away!** gå vekk! 156
**gold** gull *nt* 121, 122
**golden** gullfarget 113
**gold plated** gullbelagt 122
**golf** golf *c* 89
**golf course** golfbane *c* 89
**good** bra 14, 101; god 10
**good afternoon** god dag 10
**goodbye** adjø 10
**good evening** god aften 10
**Good Friday** langfredag *c* 152
**good morning** god morgen 10
**good night** god natt 10
**goods** vare *c* 16
**goose** gås *c* 50
**gooseberry** stikkelsbær *nt* 54
**go, to** gå 163
**go out, to** gå ut 96
**gram** gram *nt* 120
**grammar book** grammatikk *c* 105
**grape** drue *c* 54, 64
**grapefruit** grapefrukt *c* 54
**grapefruit juice** grapefruktjuice *c* 38, 59
**gravel** grus *c* 79
**gravy** brun saus *c* 52
**gray** grå 113
**graze** skrubbsår *nt* 139
**greasy** fet 30, 111
**Great Britain** Storbritannia 146
**green** grønn 113
**green bean** brekkbønne *c* 51
**greengrocer's** grønnsakhandel *c* 98
**greeting** hilsen *c* 152
**grey** grå 113
**grilled** grillstekt 46, 49
**grocer's** matvarehandel *c* 98, 120
**grotto** grotte *c* 81
**groundsheet** teltunderlag *nt* 106
**group** gruppe *c* 82
**guesthouse** pensjonat *nt* 19, 22
**guide** guide *c* 80
**guidebook** guidebok *c* 82; reise-håndbok *c* 104, 105
**gum** (teeth) tannkjøtt *nt* 145
**gymnasium** trimrom *nt* 23
**gynaecologist** gynekolog *c* 137, 141

DICTIONARY

Ordliste

# H
**habit** vane c 34
**hail** hagl nt 94
**hair** hår nt 30, 111
**hairbrush** hårbørste c 111
**haircut** klipp c 30
**hairdresser** frisør c 98; frisørsalong c 27, 30
**hair dryer** hårføner c 119
**hair dye** hårfargingsmiddel nt 111
**hair styling gel** hårgelé c 111
**hairgrip** hårklemme c 111
**hair lotion** hårvann nt 111
**hair mousse** hårskum nt 111
**hairpin** hårnål c 111
**hair slide** hårspenne c 111
**hair spray** hårlakk c 30, 111
**half** halv 148
**half** halvpart c 148
**half an hour** halvtime c 153
**half board** halvpensjon c 24
**half price** halv pris c 69
**hall porter** portier c 26
**ham** skinke c 38, 48, 62, 64
**ham and eggs** egg og skinke 38
**hamburger** hamburger c 48
**hammer** hammer c 106
**hammock** hengekøye c 106
**hand** hånd c 138
**handbag** håndveske c 116, 156
**hand cream** håndkrem c 110
**handicrafts** kunsthåndverk nt 83, 127
**handkerchief** lommetørkle nt 116
**handmade** håndlaget 113
**hanger** (kles)henger c 27
**happy** god 152
**harbour** havn c 74, 81
**hard** hard 123
**hard-boiled** (egg) hardkokt 38
**hardware store** jernvarehandel c 98
**hare** hare c 50
**hat** hatt c 116
**have, to** ha 141, 162
**hay fever** høysnue c 141
**hazelnut** hasselnøtt c 54
**he** han 162
**head** hode nt 138, 139
**headache** hodepine c 108, 141
**headphones** høretelefoner c/pl 119
**head waiter** hovmester c 61
**health food shop** helsekostforretning c 99

**health insurance** sykeforsikring c 144
**heart** hjerte nt 138
**heart attack** hjerteslag nt 141
**heated** oppvarmet 90
**heating** varme c 23, 28
**heavy** tung 14, 101
**heel** hæl c 118
**helicopter** helikopter nt 74
**hello** hallo 10, 135
**help** hjelp c 156
**help, to** hjelpe 13, 21, 71, 100, 134; (oneself) ta selv 120
**hen** høne c 50
**her** hennes, sin, sitt (pl sine) 161
**herb** urt c 53
**here** her 14
**herring** sild c 41, 43, 46, 47
**hi** hei 10
**high** høy 85, 141
**high season** høysesong c 149
**hike, to** vandre 74
**hill** høyde c 85
**hire** utleie c 20
**hire, to** leie 19, 20, 74, 90, 91, 155
**his** hans, sin, sitt (pl sine) 161
**history** historie c 83
**hitchhike, to** haike 74
**hold on!** (phone) et øyeblikk! 136
**hole** hull nt 29
**holiday** helligdag c 151
**holidays** ferie c 16, 151, 152; (school) skoleferie c 151
**home address** hjemstedsadresse c 31
**home town** hjemsted nt 25
**honey** honning c 38
**hope, to** håpe 96
**horseback riding** ridning c 90
**horse racing** hesteveddeløp nt 89
**horseradish** pepperrot c 52
**hospital** sykehus nt 99, 144
**hot** varm 14, 25, 38, 59, 94, 155
**hotel** hotell nt 19, 21, 22
**hotel directory/guide** hotellfortegnelse c 19
**hotel reservation** værelsesbestilling c 19
**hot water** varmt vann nt 23, 28
**hot-water bottle** varmeflaske c 27
**hour** time c 80, 90, 143, 153
**house** hus nt 83, 85
**how** hvordan 11
**how far** hvor langt 11, 76, 85
**how long** hvor lenge 11, 24

**how many** hvor mange 11
**how much** hvor mye 11, 24, 102
**hundred** hundre 147
**hungry** sulten 13, 35
**hunting knife** jaktkniv *c* 127
**hurry** *(to be in a)* ha det travelt 21
**hurt, to** gjøre vondt 139; ha vondt
140; verke 145; *(oneself)* slå seg
139
**husband** mann *c* 93
**hydrofoil** hydrofoil *c* 74

**I**
**I** jeg 162
**ice** is *c* 94
**ice chest** kjøleboks *c* 106
**ice cream** is(krem) *c* 55, 62
**ice cube** isbit *c* 27
**iced tea** iste *c* 59
**ice hockey** ishockey *c* 89
**Iceland** Island 146
**ice pack** kjøleelement *nt* 106
**ignition** tenning *c* 78
**ill** syk 140, 156
**illness** sykdom *c* 140
**important** viktig 13
**imported** importert 113
**impressive** imponerende 84
**in** i 15
**include, to** inkludere 24
**included** inkludert 20, 31, 40, 61, 80
**India** India 146
**indicator** *(car)* blinklys *nt* 78
**indigestion** fordøyelsesbesvær *nt*
141
**indoor** innendørs 90
**inexpensive** rimelig 35, 124
**infected** infisert 140
**infection** betennelse *c* 141
**inflammation** betennelse *c* 142
**inflation** inflasjon *c* 131
**influenza** influensa 142
**information** informasjon *c* 67
**information desk** informasjons-
skranke *c* 18
**initial** *(letter)* initial *c* 121
**injection** sprøyte *c* 142, 144
**injure, to** skade 139
**injured** skadet 79, 139
**injury** skade *c* 139
**ink** blekk *nt* 105
**inlet** vik *c* 85
**inquiry** forespørsel *c* 68
**insect bite** innsektstikk *nt* 108
**insect killer** insektgift *c* 106

**insect repellent** insektmiddel *nt*
109
**insect spray** insektgift *c* 106
**inside** inne 15
**insole** innleggssåle *c* 118
**instant coffee** pulverkaffe *c* 64
**instead** i stedet 37
**insurance** forsikring *c* 20, 71, 144
**insurance company** forsikrings-
selskap *nt* 79
**interest** *(finance)* rente *c* 131
**interested, to be** være interessert
83
**interesting** interessant 84
**international** internasjonal 133
**interpreter** tolk *c* 131
**intersection** *(vei)kryss *nt* 77
**introduce, to** presentere 92
**introduction** *(social)* presentasjon
*c* 92
**investment** investering *c* 131
**invitation** innbydelse *c* 94
**invite to, to** by på 94
**invoice** faktura *c* 131
**iodine** jod *c* 109
**Ireland** Irland 146
**Irish** irlender *c* 93
**iron** *(for laundry)* strykejern *nt* 119
**iron, to** stryke 29
**ironmonger's** jernvarehandel *c* 99
**island** øy *c* 85
**Israel** Israel 146
**its** dens/dets, sin, sitt *(pl* sine) 161

**J**
**jack** *(tool)* jekk *c* 78
**jacket** jakke *c* 116
**jam** *(preserves)* syltetøy *nt* 38, 63
**jam, to** sitte fast 28, 125
**January** januar *(c)* 150
**Japan** Japan 146
**jar** *(container)* glass *nt* 120
**jaundice** gulsott *c* 142
**jaw** kjeve *c* 138
**jeans** jeans *c/pl* 116
**jerry can** bensinkanne *c* 78
**jetty** brygge *c* 74
**jewel box** smykkeskrin *nt* 121
**jeweller's** gullsmed *c* 99, 121
**jewellery** smykke *nt* 121
**joint** ledd *nt* 138
**juice** juice *c* 37, 38, 59
**July** juli *(c)* 150
**June** juni *(c)* 150
**just** *(only)* bare 16, 37, 100

DICTIONARY

# K

**kayak** kajakk *c* 74
**keep, to** beholde 61
**kerosene** parafin *c* 106
**key** nøkkel *c* 27
**kidney** nyre *c* 48, 138
**kilo(gram)** kilo *nt* 120
**kilometre** kilometer *c* 20, 79
**kind** snill 96
**kind** *(type)* slags *nt/pl* 47, 140
**knee** kne *nt* 138
**kneesocks** knestrømper *c/pl* 116
**knife** kniv *c* 36, 60, 107
**know, to** kjenne 114; vite 16, 24, 96
**krone** *(money)* krone *c* 18, 101, 129

# L

**label** etikett *c* 105, 133
**lace** knipling *c* 114
**lady** dame *c* 155
**lake** (inn)sjø *c* 81, 90
**lamb** *(meat)* lammekjøtt *nt* 47; lamme- 48
**lamp** lampe *c* 29, 106, 119
**landmark** landemerke *nt* 85
**language** språk *nt* 104, 159
**lantern** lykt *c* 106
**large** stor 20, 101, 118, 130
**last** forrige 150, 151; siste 14, 68
**last, to** vare 87
**late** forsinket 69, 70; sen 14
**later** senere 136
**laugh, to** le 95
**launderette** selvbetjeningsvaskeri *nt* 99
**laundry** *(place)* vaskeri *nt* 99; *(clothes)* vask *c* 29
**laundry service** vaskeri-service *c* 23
**laxative** laksermiddel *nt* 109
**lead** *(metal)* bly *nt* 75
**leap year** skuddår *nt* 149
**leather** lær *nt* 114, 118
**leave, to** *(depart)* gå 68, 69, 74, 95; reise 31; *(deposit)* deponere 26; *(hand in)* levere inn 71; *(return)* levere tilbake 20
**leave alone, to** la være i fred 156
**leek** purre *c* 51
**left** venstre 21, 62, 69, 77
**left-luggage office** bagasje-oppbevaring *c* 67, 71
**leg** ben *nt* 138
**legal holiday** offentlig høytidsdag *c* 152

**lemon** sitron *c* 38, 54, 59
**lemonade** sitronbrus *c* 59
**lend, to** låne 78
**lens** *(for glasses)* glass *nt* 123; *(for camera)* objektiv *nt* 125
**lens cap** linsebeskytter *c* 125
**lentil** linse *c* 51
**less** mindre 14
**lesson** time *c* 90
**let, to** *(hire out)* til leie 155
**letter** brev *nt* 28, 132
**letter box** postkasse *c* 132
**letter of credit** kredittbrev *nt* 130
**lettuce** hodesalat *c* 51
**library** bibliotek *nt* 81, 99
**licence** *(driving)* førerkort *nt* 20, 79
**lie down, to** legge seg ned 142
**life belt** livbelte *nt* 74
**life boat** livbåt *c* 74
**life jacket** flytevest *c* 74
**lift** *(elevator)* heis *c* 27, 100, 155
**ligament** leddbånd *nt* 140
**light** *(weight)* lett 14, 55, 101; *(colour)* lys 101, 112, 113
**light** lys *nt* 28, 124; *(for cigarette)* fyr *c* 95
**light bulb** lyspære *c* 28, 75, 119
**lighter** lighter *c* 126
**lighter fluid** lighterbensin *c* 126
**lighter gas** lightergass *c* 126
**light meter** lysmåler *c* 125
**lightning** lyn *nt* 94
**like, to** like 25, 92, 102, 112; ha lyst på 96; *(want)* ville 20
**line** linje *c* 73
**linen** *(cloth)* lin *nt* 114
**lip** leppe *c* 138
**lipsalve** leppepomade *c* 110
**lipstick** leppestift *c* 110
**liqueur** likør *c* 58
**liquid** *(fluid)* væske *c* 123
**liquor store** vinmonopol *nt* 99
**listen to, to** høre på 128
**litre** liter *c* 75, 120
**little** *(a little)* lite 14
**live, to** leve 83; *(reside)* bo 83
**liver** lever *c* 48, 64, 138
**loan** lån *nt* 131
**lobster** hummer *c* 43, 45
**local** lokal 36
**local train** lokaltog *nt* 66, 69
**long** lang 116
**long time** lang tid 60, 76, 116; lenge 77, 92, 144
**long-sighted** langsynt 123

Ordliste

**look, to** se 100, 123
**look for, to** se etter 13
**look out!** se opp! 156
**loose** løs 145; *(clothes)* vid 116
**lose, to** miste 123, 156
**loss** tap *nt* 131
**lost, to be** gå seg bort 13, 156
**lost and found office** hittegods-kontor *nt* 67, 156
**lost property office** hittegods-kontor *nt* 67, 156
**lot** *(a lot)* mye 14
**loud** *(voice)* høy 135
**lovely** herlig 94
**low** lav 141
**lower** under- 69, 71
**low season** lavsesong *c* 149
**luggage** bagasje *c* 18, 26, 31, 71; *(registered)* reisegods *nt/pl* 71
**luggage insurance** reisegods-forsikring *c* 71
**luggage locker** oppbevaringsboks *c* 18, 67, 71
**luggage trolley** bagasjetralle *c* 18, 71
**lunch** lunsj *c* 27, 34, 80, 94
**lung** lunge *c* 138

**M**

**machine** maskin *c* 114
**magazine** ukeblad *nt* 105
**magnificent** storslagen 84
**maid** værelsespike *c* 26
**mail** post *c* 28, 132, 133
**mail, to** poste 28
**mailbox** postkasse *c* 132
**main** hoved- 80; størst 100
**main course** hovedrett *c* 40
**make, to** lage 113, 114
**make up, to** *(prepare)* gjøre i stand 71, 108
**make-up bag** sminkepung *c* 110
**man** mann *c* 115, 156; herre *c* 155
**manager** bestyrer *c* 61; direktør *c* 26
**manicure** manikyr *c* 30
**man's ...** herre- 116
**many** mange 11, 14
**map** kart *nt* 76, 105
**March** mars *(c)* 150
**marinated** marinert 46
**maritime history** sjøfartshistorie *c* 83
**market** torghandel *c* 81, 99

**marmalade** appelsinmarmelade *c* 38
**married** gift 93
**marzipan** marsipan *c* 63
**mascara** øyensverte *c* 110
**mashed potatoes** potetstappe *c* 52, 62
**mass** *(church)* messe *c* 84
**match** *(matchstick)* fyrstikk *c* 106, 126; *(sport)* kamp/match *c* 89
**matinée** matiné *c* 87
**mattress** madrass *c* 106
**May** mai *(c)* 150
**may** *(can)* kunne 12, 162
**meadow** eng *c* 85
**meal** måltid *nt* 24, 143
**mean, to** bety 11, 26
**measles** meslinger *c/pl* 142
**measure, to** ta mål av 114
**meat** kjøtt *nt* 47, 60
**meatball** frikadelle *c* 47; kjøttbolle *c* 48
**mechanic** mekaniker *c* 78
**mechanical pencil** skrublyant *c* 105, 121
**medical certificate** legeattest *c* 144
**medicine** medisin *c* 83, 143
**medium** *(meat)* medium stekt 49
**medium-sized** mellomstor 20
**meet, to** møtes 96; treffes 92; ses 96
**melon** melon *c* 54
**memorial** minnesmerke *nt* 81
**mend, to** lappe 29; reparere 75
**menstrual pains** menstruasjons-smerter *c/pl* 141
**menthol** mentol *c* 126
**menu** meny *c* 36, 37, 39; *(printed)* spisekart *nt* 36, 39, 40
**message** beskjed *c* 28, 136
**metre** meter *c* 112
**mezzanine** *(theatre)* balkong *c* 87
**middle** midten 69, 87, 150
**midnight** midnatt *c* 153
**midnight sun** midnattssol *c* 94
**mild** mild 126
**mileage** kjørelengde *c* 20
**milk** melk *c* 38, 59, 64
**milkshake** milkshake *c* 59
**milliard** milliard *c* 148
**million** million *c* 148
**mineral water** naturlig mineral-vann *nt* 59

**minister** *(religion)* protestantisk prest *c* 84
**minute** minutt *nt* 21, 153
**mirror** speil *nt* 115, 123
**miscellaneous** forskjellig 127
**Miss** frøken *c* 92
**miss, to** mangle 18, 29, 60
**mistake** feil *c* 31, 61, 102;
   *(misunderstanding)*
   misforståelse *c* 60
**modern** moderne 83
**modified American plan** halvpensjon *c* 24
**moisturizing cream** fuktighetskrem
   *c* 110
**moment** øyeblikk *nt* 12, 136
**monastery** kloster *c* 81
**Monday** mandag *c* 150
**money** penger *c/pl* 129, 130
**money order** postanvisning *c* 133
**month** måned *c* 16, 150
**monument** monument *nt* 81
**moon** måne *c* 94
**moped** moped *c* 74
**more** mer 14
**morning** morgen *c* 31, 151, 153
**mortgage** hypotek *nt* 131
**mosque** moské *c* 84
**mosquito net** myggnett *nt* 106
**mother** mor *c* 93
**motorbike** motorsykkel *c* 74
**motorboat** motorbåt *c* 74
**motorway** motorvei *c* 76
**mountain** fjell *nt* 85
**moustache** bart *c* 31
**mouth** munn *c* 138
**mouthwash** munnvann *nt* 109
**move, to** bevege 139
**movie** film *c* 86
**movies** kino *c* 86, 96
**Mr.** herr *c* 92
**Mrs.** fru *c* 92
**much** mye 11, 14
**mug** krus *nt* 107
**muscle** muskel *c* 138
**museum** museum *nt* 81
**mushroom** sopp *c* 51
**music** musikk *c* 83, 128
**musical** musikal *c* 86
**music box** spilledåse *c* 121
**mussel** blåskjell *c* 43, 45
**must** *(have to)* måtte 23, 31, 95
**mustard** sennep *c* 64
**mutton** fårekjøtt *nt* 42, 47, 49
**my** min, mitt *(pl* mine) 161

**N**
**nail** *(human)* negl *c* 110
**nail brush** neglebørste *c* 110
**nail clippers** negleklipper *c* 110
**nail file** neglefil *c* 110
**nail polish** neglelakk *c* 110
**nail polish remover** neglelakk-
   fjerner *c* 110
**nail scissors** neglesaks *c* 110
**name** navn *nt* 23, 79, 133;
   *(surname)* etternavn *nt* 25
**napkin** serviett *c* 36, 105, 106
**nappy** bleie *c* 111
**narrow** trang 118
**nationality** nasjonalitet *c* 25, 92
**natural history** naturhistorie *c* 83
**nauseous** kvalm 140
**near** i nærheten av 19; nær 14
**nearby** i nærheten 77
**nearest** nærmeste 73, 75, 78, 132
**neat** *(drink)* bar 58
**neck** nakke *c* 30, 138
**necklace** halskjede *nt* 121
**need, to** trenge 29, 118, 137
**needle** nål *c* 27
**negative** negativ *nt* 124, 125
**nephew** nevø *c* 93
**nerve** nerve *c* 138
**nervous system** nervesystem *nt*
   138
**never** aldri 15
**new** ny 14, 118, 149
**newspaper** avis *c* 104, 105
**newsstand** aviskiosk *c* 19, 67, 104
**New Year** nyttår *nt* 152
**New Zealand** Ny-Zealand 146
**next** neste 14, 65, 68, 73, 76, 149
**next time** neste gang 95
**next to** ved siden av 15, 77
**nice** *(beautiful)* pen 94
**niece** niese *c* 93
**night** natt *c* 10, 24, 151
**nightclub** nattklubb *c* 88
**night cream** nattkrem *c* 110
**nightdress/-gown** nattkjole *c* 116
**nine** ni 147
**nineteen** nitten 147
**ninety** nitti 147
**no** nei 10
**noisy** støyende 25
**nonalcoholic** alkoholfri 56, 57, 59
**none** ingen 15
**nonsmoker** ikke-røyker *c* 36
**noodle** nudel *c* 52
**noon** klokken tolv (om dagen) 153

**normal** normal 30
**north** nord 77
**North America** Nord-Amerika 146
**Norway** Norge 113, 146
**Norwegian** norsk 11, 12, 18, 95, 114, 127
**nose** nese c 138
**nosebleed** neseblødning c 141
**nose drops** nesedråper c/pl 109
**not** ikke 15, 163
**note** (banknote) seddel c 130
**notebook** notisbok c 105
**note paper** brevpapir nt 105
**nothing** ikke noe 15, 17; ingenting 15, 16
**notice** (sign) oppslag nt 155
**notify, to** underrette 144
**November** november (c) 150
**now** nå 15
**number** nummer nt 25, 134, 135, 136; tall nt 147
**nurse** sykepleier c 144
**nut** (fruit) nøtt c 54, 62

## O

**observatory** observatorium nt 81
**occupation** (profession) yrke nt 25
**occupied** opptatt 14, 155
**ocean** hav nt 85
**o'clock** kl./klokken c 154
**October** oktober (c) 150
**office** kontor nt 22, 67, 80, 132
**oil** olje c 37, 75, 111
**oily** (greasy) fet 30, 111
**ointment** salve c 109
**old** gammel 14, 149
**old town** gamleby c 81
**omelet** omelett c 38, 45
**on** på 15
**once** en gang 148
**one** en 147
**one-way ticket** enkeltbillett c 65, 69
**on foot** til fots 76
**onion** løk c 51, 62
**only** bare 15, 24
**on time** i rute 68
**open** åpen 14, 82, 129, 155
**open, to** åpne 11, 17, 82, 108, 130
**open-air** utendørs 90
**opening hours** åpningstider c/pl 155
**opera** opera c 88
**opera house** operahus nt 81, 88
**operation** operasjon c 144

**operator** telefonist c 134
**operetta** operette c 88
**opposite** midt imot 77
**opposite** motsetning c 14
**optician** optiker c 99, 123
**or** eller 15
**orange** oransje 113
**orange** appelsin c 54, 64
**orange juice** appelsinjuice c 38, 59
**orchestra** orkester nt 88; (seats) parkett c 87
**order, to** (goods, meal) bestille 36, 60, 102, 103
**ornithology** ornitologi c 83
**other** andre 58, 74, 101
**our** vår, vårt (pl våre) 161
**out of order** i uorden 136
**out of stock** utsolgt 103
**outlet** (electric) stikkontakt c 27
**outside** ute 15, 36
**oval** oval 101
**overalls** overall c 116
**overdone** for mye stekt 60
**overheat, to** (engine) gå varm 78
**overnight** (stay) natten over 24
**overtake, to** kjøre forbi 79
**owe, to** skylde 144
**oyster** østers c 43, 46

## P

**pacifier** (baby's) narresmokk c 111
**packet** pakke c 120, 126
**pail** spann nt 128
**pain** smerte c 140, 141, 143, 144
**painkiller** smertestillende middel nt 109
**paint, to** male 83
**paintbox** malerskrin nt 105
**painter** maler c 83
**pair** par nt 116, 118, 148
**pajamas** pyjamas c 117
**palace** slott nt 81
**palpitation** hjerteklapp c 141
**pancake** pannekake c 45
**panties** truser c/pl 116
**pants** (trousers) langbukser c/pl 117
**panty hose** strømpebukse c 117
**paper** papir nt 105
**paperback** pocketbok c 105
**paperclip** binders c 105
**paper napkin** papirserviett c 105
**paper towel** husholdningspapir nt 106
**paraffin** (fuel) parafin c 106

**parcel** pakke *c* 132
**pardon** unnskyld 10
**parents** foreldre *c/pl* 93
**park** park *c* 81
**park, to** parkere 26, 77
**parka** anorakk *c* 117
**parking** parkering *c* 77, 79
**parking garage** parkeringshus *nt* 77
**parking lot** parkeringsplass *c* 77
**parking meter** parkometer *nt* 77
**parliament building** storting *nt* 81
**parsley** persille *c* 53
**part** del *c* 138
**partridge** rapphøne *c* 50
**party** *(social gathering)* fest *c* 95
**pass, to** *(driving)* kjøre forbi 79
**passport** pass *nt* 16, 17, 25, 26, 156
**passport photo** passfoto *nt* 124
**pass through, to** være på gjennomreise 16
**pastry** bakverk *nt* 63
**pastry shop** konditori *nt* 99
**path** sti *c* 85
**patient** pasient *c* 144
**pattern** mønster *nt* 112
**pay, to** betale 31, 61, 100, 102
**payment** betaling *c* 131
**pea** ert *c* 51
**peach** fersken *c* 54
**peak** topp *c* 85
**pear** pære *c* 54
**pearl** perle *c* 122
**pearl strand** perlekjede *nt* 121
**peg** *(tent)* plugg *c* 107
**pen** penn *c* 105
**pencil** blyant *c* 105
**pendant** hengesmykke *nt* 121
**penicillin** penicillin *nt* 143
**penknife** lommekniv *c* 106
**pensioner** pensjonist *c* 82
**people** folk *nt/pl* 92
**pepper** pepper *c* 37, 38, 53, 64
**per cent** prosent *c* 148
**percentage** prosentsats *c* 131
**per day** pr. dag 20, 32, 90
**perfume** parfyme *c* 110
**perfumery** parfymeri *nt* 99
**perhaps** kanskje 15
**per hour** pr. time 77, 90
**period** *(monthly)* menstruasjon *c* 141
**period pains** menstruasjons-smerter *c/pl* 141
**permanent wave** permanent *c* 30

**per night** pr. natt 24
**per person** pr. person 32
**person** person *c* 32
**personal** personlig 17
**personal call** personlig samtale *c* 134
**person-to-person call** personlig samtale *c* 134
**per week** pr. uke 20, 24
**petrol** bensin *c* 75, 78
**pewter** tinn *nt* 122
**pharmacy** apotek *nt* 99, 108
**pheasant** fasan *c* 50
**photo** bilde *nt* 125; foto *nt* 124
**photocopy** fotokopi *c* 131
**photograph, to** fotografere 82
**photographer** fotograf *c* 99
**photography** fotografering *c* 124
**phrase** uttrykk *nt* 12
**phrase book** parlør *c* 105
**pick up, to** *(person)* hente 80, 96
**pickled gherkin** sylteagurk *c* 51, 64
**picnic** picnic *c* 64
**picture** bilde *nt* 83
**picture-book** billedbok *c* 105
**piece** stykke *nt* 63, 120
**pier** pir *c* 74
**pill** pille *c* 109; *(contraceptive)* p-pille *c* 141
**pillow** pute *c* 27
**pin** nål *c* 110, 111, 122
**pineapple** ananas *c* 54
**pink** rosa 113
**pipe** pipe *c* 126
**pipe cleaner** piperenser *c* 126
**place** sted *nt* 25, 76
**place of birth** fødested *nt* 25
**plane** fly *nt* 65
**plaster, to put in** gipse 140
**plastic** plast *c* 107
**plastic bag** plastpose *c* 107
**plate** asjett *c* 127; tallerken *c* 36, 60, 107
**platform** *(station)* perrong *c* 67, 68, 69, 70
**play** *(theatre)* stykke *nt* 86, 87
**play, to** spille 86, 88, 89, 93
**playground** lekeplass *c* 32
**playing card** spillkort *c* 105
**please** vær (så) snill å ... 10; ... takk 10
**pliers** tang *c* 78, 107
**plimsoll** turnsko *c* 118
**plug** *(electric)* støpsel *nt* 29
**plum** plomme *c* 54

**pneumonia** lungebetennelse c 142
**poached** pochert 46; *(egg)* forlorent 45
**pocket** lomme c 117
**pocket calculator** lommekalkulator c 105
**pocket dictionary** lommeordbok c 104
**pocketknife** lommekniv c 107
**pocket radio** lommeradio c 119
**pocket watch** lommeur nt 121
**point, to** peke 12
**poison** gift c 109, 156
**poisoning** forgiftning c 142
**pole** *(ski)* stav c 91; *(tent)* stang c 107
**police** politi nt 79, 156
**police station** politistasjon c 99, 156
**polo-neck** høyhalset 117
**pond** dam c 85
**pork** svinekjøtt nt 47; svine- 48
**porridge** grøt c 38
**port** havn c 74; *(wine)* portvin c 58
**portable** bærbar 119
**porter** bærer c 18, 26, 71
**portion** porsjon c 37, 60
**possible** mulig 137
**post** *(mail)* post c 28, 133
**post, to** poste 28
**postage** porto c 132
**postage stamp** frimerke nt 28, 126, 132, 133
**postcard** postkort nt 105, 126, 132
**poste restante** poste restante 133
**post office** postkontor nt 99, 132
**pot** kanne c 59
**potato** potet c 52
**pottery** pottemakerkunst c 83
**poultry** fugl c 50
**pound** pund nt *(money)* 18, 102, 130, *(weight)* 120
**powder** pudder nt 110
**powder compact** pudderdåse c 121
**prawn** reke c 43, 46
**prefer, to** foretrekke 101
**pregnant** gravid 141
**premium** *(gasoline)* super 75
**prescribe, to** skrive ut 143
**prescription** resept c 108, 143
**present** presang c 121
**press, to** *(iron)* presse 29
**press stud** trykknapp c 117
**pressure** trykk nt 75, 141

**pretty** søt 84
**price** pris c 69, 124
**priest** katolsk prest c 84
**primus stove** primus c 107
**print** *(photo)* kopi c 125
**private** privat 80, 155
**processing** *(photo)* fremkalling c 124
**profit** utbytte nt 131
**programme** program nt 87
**pronounce, to** uttale 12
**pronunciation** uttale c 6
**propelling pencil** skrublyant c 105
**propose, to** anbefale 40
**Protestant** protestantisk 84
**provide, to** skaffe 131
**prune** sviske c 54
**ptarmigan** rype c 50
**public holiday** offentlig høytidsdag c 152
**pull, to** trekke 155
**pullover** genser c 117
**pump** pumpe c 107
**puncture** punktering c 75
**purchase** kjøp nt 131
**pure** ren 114
**purple** fiolett 113
**push, to** *(open)* skyve 155
**put, to** sette 24
**pyjamas** pyjamas c 117

**Q**

**quail** vaktel c 50
**quality** kvalitet c 113
**quantity** mengde c 14
**quarter** fjerdedel c 148; *(district of town)* kvarter nt 81
**quarter of an hour** kvarter nt 153
**question** spørsmål nt 11
**quick** rask 14
**quickly** øyeblikkelig 137, 156
**quiet** rolig 23, 25
**quilt** dyne c 27

**R**

**rabbi** rabbiner c 84
**rabbit** kanin c 50
**race** *(vedde)*løp nt 89
**race course/track** heste-veddeløpsbane c 89
**racket** *(sport)* racket c 90
**radiator** *(car)* kjøler c 78
**radio** radio c 23, 28, 119

**radio cassette recorder** radio-kassettopptaker c 119
**railway** jernbane c 67, 154
**railway station** jernbanestasjon c 19, 21, 67
**rain** regn nt 94
**rain, to** regne 94
**rainbow trout** regnbueørret c 46
**raincoat** regnfrakk c 117
**rainy** regnfull 94
**raisin** rosin c 54, 63
**rangefinder** avstandsmåler c 125
**rare** (meat) blodig 60; råstekt 49
**rash** utslett nt 139
**raspberry** bringebær nt 54
**rate** (of exchange) kurs c 18, 130
**razor** barberhøvel c 110
**razor blade** barberblad nt 110
**read, to** lese 27
**reading lamp** leselampe c 27
**ready** ferdig 118, 123, 125, 145; klar 29, 31
**real** (genuine) ekte 118, 121
**rear** bak 69, 75
**reason** (purpose) hensikt c 25
**receipt** kvittering c 102, 103, 144
**reception** resepsjon c 23
**receptionist** resepsjonist c 26
**recommend, to** anbefale 35, 36, 80, 145; (suggest) foreslå 44
**record** (disc) plate c 127, 128
**record player** platespiller c 119
**rectangular** rektangulær 101
**red** rød 113
**redcurrant** rips c 54
**reduction** rabatt c 82; reduksjon c 24
**refill** (pen) refill c 105
**refrigerator** kjøleskap nt 28
**refund, to get a** få pengene tilbake 103
**regards** hilsen c 152
**register, to** (luggage) ekspedere 71; (mail) rekommandere 132
**registered mail** rekommandert 132
**registration** innskriving c 25
**registration form** meldeskjema nt 25
**regular** (petrol) normal 75
**reindeer** reinsdyr nt 50
**reindeer skin** reinsdyrskinn nt 127
**religion** religion c 83
**religious service** gudstjeneste c 84
**rent, to** leie 19, 20, 74, 90, 91, 155
**rental** utleie c 20

**repair** reparasjon c 125
**repair, to** reparere 29, 118, 119, 121, 123, 125, 145
**repeat** gjenta 12
**report, to** (a theft) anmelde 156
**reservation** bestilling c 19, 69; reservasjon c 65
**reserve, to** bestille 19, 23, 35, 87; reservere 69, 155
**restaurant** restaurant c 33, 35, 67
**return ticket** tur-returbillett c 65, 69
**return, to** (come back) være tilbake 21, 80; (give back) levere tilbake 103
**reverse-charge call** noterings-overføring c 135
**revue** revy c 86
**rheumatism** reumatisme c 141
**rib** ribben nt 138
**ribbon** bånd nt 105
**rice** ris c 52
**ridge** ås c 85
**right** (correct) 14; (direction) høyre 21, 62, 69, 77
**ring** (jewellery) ring c 122
**river** elv c 85, 90
**road** vei c 76, 77
**road assistance** hjelp på veien c 78
**road map** veikart nt 105
**road sign** trafikkskilt nt 79
**roast** ovnsstekt 49
**roast** stek c 47, 48
**roast beef** oksestek c 48; roastbiff c 48
**roll** rull c 109; (bread) rundstykke nt 38, 64
**roller skates** rulleskøyter c/pl 128
**roll film** rullefilm c 124
**romantic** romantisk 84
**room** rom nt 19, 23, 24, 25; (space) plass c 32
**room number** romnummer nt 26
**rope** tau nt 107
**rosé** rosévin c 58
**round** rund 101
**round** (golf) runde c 90
**round-trip ticket** tur-returbillett c 65, 69
**route** vei c 85
**rowing boat** robåt c 74
**royal** kongelig 81
**rubber** (eraser) viskelær nt 105; (material) gummi c 118
**rubber band** gummistrikk c 105

**rucksack** ryggsekk *c* 107
**ruin** ruin *c* 82
**ruler** *(for measuring)* linjal *c* 105
**rum** rom *c* 58
**running water** rennende vann *nt* 23

**S**
**safe** *(free from danger)* trygg 90
**safe** safe *c* 26
**safety pin** sikkerhetsnål *c* 110
**sailing boat** seilbåt *c* 74
**salad** salat *c* 44, 51
**sale** salg *nt* 131; *(bargains)* (ut)salg *nt* 100, 155
**sales tax** moms *c* 24, 102, 154
**salmon** laks *c* 43, 46, 47
**salt** salt *nt* 37, 38, 53, 64
**salty** salt 60
**same** samme 118
**sand** sand *c* 90
**sandal** sandal *c* 118
**sandwich** smørbrød *nt* 41, 62
**sanitary napkin/towel** sanitetsbind *nt* 109
**Saturday** lørdag *c* 150
**sauce** saus *c* 52
**saucepan** kasserolle *c* 107
**saucer** skål (til kopp) *c* 107
**sauna** badstue *c* / sauna *c* 23, 32
**sausage** pølse *c* 48, 62, 64
**Scandinavia** Skandinavia 25
**scarf** skjerf *nt* 117
**scenery** *(landscape)* natur *c* 92
**scenic** naturskjønn 85
**school** skole *c* 151
**school holidays** skoleferie *c* 151
**scissors** saks *c* 107, 110
**scooter** scooter *c* 74
**Scotland** Skottland 146
**scrambled egg** eggerøre *c* 38
**screwdriver** skrutrekker *c* 107
**sculptor** billedhugger *c* 83
**sculpture** skulptur *c* 83
**sea** sjø *c* 85, 90
**seafood** skalldyr *nt/pl* 45
**sealskin** selskinn *nt* 127
**search for, to** lete etter 13
**season** årstid *c* 149
**seasoning** krydder *nt* 37
**seat** plass *c* 69, 70, 87
**seat belt** bilbelte *nt* 75
**second** andre 148; annen 148
**second** sekund *nt* 153

**second class** andre klasse *c* 69; annen klasse *c* 69
**second hand** sekundviser *c* 122
**second-hand shop** marsjandise-forretning *c* 99
**secretary** sekretær *c* 27, 131
**see, to** se 12, 80; *(examine)* undersøke 137
**self-adhesive** selvklebende 105
**sell, to** selge 100
**send, to** sende 78, 102, 132, 133
**send up, to** bringe opp 26
**senior citizen** pensjonist *c* 82
**sentence** setning *c* 12
**September** september *(c)* 150
**serve, to** servere 27, 40
**service** *(church)* gudstjeneste *c* 84
**service charge** service *c* 61
**serviette** serviett *c* 36
**set menu** meny *c* 36
**setting lotion** leggevann *nt* 30, 111
**seven** sju 147
**seventeen** sytten 147
**seventy** sytti 147
**sew, to** sy 29
**shade** *(colour)* nyanse *c* 112
**shallow** langgrunt 91
**shampoo** sjampo *c* 30, 111
**shampoo and set** vask og legg *c* 30
**shape** form *c* 103
**share** *(finance)* aksje *c* 131
**shave** barbering *c* 31
**shaver** barbermaskin *c* 27, 119
**shaving cream** barberkrem *c* 111
**she** hun 162
**shellfish** skalldyr *nt/pl* 45
**sherbet** sorbett *c* 55
**ship** skip *nt* 74
**shirt** skjorte *c* 117
**shoe** sko *c* 118
**shoelace** skolisse *c* 118
**shoemaker's** skomaker *c* 99
**shoe polish** skokrem *c* 118
**shoe shop** skoforretning *c* 99
**shop** butikk *c* / forretning *c* 98, 99
**shopping** shopping *c* 97
**shopping area** handlestrøk *nt* 82, 100
**shopping centre** butikksenter *nt* 99
**shop window** (utstillings)vindu *nt* 100, 112
**short** kort 30, 116
**shorts** shorts *c/pl* 117
**short-sighted** nærsynt 123

DICTIONARY

**shoulder** skulder *c* 138
**shovel** spade *c* 128
**show** show *nt* 88; *(theatre)* forestilling *c* 87
**show, to** vise 13, 76, 100, 101, 119
**shower** dusj *c* 23, 32
**shrimp** reke *c* 43, 46
**shrink, to** krympe 114
**shut** stengt 14
**shutter** *(camera)* lukker *c* 125
**sick** *(ill)* syk 140, 156
**sickness** *(illness)* sykdom *c* 140
**side** side *c* 31
**sideboards/-burns** kinnskjegg *nt* 31
**side dish** tilbehør *nt* 40
**sightseeing** sightseeing *c* 80
**sightseeing tour** sightseeingtur *c* 80
**sign** *(notice)* skilt *nt* 79, 155
**sign, to** undertegne 26, 130
**signature** underskrift *c* 25
**signet ring** signetring *c* 122
**silk** silke *c* 114
**silver** *(colour)* sølvfarget 113
**silver** sølv *nt* 121, 122
**silver plate** sølvplett *c* 122
**silverware** sølvtøy *nt* 122
**simple** enkel 124
**since** siden 15, 150
**sing, to** synge 88
**single** enkel 74; *(unmarried)* ugift 93
**single room** enkeltrom *nt* 19, 23
**single ticket** enkeltbillett *c* 65, 69
**sink** vask *c* 28
**sister** søster *c* 93
**sit down, to** sette seg 95, 142
**six** seks 147
**sixteen** seksten 147
**sixty** seksti 147
**size** *(clothes)* størrelse *c* 114, 115; *(film)* format *nt* 124; *(shoes)* nummer *nt* 118
**skate** skøyte *c* 91
**skating rink** skøytebane *c* 91
**ski** ski *c* 91
**ski, to** gå på ski 91
**ski boot** skistøvel *c* 91
**ski jumping** skihopping *c* 89
**ski lift** skiheis *c* 91
**skin** hud *c* 138
**ski race** skirenn *nt* 89
**skirt** skjørt *nt* 117
**ski run** skibakke *c* 91

**ski track/trail** skiløype *c* 91
**sky** himmel *c* 94
**sleep, to** sove 144
**sleeping bag** sovepose *c* 107
**sleeping car** sovevogn *c* 68, 72
**sleeping pill** sovetablett *c* 143
**sleeve** erme *nt* 116
**slice** skive *c* 62, 120
**sliced** oppskåret 120
**slide** *(photo)* lysbilde *nt* 124
**slide film** film for lysbilder *nt/p* 124
**slide projector** lysbildeapparat *nt* 125
**slip** *(underwear)* underkjole *c* 117
**slipper** tøffel *c* 118, 127
**slow** sakte 14
**slowly** langsom 12, 135; sakte 21
**small** liten 14, 20, 25, 101, 118, 130
**smoke, to** røyke 95
**smoked** røkt 42, 43, 46, 49
**smoker** røyker *c* 36
**smorgasbord** koldtbord *nt* 41
**snack** småretter *c/pl* 62
**snack bar** snackbar *c* 67
**snail** snegle *c* 43
**snap fastener** trykknapp *c* 117
**snorkel** snorkel *c* 128
**snow** snø *c* 94
**snow, to** snø 94
**snuff** snus *c* 126
**soap** såpe *c* 27, 111
**soccer** fotball *c* 89
**sock** sokk *c* 117
**socket** *(electric)* stikkontakt *c* 27
**soda water** sodavann *nt* 58
**soft** myk 123
**soft-boiled** *(egg)* bløtkokt 38
**soft drink** leskedrikk 40, 59, 64
**soft ice cream** softis *c* 62
**sold out** utsolgt 87, 155
**sole** *(fish)* sjøtunge *c* 46; *(shoe)* såle *c* 118
**soloist** solist *c* 88
**some** litt 15; noe 15
**someone** noen 95
**something** noe 29, 36, 55, 108
**son** sønn *c* 93
**song** sang *c* 128
**soon** snart 15, 137
**sorbet** sorbett *c* 55
**sore** *(painful)* sår 141, 145
**sorry, to be** beklage 10, 16, 103
**sort** *(kind)* slags *nt/pl* 86, 120
**soup** suppe *c* 44
**south** sør 77

Ordliste

**South Africa** Sør-Afrika 146
**South America** Sør-Amerika 146
**souvenir** suvenir c 127
**souvenir shop** suvenirbutikk c 99
**spade** spade c 128
**spanner** skrunøkkel c 78
**sparerib** svineribbe c 48
**spare tyre** reservedekk nt 75
**spark(ing) plug** tennstift c 75
**sparkling** (spring water) med kullsyre 59; (wine) musserende 58
**speak, to** snakke 12, 135
**speaker** (loudspeaker) høyttaler c
119
**special** spesial- 20, 37; spesiell 80
**specialist** spesialist c 142
**speciality** spesialitet c 36, 40, 42
**specimen** (medical) prøve c 142
**spell, to** bokstavere 12
**spend, to** gi 101
**spice** krydder nt 53
**spinach** spinat c 51
**spine** ryggrad c 138
**sponge** svamp c 111
**sponge bag** toalettmappe c 111
**spoon** skje c 36, 60, 107
**sport** sport c 89
**sporting event** sportsstevne nt
89
**sporting goods shop** sports-
forretning c 99
**sportswear** sportsklær pl 117
**sprain, to** vrikke 140
**spring** (season) vår c 149; (water)
kilde c 85
**spring water** naturlig mineralvann
nt 59
**square** firkantet 101
**square** plass c 82; torg nt 82
**stadium** stadion nt 82
**staff** (personnel) personale nt 26
**stain** flekk c 29
**stainless steel** rustfritt stål nt 107
**stalls** (theatre) parkett c 87
**stamp** (postage) frimerke nt 28,
126, 132, 133
**staple** heftestift c 105
**stapler** heftemaskin c 105
**star** stjerne c 94
**start, to** starte 78, 80
**starter** (meal) forrett c 43
**station** stasjon c; (railway)
jernbanestasjon 19, 21, 67, 70;
(underground/subway)
T-banestasjon 73

**stationer's** papirhandel c 99, 104
**statue** statue c 82
**stave church** stavkirke c 82
**stay** opphold nt 31
**stay, to** bli 16, 24; (reside) bo 93
**steak** biff c 47
**steal, to** stjele 156
**steamed** dampkokt 46
**steamer** dampbåt c 74
**steering** (car) styring c 78
**stew pot** gryte c 107
**stiff** stiv 141
**still** (mineral water) uten kullsyre
59
**sting** stikk nt 139
**sting, to** bite 139
**stitch, to** sy sammen 29, 118
**stock exchange** børs c 82
**stocking** strømpe c 117
**stomach** mage c 138
**stomach ache** magesmerte c 141
**stools** avføring c 142
**stop** (place) holdeplass c, 72
**stop, to** stanse 21, 68, 72; stå 70
**stop thief!** stopp tyven! 156
**store** (shop) butikk c 98, 99;
forretning c 98, 99
**straight** (drink) bar 58
**straight ahead** rett frem 21, 77
**strange** underlig 84
**strawberry** jordbær nt 54, 55
**stream** bekk c 85
**street** gate c 77
**streetcar** trikk c 72
**street map** kart nt 19, 105
**string** hyssing c 105; (of pearls)
perlekjede nt 121
**strong** sterk 126, 143
**student** student c 82, 93
**study, to** studere 93
**stuffed** fylt 49, 51
**sturdy** robust 101; solid 101
**styling gel** hårgelé c 111
**subway** (railway) T-bane c 73
**suede** semsket skinn nt 114, 118
**sugar** sukker nt 37, 64
**suit** (man's) dress c 117;
(woman's) drakt c 117
**suitcase** koffert c 18
**summer** sommer c 149
**sun** sol c 94
**sunburn** solforbrenning c 108, 141
**Sunday** søndag c 150
**sunglasses** solbriller c/pl 123
**sunshade** (beach) parasoll c 91

**sun-tan cream** solkrem *c* 110
**sun-tan oil** sololje *c* 111
**super** *(petrol)* super 75
**superb** ypperlig 84
**supermarket** supermarked *nt* 99
**suppository** stikkpille *c* 109
**surgery** *(consulting room)* legekontor *nt* 137
**surname** etternavn *nt* 25
**suspenders** *(Am.)* (bukse)seler *c/pl*
117
**swallow, to** svelge 143
**sweater** genser *c* 117
**sweat suit** treningsdrakt *c* 117
**Sweden** Sverige 146
**sweet** søt 58, 60
**sweet** *(confectionery)* godter *nt/pl*
126
**sweet corn** mais *c* 51
**sweetener** søtningsmiddel *nt* 37
**sweet pepper** paprika *c* 51
**sweet shop** godtebutikk *c* 99
**swelling** hevelse *c* 139
**swim, to** bade 90; svømme 90
**swimming** svømming *c* 90
**swimming pool** badebasseng *nt*
32; svømmebasseng *nt* 23, 90
**swimming trunks** badebukse *c* 117
**swimsuit** badedrakt *c* 117
**switch** *(electric)* bryter *c* 29
**switch on, to** sette i gang 119
**switchboard operator** sentralbord-
betjent *c* 26
**swollen** hoven 139
**synagogue** synagoge *c* 84
**synthetic** syntetisk 114
**system** system *nt* 138

**T**
**table** bord *nt* 36; *(list)* tabell *c* 157
**tablet** *(medical)* tablett *c* 109, 143
**tailor's** skredder *c* 99
**tail pipe** eksosrør *nt* 78
**take, to** ta 18, 25, 60, 73, 76, 102
**take away, to** *(carry)* ta med seg
62
**talcum powder** talkum *c* 111
**tampon** tampong *c* 109
**tap** *(water)* kran *c* 28
**tap beer** fatøl *nt* 56
**taste, to** smake 60
**tax** skatt *c* 131
**tax-free shop** tax-free-butikk *c* 19
**taxi** drosje *c* 18, 19, 21, 31, 67

**taxi rank/stand** drosjeholdeplass *c*
21
**tea** te *c* 38, 59, 64
**teashop** konditori *nt* 33
**teaspoon** teskje *c* 107, 143
**team** lag *nt* 89
**telegram** telegram *nt* 133
**telegraph office** telesenter *nt* 99,
133
**telephone** telefon *c* 27, 28, 79, 134
**telephone, to** *(call)* ringe 134, 136
**telephone booth** telefonkiosk *c* 134
**telephone call** (telefon)samtale *c*
136; telefon *c* 136
**telephone directory** telefonkatalog
*c* 134
**telephone number** (telefon-
nummer *nt* 134, 135, 136
**telephoto lens** teleobjektiv *nt* 125
**television** TV *c* 23, 28, 119
**telex** telex *c* 133
**telex, to** sende telex 130
**tell, to** si 13, 76, 153
**temperature** temperatur *c* 142;
*(fever)* feber *c* 140
**temporary** provisorisk 145
**ten** ti 147
**tendon** sene *c* 138
**tennis** tennis *c* 89
**tennis court** tennisbane *c* 89
**tennis match** tenniskamp *c* 89
**tennis racket** (tennis)racket *c* 90
**tent** telt *nt* 32, 107
**tent peg** teltplugg *c* 107
**tent pole** teltstang *c* 107
**terrible** forferdelig 84
**tetanus** stivkrampe *c* 140
**than** enn 14
**thank, to** takke 10, 95, 96
**that** den 161; det 11, 100, 161
**theatre** teater *nt* 82, 86
**theft** tyveri *nt* 156
**their** deres 161
**then** da 15
**there** der 14
**thermometer** termometer *nt* 109
**these** disse 62, 161
**they** de 162; dem 162
**thief** tyv *c* 156
**thigh** lår *nt* 138
**thin** tynn 113
**think, to** *(believe)* tro 31, 94
**thirsty** tørst 13, 35
**thirteen** tretten 147
**thirty** tretti 147

**this** denne 161; dette 11, 100, 161
**those** dem 62, 120; de 161
**thousand** tusen 148
**thread** tråd c 27
**three** tre 147
**throat** hals c 138, 141
**throat lozenge** halstablett c 109
**through** gjennom 15; til 151
**through train** gjennomgående tog nt 68, 69
**thumb** tommel c 138
**thumbtack** tegnestift c 105
**thunder** torden c 94
**thunderstorm** tordenvær nt 94
**Thursday** torsdag c 150
**ticket** billett c 65, 69, 72, 87, 89
**ticket office** billettluke c 67
**tie** slips nt 117
**tie clip** slipsklype c 122
**tie pin** slipsnål c 122
**tight** (close-fitting) trang 116
**tights** strømpebukse c 117
**time** tid c 80; (occasion) gang c 95, 148; (clock) klokken 153
**timetable** rutetabell c 68
**tin** (container) boks c 120
**tin opener** boksåpner c 107
**tint** hårtoningsmiddel nt 111
**tinted** farget 123
**tire** dekk nt 75
**tired** trett 13
**tissue** (handkerchief) papir-lommetørkle nt 111
**tissue paper** silkepapir nt 105
**to** til 15; å 162
**toast** ristet brød nt 38
**tobacco** tobakk c 126
**tobacconist's** tobakkshandel c 99, 126
**today** i dag 29, 150, 151
**toe** tå c 138
**toilet paper** toalettpapir nt 111
**toiletries bag** toalettmappe c 111
**toiletry** toalettartikkel c 110
**toilets** toalett nt 27, 32, 67
**toilet water** eau de toilette c 111
**tomato** tomat c 51
**tomato juice** tomatjuice c 43
**tomb** grav c 82
**tomorrow** i morgen 29, 94, 96, 151
**tongue** tunge c 48, 138
**tonic** tonic c 58
**tonight** i kveld 29, 86, 87, 88, 96
**tonsils** mandler c/pl 138
**too** for 15, 19; (also) også 15, 75

**tool** verktøy nt 78
**too much** for mye 15
**tooth** tann c 145
**toothache** tannpine c 145
**toothbrush** tannbørste c 111, 119
**toothpaste** tannpasta c 111
**torch** (flashlight) lommelykt c 107
**torn** avslitt 140
**tough** (meat) seig 60
**tour** tur c 74, 80
**tourist office** turistkontor nt 22, 80
**towards** mot 15
**towel** håndkle nt 111
**tower** tårn nt 82
**town** by c 19, 88
**town hall** rådhus nt 82
**towrope** slepetau nt 78
**tow truck** kranbil c 78
**toy** leke c 128
**toy shop** leketøysbutikk c 99
**track** (railway) spor nt 67, 68, 69
**track-and-field meeting** friidretts-stevne nt 89
**tracksuit** treningsdrakt c 117
**traffic** trafikk c 76
**traffic light** trafikklys nt 77
**trailer** campingvogn c 32
**train** tog nt 66, 67, 68, 69, 70
**tram** trikk c 72
**tranquillizer** beroligende middel nt 143
**transfer** (finance) overføring c 131
**transformer** transformator c 119
**translate, to** oversette 12
**translation** oversettelse c 131
**translator** oversetter c 131
**transport** transport c 74
**travel, to** reise 93
**travel agency** reisebyrå nt 99
**travel guide** reisehåndbok c 105
**traveller's cheque** reisesjekk c 18, 61, 102, 130
**travel sickness** reisesyke c 108
**treatment** behandling c 143
**tree** tre nt 85
**tremendous** forskrekkelig 84
**trim, to** (a beard) stusse 31
**trip** reise c 93, 152; tur c 74
**troll** troll nt 127
**trolley** tralle c 18, 71
**trousers** langbukser c/pl 117
**trout** ørret c 46; aure c 45
**try, to** forsøke 136; (sample) prøve 42, 57
**try on, to** prøve 115

DICTIONARY

**T-shirt** T-skjorte *c* 117
**tube** tube *c* 120
**Tuesday** tirsdag *c* 150
**tumbler** drikkeglass *nt* 107
**turkey** kalkun *c* 50
**turn, to** *(change direction)* svinge 21
**turtleneck** høyhalset 117
**tweezers** pinsett *c* 111
**twelve** tolv 147
**twenty** tjue 147
**twice** to ganger 148
**twin beds** to senger *c/pl* 23
**two** to 147
**typewriter** skrivemaskin *c* 27
**typically** typisk 127
**typing paper** skrivemaskinpapir *nt* 105
**tyre** dekk *nt* 75

## U

**ugly** stygg 14, 84
**umbrella** paraply *c* 117
**uncle** onkel *c* 93
**unconscious** bevisstløs 139
**under** under 15
**underdone** *(meat)* råstekt 49; for lite stekt 60
**underground** *(railway)* T-bane *c* 73
**underpants** underbukse *c* 117
**undershirt** trøye *c* 117
**understand, to** forstå 12, 16
**undress, to** kle av seg 142
**United States** USA 146
**university** universitet *nt* 82
**unleaded** blyfri 75
**until** til 15, 150
**up** opp 15, 155
**upper** over- 69
**upset stomach** urolig mage *c* 108
**upstairs** oppe 15; opp trappen 69
**urgent, to be** haste 13
**urine** urin *c* 142
**use** bruk *c* 17, 109
**useful** nyttig 15
**usual** vanlig 143

## V

**vacancy** ledig rom *nt* 23
**vacant** ledig 14
**vacation** ferie *c* 16, 151, 152
**vaccinate, to** vaksinere 140
**vacuum flask** termosflaske *c* 107
**vaginal infection** underlivsbetennelse *c* 141

**valid** gyldig 65
**valley** dal *c* 85
**value** verdi *c* 131
**value-added tax** moms *c* 24, 102
**vanilla** vanilje *c* 55
**VAT** *(sales tax)* moms *c* 154
**veal** kalvekjøtt *nt* 47; kalve- 48
**vegetable** grønnsak *c* 40, 51
**vegetable store** grønnsakhandel *c* 99
**vegetarian** vegetar(isk) 37, 40
**vein** vene *c* 138; åre *c* 138
**venereal disease** kjønnssykdom *c* 142
**venetian blind** persienne *c* 29
**venison** rådyr *nt* 50
**very** meget 15
**vest** trøye *c* 117; *(Am.)* vest *c* 117
**veterinarian** dyrlege *c* 99
**video camera** videokamera *nt* 124
**video cassette** videokassett *c* 119, 124, 127
**video recorder** videokassettopptaker *c* 119
**view** *(panorama)* utsikt *c* 23, 25
**viking ship** vikingskip *nt* 127
**village** tettsted *nt* 76
**vinegar** eddik *c* 37
**visit** besøk *nt* 92; *(stay)* opphold *nt* 25
**visiting hours** besøkstid *c* 144
**visit, to** *(a person)* besøke 95; *(a place)* se 84
**vitamin pill** vitaminpille *c* 109
**voltage** strømstyrke *c* 119
**vomit, to** kaste opp 140

## W

**waffle** vaffel *c* 55
**waistcoat** vest *c* 117
**wait, to** vente 108
**wait for, to** vente på 21, 95
**waiter** kelner *c* 26; servitør *c* 26
**waiting room** venteal *c* 67
**waitress** serveringsdame *c* 26; servitør *c* 26
**wake, to** vekke 27, 71
**Wales** Wales 146
**walk, to** spasere 74, 85
**wall** mur *c* 85
**wallet** lommebok *c* 156
**walnut** valnøtt *c* 53
**want, to** *(wish)* ønske 13
**warm** varm 94
**wash, to** vaske 29

Ordliste

**washbasin** vask *c* 28
**washcloth** ansiktsklut *c* 111
**washing powder** vaskepulver *nt* 107
**watch** klokke *c* 121, 122
**watchmaker's** urmaker *c* 99, 121
**watchstrap** klokkerem *c* 122
**water** vann *nt* 23, 28, 32, 38, 75, 91
**watercolors** *(box of)* malerskrin *nt* 105
**waterfall** foss *c* 85
**water flask** feltflaske *c* 107
**watermelon** vannmelon *c* 54
**waterproof** vanntett 122
**water-ski** vannski *c* 91
**way** vei *c* 76, 77
**we** vi 162
**weak** svak 140
**weather** vær *nt* 94
**weather forecast** værutsikter *c/pl* 94
**wedding ring** giftering *c* 122
**Wednesday** onsdag *c* 150
**week** uke *c* 16, 20, 24, 80, 151
**weekday** hverdag *c* 151
**weekend** helg *c* 24; weekend *c* 20, 151
**well** bra 10
**well** brønn *c* 85
**well-done** *(meat)* godt stekt 49
**west** vest 77
**what** hva 11
**wheel** hjul *nt* 78
**when** når 11
**where** hvor 11
**which** hvilken 11
**whipped cream** pisket krem *c* 55
**white** hvit 113
**Whit Monday** 2. pinsedag *c* 152
**who** hvem 11
**whole** hel 49
**why** hvorfor 11
**wick** veke *c* 126
**wide** vid 118
**wide-angle lens** vidvinkelobjektiv *nt* 125
**wife** kone *c* 93
**wig** parykk *c* 111
**wild duck** villand *c* 50
**wind** vind *c* 94
**window** vindu *nt* 28, 36, 100, 112
**window seat** vindusplass *c* 65, 69
**windscreen/shield** frontrute *c* 76
**windsurfer** seilbrett *nt* 91
**wine** vin *c* 57, 60, 64

**wine list** vinkart *nt* 57
**wine merchant's** vinmonopol *nt* 99
**winter** vinter *c* 149
**winter sports** vintersport *c* 91
**wiper** *(car)* vindusvisker *c* 75
**wish** gratulasjon *c*/ønske *nt* 152
**with** med 15
**withdraw, to** *(from account)* ta ut 130
**without** uten 15
**woman** kvinne *c* 115, 156
**woman's ...** dame- 117
**wood** *(material)* tre *nt* 127
**woodcock** rugde *c* 50
**woodgrouse** tiur *c* 50
**wool** ull *c* 114
**word** ord *nt* 12, 15, 133
**work** arbeid *nt* 79
**work, to** *(function)* fungere 119; virke 28
**working day** arbeidsdag *c* 151
**worse** verre 14
**wound** sår *nt* 139
**wrap up, to** pakke inn 103
**wrapping paper** innpakningspapir *nt* 105
**wrinkle-free** krøllfri 114
**wristwatch** armbåndsur *nt* 122
**write, to** skrive 12, 101
**writing pad** skriveblokk *c* 105
**writing paper** skrivepapir *nt* 105
**wrong** feil 14, 135

## X
**X-ray, to** røntgenfotografere 140

## Y
**year** år *nt* 149
**yellow** gul 113
**yes** ja 10
**yesterday** i går 151
**yet** ennå 15, 16
**yoghurt** yoghurt *c* 38
**you** du 162
**young** ung 14, 149
**your** din, ditt *(pl* dine) 161
**youth hostel** vandrerhjem *nt* 22, 32

## Z
**zero** null 147
**zip(per)** glidelås *c* 117
**zoo** dyrehage *c* 82
**zoology** zoologi *c* 83

# Norsk register